T0301024

Global Services Outsourcing

Services outsourcing is an increasingly attractive option for firms seeking to reduce costs and achieve service improvements. Many organisations now choose to transfer responsibility for entire functions such as human resources, finance and information technology services to both local and global vendors. Yet outsourcing such functions is a complex process, one that is driven by factors that transcend cost considerations alone. Issues such as service design, unbundling processes, managing work across different cultures and time zones, and business process redesign have all become important elements of managing services outsourcing arrangements. This book uses tools and techniques from a variety of disciplines to show how to plan, implement and manage services outsourcing arrangements successfully. Based on in-depth analysis of large-scale outsourcing arrangements across a wide range of sectors, this is an excellent resource for both academics and practitioners who wish to understand more about this complex phenomenon.

RONAN MCIVOR is Professor of Operations Management at the University of Ulster. He has carried out extensive research in the area of outsourcing and supply chain management. He is the author of a number of books, including *The Outsourcing Process: Strategies for Evaluation and Management* (Cambridge University Press, 2005).

GLOBAL SERVICES OUTSOURCING

Ronan McIvor

CAMBRIDGE
UNIVERSITY PRESS

CAMBRIDGE
UNIVERSITY PRESS

University Printing House, Cambridge CB2 8BS, United Kingdom

One Liberty Plaza, 20th Floor, New York, NY 10006, USA

477 Williamstown Road, Port Melbourne, VIC 3207, Australia

314-321, 3rd Floor, Plot 3, Splendor Forum, Jasola District Centre, New Delhi - 110025, India

103 Penang Road, #05-06/07, Visioncrest Commercial, Singapore 238467

Cambridge University Press is part of the University of Cambridge.

It furthers the University's mission by disseminating knowledge in the pursuit of education, learning and research at the highest international levels of excellence.

www.cambridge.org
Information on this title: www.cambridge.org/9780521765466

First published 2010

A catalogue record for this publication is available from the British Library

ISBN 978-0-521-76546-6 Hardback

Contents

Figures

Tables

Illustrations

Acknowledgements

I would like to thank the many people who have helped in the writing of this book. A significant part of the book is based on in-depth analysis of services outsourcing in a range of organisations. This analysis involved carrying out interviews with a range of individuals in these organisations. I would like to thank the individuals in these organisations who facilitated the interviews and who participated in the interview process. These interviews were an important influence on the structure and analysis presented in the book. I would also like to thank a number of colleagues who contributed support to the book. In particular, I would like to thank Paul Humphreys, Alan McKittrick and Tony Wall for their contribution to the collection and analysis of data in the financial services organisation presented in Chapter 7. Martina Gerbl provided valuable feedback on the structure and content of certain chapters of the book. I would also like to thank the following colleagues for providing both direct and indirect support throughout the writing process: Paul Humphreys, Marie McHugh, Jim Bell and Liam Maguire. I would like to thank those academics and researchers whose work I have cited. Students at the University of Ulster provided valuable feedback on various ideas and concepts in the book, and also contributed to its development. Also, Paula Parish at Cambridge University Press provided helpful advice on the structure of the book, and useful comments at various stages in the writing process. The three anonymous reviewers of the proposal for the book provided valuable guidance and suggestions for improvement. Finally, I would like to thank my family, in particular Deirdre and Nathan, who contributed support and encouragement throughout the preparation of this book.

Introduction

Outsourcing has become a strategic imperative as organisations seek to reduce costs and specialise in a limited number of core areas. Increasingly, organisations are looking beyond the traditional boundaries of the firm to reduce costs and achieve performance improvements. Services outsourcing has grown as organisations have been transferring responsibility for entire functions such as human resources, finance and information technology services to both local and global vendors. Business services are services provided by businesses to other businesses and include legal services, consultancy, customer contact, human resource services, and research and development. The growth of services outsourcing has generated considerable debate among economists and policymakers. Much of this debate has focused on issues such as labour costs, tax incentives and location advantages. However, while this debate has continued, practitioners have had to get on with the job of implementing services outsourcing arrangements. Services outsourcing is often a complex phenomenon, which is driven by factors that transcend cost considerations alone. Issues such as service design, unbundling processes, managing work across different cultures and time zones, and business process redesign have become important elements of managing services outsourcing arrangements.

The analysis presented in this book focuses on the implications of planning, implementing and managing services outsourcing arrangements. Services outsourcing arrangements encompass a range of areas including continuous improvement, change management, stakeholder management, knowledge management, information technology, contracting and performance management. These areas are integrated into the book by providing insights into their application in outsourcing arrangements in practice. The author has undertaken in-depth, longitudinal case-study analysis of a number of large-scale outsourcing arrangements across a range of sectors including utility services, financial services, human resource management, research and development and information technology. In-depth interviews were carried out with senior and middle managers to understand how organisations approached the outsourcing process. This involved exploring different sourcing strategies, and identifying the benefits and risks of particular sourcing strategies. This analysis forms a central part of the book.

Particular attention is given to the global dimension, and the impact upon services outsourcing. A comprehensive discussion of the key factors involved in selecting the location and sourcing model for global services outsourcing arrangements is provided (Chapter 4). Challenges such as those of intellectual property rights, legal issues, security, language, culture, quality, politics, time zones and company reputation are considered. Particular attention is given to the issues involved in managing global services arrangements (Chapter 5). Significant emphasis is placed on how strategies can be employed to achieve the benefits and reduce the risks of global services outsourcing. It is shown how emerging economies such as India's are developing their competitiveness to increase their attractiveness as locations for a range of business services including customer contact, legal services and information technology. The book also intersperses global issues throughout a number of the chapters. Insights are provided into the factors that influence the mobility of service processes in the global economy, and how the distinctive characteristics of services create challenges in services outsourcing (Chapter 2).

The book synthesises and integrates contemporary research and practice in services outsourcing and related disciplines in a way that is readily accessible to students. Each chapter includes illustrations developed both from empirical research undertaken by the author and contemporary research in the area. The writing style of the book is suitable for both business/economics students and those from other disciplines such as engineering and information technology. Theoretical frameworks are introduced in a way that is accessible to students from these disciplines. These theories include transaction cost economics, the resource-based view, eclectic theory, social exchange theory and organisation behaviour theory. Contemporary management techniques being employed in services outsourcing such as Six Sigma, process analysis, workflow mapping, knowledge management and project management are introduced. Summaries are included at the end of each chapter, outlining the implications of the analysis presented. A 'Recommended key reading' section is included at the end of each chapter, identifying key sources and useful additional reading in the relevant subject area. A glossary is included at the end of the book, defining and explaining key terms associated with services outsourcing.

This book is intended for readers in the academic market who require an up-to-date understanding of the issues involved in global services outsourcing. It will be of interest to students on postgraduate (MBA, MA and MSc) programmes studying the subject of services outsourcing, and can be used as a supplementary text on modules such as business strategy, international business, global sourcing, management information systems, operations management and services management where significant attention is given to outsourcing. The book is also of value to students who are researching the area of outsourcing. Theoretical models are introduced throughout to explain particular aspects of services outsourcing.

The book is of value to practitioners who are involved in or considering outsourcing business services. It is based on contemporary research, which has focused on examining the challenges, risks and benefits of planning and implementing business services outsourcing arrangements. Insights are provided into tools and techniques employed by organisations to manage business services outsourcing arrangements. Although the analysis presented employs a number of the theoretical models, these are particularly valuable for strategic decision-making. Theoretical models are presented in a manner that can be easily understood by practitioners. In addition, integrating contemporary practice with theory assists in stimulating a deeper understanding of the key issues associated with services outsourcing. The book alerts practitioners to the key issues that should be addressed if they are approaching the problem themselves.

The book is timely because of the growing trend towards global outsourcing of business services. Through extensive research and teaching in this area, I have found that there is no single text that adequately addresses the topic of services outsourcing. Many texts in this area are focused on the global outsourcing of information technology services. A number of books focus only on a single business service area such as human resource management or research and development. This book considers business services outsourcing in a number of areas, including financial services, utility services, order processing, customer contact, legal services, information technology and human resource services. It has been made as interesting as possible through the use of illustrations and empirical research. The illustrations in each chapter are intended to enrich the content and provide support for the analysis and insights outlined. The book is strengthened through reference to contemporary research in the area of outsourcing in a range of leading international journals. It is structured as follows.

Chapter 2: Global services outsourcing overview – presents an overview of services outsourcing, which includes the types of services outsourcing arrangement, stages in the outsourcing process, drivers of services outsourcing, and the arguments for and against services outsourcing. The influence of service design principles on services outsourcing is examined, which involves considering the influences on the mobility of service processes and the distinctive challenges of outsourcing service processes.

Chapter 3: Making the services outsourcing decision – presents a framework that identifies suitable outsourcing strategies for service processes. The framework provides a mechanism for understanding which processes should be kept internal and which should be outsourced based on both organisational capability and opportunism considerations. The framework outlines a number of potential outsourcing relationships and the key aspects of each. The logic of the framework and the sourcing strategies is illustrated through providing real case illustrations both in a local and global context.

Chapter 4: Location and sourcing model choice in global services outsourcing – provides a structured approach for understanding the issues involved in selecting the location and sourcing model. Making the location decision involves consideration of a range of factors including culture, language and geographical distance, infrastructure, political risk, legal matters, government policy and labour issues. Selecting the appropriate sourcing model is closely linked to the location choice. The influences on sourcing model choice are the characteristics of the service process and include process interdependencies, performance measurement, risk and knowledge intensity.

Chapter 5: Managing global services outsourcing arrangements – focuses on the area of software development to illustrate the issues involved in managing global services outsourcing arrangements. Software development is one of the most challenging areas of global outsourcing, and provides an illustration of the complexity of managing such arrangements. This is a well-developed area in practice where companies have been adopting innovative and novel practices to obtain the potential benefits and mitigate the risks. An overview of the key issues involved in effectively managing global software development outsourcing projects is provided. Throughout this analysis, illustrations of how clients and vendors manage the challenges of global software development outsourcing are introduced.

Chapter 6: Creating shared services arrangements – focuses on the planning and implementation phases of a major outsourced shared services arrangement in the public sector. A detailed overview of the key tasks involved in planning and implementing outsourced shared services arrangements is provided. These tasks include a structured approach to project management, business case development, vendor engagement, contracting, change management, stakeholder engagement, business process redesign and strategic partnership development. Important insights are provided on the implications of creating outsourced shared services arrangements.

Chapter 7: Services outsourcing and performance management – focuses on performance management and the outsourcing process. A framework is presented which provides an outline of the stages involved in integrating performance management into the outsourcing process. The framework integrates a number of performance management techniques into the outsourcing process including cost analysis, benchmarking, workflow mapping and continuous improvement. Illustrations from a financial services organisation are introduced throughout to demonstrate the practical implications of performance management and the outsourcing process. The challenges and benefits of performance management and outsourcing are outlined.

Chapter 8: Services outsourcing and the spin-off arrangement – provides detailed insights into the development and implementation of spin-off arrangements. The content of the chapter is enriched by integrating the experiences of a utility company that spun off a number of functions into a separate commercial business. The following issues are considered: motives for spinning off functions; assessing capabilities of internal functions prior to the spin-off; preparation strategies prior to spin-off; potential governance structures between the spin-off and the parent company; strategies for allowing the spin-off to grow; developing an entrepreneurial culture in the spin-off; and managing the outsourcing relationship between the parent company and the spin-off.

Chapter 9: Learning from failure and strategies for recovery in business process outsourcing – considers the common causes of failure in business process outsourcing (BPO) and strategies for recovery. The analysis is enriched through analysing the experiences of a global software provider in a major BPO arrangement. The experiences of the company, along with illustrations from the existing literature, are used to outline the common causes of failure in BPO. The chapter focuses on strategies for recovering failing BPO arrangements including developing an effective sourcing strategy, business process analysis and redesign, knowledge management, and employing formal contracting and collaboration as complements. Illustrations are provided on how knowledge management tools, information technology applications and continuous improvement techniques can be employed to reduce transaction costs in BPO arrangements.

Chapter 10: Conclusion – This chapter summarises some of the key challenges of services outsourcing and outlines key aspects of effective services outsourcing based upon the analysis presented in the book.

Global services outsourcing overview

2.1 Introduction

Services outsourcing has become an important feature of the global economy. Globalisation and advances in technology have allowed companies to transfer information technology, human resource, legal and accounting services to local and foreign vendors. Services outsourcing poses considerable challenges, and is more complex than manufacturing outsourcing. The unique features of services, such as the involvement of the customer in service delivery, service customisation and the need for physical contact, make services outsourcing extremely challenging. However, organisations have been pursuing a range of strategies to reduce the risks, and achieve the benefits that services outsourcing offers. Organisations have been redesigning business processes to retain customer contact services locally and to outsource routine, labour-intensive back-office services. This has involved adopting sourcing models with vendors to maintain control over critical outsourced processes, whilst leveraging the lower costs of vendors in emerging economies. Moreover, organisations have been increasingly looking beyond labour cost advantages and using global services outsourcing to access highly qualified staff in knowledge-intensive services.

This chapter provides an overview of the global services outsourcing phenomenon. A background to the growth in business services is outlined. An overview of services outsourcing is presented, which includes the types of outsourcing arrangement being adopted by organisations, stages in the outsourcing process, drivers of services outsourcing and the arguments for and against services outsourcing. The influence of service design principles on services outsourcing is examined. This involves considering influences on the mobility of service processes in the global economy, and how the distinctive characteristics of services create challenges in services outsourcing.

2.2 The services revolution

Developed economies such as those of the USA and UK have witnessed tremendous growth in the trading of services. These economies have experienced the hollowing out of their manufacturing bases, as product manufacture has been outsourced to economies such as those of China, South America and Eastern Europe. The services sectors have become a critical driving force of these developed economies. As manufacturing has contracted, productivity and employment levels have increased in the service sectors of these economies. Services can be categorised into those used by individual consumers and those used by businesses – referred to as business services. Business services can be divided into information technology (IT) services and the rapidly growing area of IT-enabled services as shown in Figure 2.1.[1] IT services include hardware and software consultancy, computer maintenance and repair, data processing and database activities. IT-enabled services include professional services (legal, accountancy, market research, technical, engineering, advertising, human resources and consultancy), research and development, recruitment agencies and call centres.

There are a number of reasons for the growing importance of services. Firstly, manufacturing companies have focused on services as product markets have become saturated, and used it as a defence against the increasing commoditisation of many products.[2] Organisations have been using

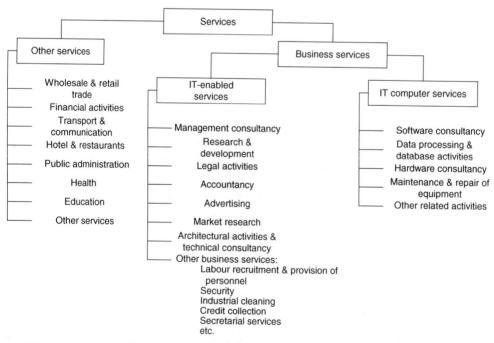

Figure 2.1   Categories of business services

services to complement their core product offerings and diversify into other service areas in order to achieve further growth. Automotive companies have been offering a range of complementary services to customers including financing, insurance and roadside assistance, whilst GE has been offering financial services to complement its existing product range, and diversify into other service markets.

Secondly, advances in information and communication technologies (ICTs) have allowed organisations to extend their reach into a range of service areas. High-street retailers now offer a range of online services such as insurance, credit and banking services. In addition, developments in ICTs have led to the offering of a range of services that previously did not exist. For example, in the field of mobile communications, specialist providers have emerged offering digitised services such as broadband access, web browsing, messaging and document management.

Thirdly, as a result of competitive pressures and more demanding consumers, organisations have been restructuring their organisations to remove highly fragmented business processes. Fragmented and widely dispersed processes have led to increased costs, duplication of resource and a lack of consumer responsiveness across a range of industry sectors as shown in Table 2.1. Organisations have been redesigning business processes and using ICTs to improve process performance and deliver services digitally. These initiatives have focused not only on better serving the needs of consumers, but also on meeting the needs of organisational employees – internal

Table 2.1 Examples of process deficiencies

Industry sector	End-to-end business process deficiencies
Automotive	Poor integration of systems and software from multiple vendors
Electronics	Challenges in move from mass production to build-to-order supply chains to achieve productivity and customer responsiveness
Health care	Fragmented processes across users, providers and hospitals
	Poor quality of patient records
	Increasing costs and slow responsiveness
Banking	Under-utilised data and functional silos
	Poor customer loyalty with deficient products and services
Retailing	Fragmented systems and under-utilised data across supply chains
Telecommunications	Incomplete view of customer as a result of fragmented systems for billing, customer care, self-service etc.

Source: Adapted from Rai, A. and Sambamurthy, V. (2006). The Growth of Interest in Services Management: Opportunities for Information Systems Scholars, *Information Systems Research*, 17(4), 327–31.

customers. Many organisations have been transforming their human resource and finance functions from purely transaction-based roles into providers of high-quality value-added services to employees.

2.3 Services outsourcing

As the services sectors of developed economies have grown in importance, the trend towards services outsourcing, both domestically and globally, has become more prominent. Services outsourcing can be either task-oriented or business-process-oriented. Task-oriented outsourcing involves the vendor completing tasks such as data entry and technical support for the client. Process-oriented outsourcing involves the vendor taking responsibility for executing a business process such as customer contact, and delivering it to the client as a service, often referred to as business process outsourcing (BPO). Organisations can pursue three different models for business process outsourcing. *Selective outsourcing* involves outsourcing a limited number of activities associated with the business process. *Transitional outsourcing* involves outsourcing the process to a vendor on a temporary basis. *Total outsourcing* involves outsourcing the entire process to a vendor.[3]

BPO often involves outsourcing the infrastructure supporting the business process, including the IT infrastructure. BPO focuses on how the overall process methodology or function is effective, from manager to end user, rather than on the technology that supports the process. Services outsourcing also includes IT outsourcing, which involves the IT component of business operations, such as data centre and desktop operations. For example, outsourcing the data centre may involve back-office support to a number of business functions such as human resources and finance and accounting. As well as outsourcing routine processes such as data entry and transaction processing to reduce costs, organisations have increasingly been outsourcing processes that impact competitive advantage. Organisations have been outsourcing more complex processes, as vendors have upgraded their initial capabilities in cost reduction, to offering specialist knowledge and continuous improvement capabilities to transform process performance for clients (Figure 2.2).

Organisations have been outsourcing services to both local and foreign locations. Local outsourcing involves transferring a process previously carried out internally to a vendor located in the same country of operation. This can involve an organisation transferring parts of the process including staff, equipment and other assets to the vendor. Local outsourcing can also involve redeploying staff in the outsourcing organisation or redundancies. However, the negative effects of this type of outsourcing are mitigated,

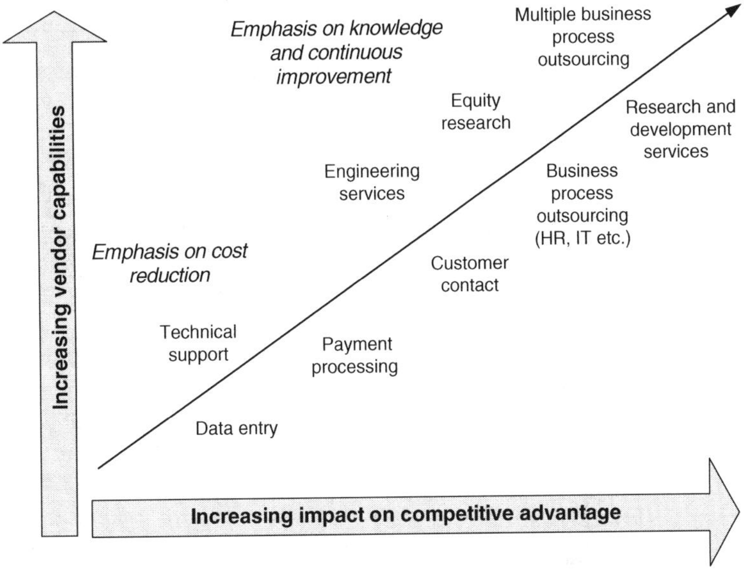
Increasing vendor capabilities
Increasing impact on competitive advantage
Emphasis on knowledge and continuous improvement
Emphasis on cost reduction
Multiple business process outsourcing
Research and development services
Equity research
Engineering services
Business process outsourcing (HR, IT etc.)
Customer contact
Technical support
Payment processing
Data entry

Figure 2.2 The relationship between competitive advantage and increasing vendor capabilities in BPO

because the displaced jobs still remain local, and are only redistributed to another local vendor. Therefore, the impact of local outsourcing on those people in services mainly involves job transfers. In contrast, foreign outsourcing involves transferring a process previously carried out locally to a vendor or a subsidiary operation owned and managed by the client organisation in a foreign country.

The terms *offshoring* and *nearshoring* are often used in the context of global outsourcing. Offshoring involves outsourcing a process to a location that is both geographically and culturally distant. An example of offshoring is when a UK financial services organisation transfers its customer service contact process to an Indian vendor. Nearshoring involves outsourcing a process to a location that is both geographically and culturally close. An example of nearshoring is when a German company outsources software development to a vendor in Hungary.

Illustration 2.1 A brief historical perspective on outsourcing

A common misconception associated with outsourcing is that it is a recent phenomenon. Rather than being totally self-sufficient, organisations have always engaged in outsourcing to some extent, whether it involved using external vendors for mail services or for contract cleaning. However, more recently, outsourcing has become an important part of an organisation's corporate strategy, and has involved more critical processes. The growth in manufacturing outsourcing pre-dated that of services outsourcing. The trend towards outsourcing manufacturing – referred to as the make-or-buy decision – can be traced back as far as the 1950s when manufacturers in a range of industries in the USA and Europe used suppliers for mainly routine, standard component manufacture in domestic and overseas locations with lower labour costs. However, the trend towards outsourcing manufacturing accelerated through the 1980s and 1990s for a number of reasons. Previously, organisations were highly vertically integrated with many activities owned and controlled internally, primarily to achieve scale economies and bargaining power – central to Michael Porter's industry view.[a] The classic example of vertical integration is the Ford Motor Company in the early twentieth century, when it owned almost the entire value chain, including manufacture, assembly, iron ore extraction, the saw mills and the car dealer network.[b]

Later, management philosophy began to change, largely influenced by the core competence concept, and many organisations moved away from inflexible, highly integrated structures, to focusing on a limited number of core areas where they excelled, and outsourcing non-core areas to vendors with superior skills and knowledge. The rise of 'lean production', a paradigm developed from analysing Japanese production and supply systems, fuelled the growth in manufacturing outsourcing in the early 1990s.[c] Companies could dramatically improve their performance by adopting the lean production approach pioneered by Toyota in its Toyota Production System (TPS). A significant part of the success of the TPS was attributed to the integration of key internal processes with those of their suppliers. In this context, outsourcing involved more critical components, and the development of longer-term, collaborative supplier relationships. Adopting collaborative buyer–supplier relationships was viewed as a means of reducing the risks associated with outsourcing in cases where the requirements of the buyer were not standardised and the transaction involved frequent changes.

Services outsourcing became more prominent in the 1980s, as a result of a number of important developments. Reforms in the public sector in the USA and UK were an important development; in this context, outsourcing was used to reduce costs, union power and labour levels. Outsourcing was viewed as an instrument for reducing bureaucracy and using competitive market mechanisms to reduce costs and improve service quality. An important outcome of outsourcing in the public sector was the growth in specialist vendors for services such as facilities maintenance, security and contract cleaning. A further development was the growth in information technology (IT) outsourcing. Although companies had outsourced routine IT services, such as data processing, since the 1960s, the landmark outsourcing deal, where Kodak outsourced a wide range of IT services in 1989, led to an explosion in the growth of IT outsourcing in the 1990s – sometimes referred to as the 'Kodak effect'.[d] Organisations such as British Petroleum and Bank of America outsourced their IT departments, which in turn led to the growth of large IT vendors such as Accenture, IBM and EDS.

Falling trade barriers and developments in information and communication technologies were key developments in the growth of the outsourcing of services to foreign locations. Increasingly, organisations have been moving beyond cost motives alone, to use services outsourcing as a means of accessing skilled foreign labour pools, and reduce development times in knowledge-intensive services such as IT and research and development.[e] Crucially, the development of services outsourcing exhibits some important differences from that of manufacturing outsourcing. Global services outsourcing has evolved much more quickly than that of manufacturing outsourcing, primarily because many services can be traded digitally, and trade in services is not impacted by trade tariffs to the same extent as manufacturing. Moreover, whereas manufacturing outsourcing impacted lower-skilled, blue-collar workers, global services outsourcing has impacted highly educated, white-collar workers.

Notes:
[a] The 'industry view' is often used to describe the seminal work of Michael Porter. Key references include Porter, M. E. (1985). *Competitive Advantage: Creating and Sustaining Superior Performance*, New York: Free Press; and Porter, M. E. (1980). *Competitive Strategy*, New York: Free Press.
[b] For further information on the Ford production model, see: Chandler, A. (1977). *The Visible Hand: The Managerial Revolution in American Business*, Cambridge, Mass.: Harvard University Press.
[c] See Womack, J., Jones, D. T. and Roos, D. (1990). *The Machine that Changed the World*, New York: Rawson Associates.
[d] See Loh, L. and Venkatraman, N. (1992). Diffusion of Information Technology Outsourcing: Influence Sources and the Kodak Effect, *Information Systems Research*, 3(4), 334–58.
[e] See Couto, V., Mani, M., Lewin, A. and Peeters, C. (2006). The Globalisation of White Collar Work: The Facts and Fallout of Next-Generation Offshoring, https://offshoring.fuqua.duke.edu/pdfs/gowc_v4.pdf.

2.4 Types of services outsourcing arrangements

There is a vast array of terms used in the outsourcing literature, and there appears to be little convergence between academia and practice in the terminology. This can often create confusion around the subject. However, there are a number of configurations for managing outsourcing arrangements both locally and globally. Using the dimensions of *level of ownership* and *location*, a typology of sourcing arrangements can be created as shown in Figure 2.3. Each of these arrangements is now discussed.

Local in-house sourcing
This occurs when an organisation sources services internally from business functions such as human resources, information technology and finance and accounting.

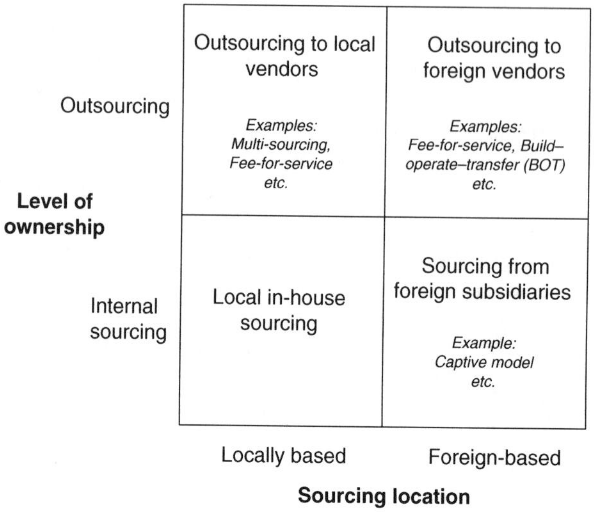

Figure 2.3   Typology of sourcing configurations

Outsourcing to local vendors

This option involves an organisation sourcing services from vendors within its national boundaries. There are a number of configurations which organisations employ for local outsourcing. Organisations are increasingly utilising multi-sourcing instead of moving directly to totally externally owned outsourcing arrangements. Multi-sourcing integrates in-house service provision with outsourced methods which include 'out-tasking' some of the steps in a process, or total business process outsourcing. Out-tasking is often a practical way of exploring the potential benefits of total outsourcing without the risks of total dependency.

Sourcing from foreign subsidiaries

This involves establishing and managing a subsidiary in a foreign location to take advantage of local skills and lower labour costs. A common sourcing model associated with this arrangement is the captive model. With the captive model, the client builds, owns, staffs and operates the global facility. The captive model offers a high level of control through ownership, but also carries high levels of risk due to the inflexibility associated with ownership. Global shared services arrangements are often established via the captive model. Shared services arrangements involve centralising processes at a single location where the geographically dispersed units of an organisation share the services centrally, rather than have all the services provided locally.[4] Multi-divisional organisations have been establishing

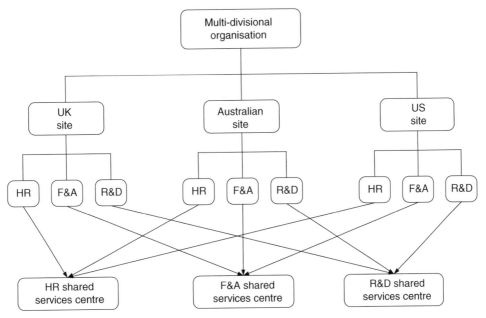

Figure 2.4   Shared services arrangement

shared services arrangements for processes in functions such as human resources (HR), finance and accounting (F&A), information technology (IT) and research and development (R&D) as shown in Figure 2.4. American Express consolidated more than forty-six transaction processing sites into three shared service centres located in the USA, UK and India.[5] The captive model allowed American Express to reduce its overall costs, primarily as a result of lower labour costs in India, and to transfer work among regional service centres to provide capacity flexibility and serve customers on a global basis twenty-four hours a day.

Outsourcing to foreign vendors

This arrangement involves sourcing services from an independent vendor in foreign locations. Again, there are a number of models employed by organisations, which are largely influenced by the level of control required. Organisations can use external vendors on a contractual basis. This is the case with fee-for-service outsourcing in areas such as software development and customer contact where the client signs a contract with a foreign vendor who owns its own facility and employs its own staff. This is the most popular global outsourcing model as it offers the lowest level of risk.[6] Another common model in global outsourcing is the joint venture where the client and vendor share ownership in the facility. Organisations often chose a joint venture over the captive model because they want to sacrifice control in exchange for the vendor taking on most of the risk. The build–operate–transfer (BOT) model is often associated with the joint venture model. This model provides an opportunity to leverage the capabilities of a vendor to establish operations in the foreign country, and then transfer the operations to the full control of the client after an agreed period of time. The BOT model has become increasingly prevalent in many industries where distinctive capabilities are built around unique knowledge bases such as design and engineering.[7]

2.5 Stages in the services outsourcing process

Decision to outsource

This stage involves analysing whether outsourcing a process is appropriate, and developing a business case to justify outsourcing. The impetus for outsourcing is often corporate restructuring initiatives and the need to reduce costs. At corporate level, this can involve distinguishing between core and non-core processes. This involves considering issues such as the capability in the process relative to competitors, the importance of the process to competitive advantage, the capability of vendors to provide the process, the level of risk in the supply market, potential workforce resistance and the impact upon employee morale. Important motives for outsourcing include consolidating processes to achieve economies of scale, accessing skills at a lower cost and improving service quality.

Select the outsourcing strategy

Once an organisation has decided to outsource a process, the next stage is the selection of a strategy, which involves location and outsourcing relationship considerations. A critical consideration at this stage is whether the organisation should select a vendor in a local or foreign location. The local outsourcing option is often chosen for reasons such as the availability of capable vendors, maintaining greater control over a complex process, the need for cultural closeness and avoiding adverse publicity from using vendors in foreign locations. In relation to the choice of the foreign location option, rather than selecting the location on the basis of costs (labour, infrastructure etc.) and risks (for example, political, legal etc.) alone, organisations are increasingly employing a wider set of business criteria, which include their strategy objectives (for example, access to new customer markets in the foreign location) and overall commitment to the location (for example, to complement existing facilities in the location). The level of control required is an important influence on the type of global sourcing model chosen – direct control with a captive facility, third-party control via outsourcing to an independent foreign vendor, or a combination of the two.[8]

Implementation

This stage involves transferring the process to the vendor. There are a number of issues relevant to both local and foreign outsourcing including vendor selection, contract negotiations, transitioning of assets and deriving performance measures. Organisations have to consider how easily the process can be codified and how precise performance measures can be developed for the service level agreement (SLA).[9] The type of business process will influence the level of risk and dependency on the vendor in the outsourcing arrangement. For example, standard processes, where tasks and performance measures can be specified, can be transferred more easily to alternative vendors than more complex processes. However, some implementation issues are further amplified in the case of global outsourcing. Problems relating to the political situation in a global location, along with cultural and language differences, are additional difficulties when transferring processes.

Management

This stage involves managing the outsourcing arrangement. Organisations often under-estimate the management resource required to effectively manage both local and foreign outsourcing arrangements. In fact, the challenges of managing foreign arrangements are quite formidable. Additional resource has to be committed to managing a vendor in a different time zone. It can often take months for the foreign facility fully to meet client requirements, because of the need to transfer domain knowledge from the sourcing organisation.[10] Managing the global arrangement can make or break the relocated process and can extend far beyond financial implications. Performance management is an important aspect of any outsourcing arrangement. Organisations track performance by employing a variety of metrics that consider costs, quality, timeliness and risk.

2.6 Drivers of services outsourcing

Business process perspective

The business process perspective championed by Hammer and Davenport and consultancy firms such as Accenture and Genpact has had a major influence on how organisations view their operations and outsource business processes. Process management is a structured approach to performance improvement that focuses on the disciplined design and careful execution of an organisation's end-to-end business processes.[11] Hammer defines a business process as an organised group of related processes that work together to create value for customers. Previously, organisations developed their own processes such as order fulfilment, customer support and order processing, which were company- and location-specific. These processes were constructed to meet the idiosyncrasies of individual organisations. However, as a result of continuous improvement, information technology implementations and total quality management (TQM) initiatives, organisations have embarked upon mapping processes and improving process performance. A major element of these initiatives has involved standardising and outsourcing processes to specialist vendors.[12]

Standardisation facilitates outsourcing for a number of reasons. Standardising a process means it can be performed successfully using a set of consistent and repeatable tasks. For example, when a customer places an order for a product with a company, there are a number of predetermined steps and a sequence involved in processing the order. The company will have a standard process for processing the order, which does not vary from customer to customer. The consistency of the process means that it is straightforward to transfer to a vendor. Standardising processes makes it easier to compare in-house costs with those of outsourcing to vendors. In addition, standardising processes makes it easier for companies to outsource, as they can establish clear interfaces between their organisations and the vendor. This means that responsibility for, and performance of, the processes can be clearly handed over to the vendor. Information technology can allow the client to implement standard interfaces with internal processes, and with those of vendors. Many processes such as labour recruitment, payroll processing and debt collection are performed in the same way by many organisations. Because of the outsourcing of processes with standard requirements, vendors can achieve economies of scale and in turn reduce costs for clients. Organisations are now outsourcing a range of service business processes (Table 2.2).

Indeed, the trend towards outsourcing these processes has been further driven by specialist vendors who continue to expand their range of capabilities in these areas. Moreover, companies have begun to exploit their capabilities in internal functions to offer services to customers outside their core markets. UPS, traditionally a parcel delivery company, has leveraged its scale and skills in logistics processes and technology. It has emerged as a specialist vendor for the entire logistics requirements of an organisation, including supply-chain design and planning, sourcing, manufacturing, order fulfilment and vendor management.[13]

Table 2.2 Typical outsourced service processes

Business process	Sub-process
Finance and accounting	General accounting, accounts payable, accounts receivable, contract maintenance, financial systems, tax and regulatory compliance, budgeting etc.
Human resources	Benefits administration, job posting, payroll processing, training administration, recruitment, assessment and selection, policy enquiries and resolution etc.
Customer relationship management	Customer acquisition, customer help-desk, cross-selling etc.
Procurement	Requisition and approval, order management, receiving, inventory and invoicing, financial reporting and analysis etc.
Transaction processing	Billing and payment services, indirect procurement, tax processing, claims and policy processing etc.
Information technology	Software and application development, systems architecture design, software implementation and integration, systems maintenance etc.
Logistics	Product selection, acquisition, delivery, inventory and warehouse management, maintenance and help-desk services etc.

Illustration 2.2 The business process perspective

The business process perspective can be traced back to the early 1990s. In the late 1980s, executives in many corporations became concerned with the return on investment from information technology (IT). Despite huge investments in IT, corporations had not achieved the anticipated improvements in performance and productivity. Various explanations were proposed, including poor implementation of IT systems or ineffective performance measurement systems to fully capture the benefits of IT. However, some argued that IT was not the problem; rather it was organisational processes and structures that were deploying IT. It was argued that IT was unlikely to deliver the required improvements if it was implemented in hierarchical organisations with functionally oriented command and control procedures. In these circumstances, IT implementations were further exacerbating the problems by automating complex structures and making them more rigid. Proponents of the business process approach such as Hammer, Champy and Davenport began to argue that corporations should radically rethink and redesign their existing organisational structures and implement IT to further improve productivity and performance. Michael Hammer in the *Harvard Business Review*, using the slogan 'Obliterate, don't automate!', argued that companies should blow up their existing processes, start from scratch, and then use IT to radically change and redesign processes. This led to the development of business process redesign (BPR), which has evolved into the process management approach, encompassing practices such as total quality management (TQM), business improvement, benchmarking and knowledge management.

Process management is a structured approach to improving performance that involves the design and execution of a company's end-to-end business processes. A business process is an organised group of related activities that work together to create value for internal customers (such as employees in other parts of the organisation) or external customers. Processes can be complex, encompassing a number of functions (such as order fulfilment, new product development), or relatively straightforward (such as order entry). An important principle of a business process is the cross-functional focus where individuals and functions work together and are aligned to serve customer needs. Figure 2.5 provides an illustration of cross-functional processes. For example, order fulfilment involves all activities from the customer order until the customer has received the product or service and paid, and therefore transcends functions and integrates customer service, logistics, finance and manufacturing to provide value for the end customer. Of course, information technologies such as electronic commerce play a pivotal role in allowing companies to link systems of internal functions with those of their customers and suppliers. This contrasts with the single functional perspective – sometimes known as the 'silo mentality' – where functions focus on narrow tasks and protect their own single functional interests. In this instance, functions often pursue differing objectives and are unaware of the needs of other functions, which ultimately leads to lower value for the company's customers.

Continuous improvement is central to business process management, which involves constant efforts to improve performance to increase customer satisfaction. Creating a common purpose and aligning functions with serving customer needs means employees will recognise that they are part of the overall organisation and thus achieve higher performance, which can be linked

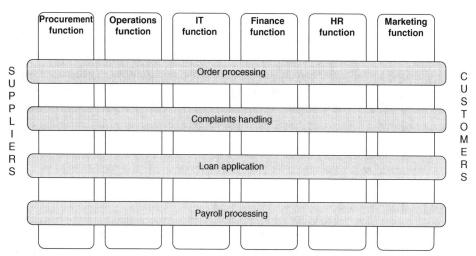

Figure 2.5   Cross-functional process examples

with incentive schemes. Consider order fulfilment for a manufacturer with multiple functions where each function has a different performance objective and no overall responsibility for the order. Adopting a process management approach and introducing metrics for the total order fulfilment cycle time will lead to each function taking responsibility for the entire process rather than blaming other functions for poor performance. An important facilitator of process improvement is the process-owner who ensures that the people performing the process understand it, are trained in it, have the required tools and are following the specified design. In the case of performance problems with the process, the process-owner is responsible for ensuring a completely new process design is introduced, which may involve a re-engineering exercise.

Sources: Davenport, T. (2005). The Coming Commoditization of Processes, *Harvard Business Review*, 83(6), 100–8; Hammer, M. (2002). Process Management and the Future of Six Sigma, *Sloan Management Review*, 43(2), 26–32.

Developments in information and communication technologies (ICTs)

The advent of relatively cheap and reliable telecommunications and information technology has facilitated the trend towards services outsourcing. The increasing importance of innovative ICTs for economies and societies has been attracting considerable attention from both academics and practitioners. In the last few decades, ICTs have transformed organisations internally, and the way in which they interact with customers and suppliers. In particular, developments in ICTs have enabled organisations to transfer responsibility for processes to vendors both locally and globally.[14] Networking, digitisation and storage technologies have been transforming business services, particularly those with standard processes, into utility-type services that can be managed and delivered from anywhere at any time. The omnipresent nature of reliable and efficient communication networks like the Internet means that for many services there is little difference whether the service is delivered from an adjacent room or from the other side of the world. In addition, ICTs are facilitating the standardisation of service processes and allowing vendors to benefit from economies of scale. Some have argued that information can be standardised, built-to-order, assembled from components, picked, packed, stored and shipped, all using processes similar to manufacturing.[15]

The work of Philip Evans and Thomas Wurster[16] provides a useful analogy for explaining how advances in ICTs are driving services outsourcing. They have argued that every organisation is composed of processes that have both physical and information elements. The consumer buying process is composed of both physical and information elements. The physical element of the process involves purchasing the product or service, whilst the information element involves evaluating the options on offer. However, the advent of ICTs makes it possible for organisations to separate the information elements from the physical elements of service processes. Service processes such as market research, customer service and product support are rich in information content, and can be sourced from vendors both locally and offshore. For example, global vendors can offer IT-enabled customer support processes to customers anywhere in the world regardless of physical location. Separating the information element from the physical element of business processes allows an organisation to fundamentally rethink and re-engineer its operations in ways that reduce costs and enhance value for its customers.[17]

Advances in technology are also impacting highly knowledge-intensive services. Radiology in the healthcare sector provides an interesting illustration. Highly skilled physician services such as radiology have been outsourced from the USA to locations such as India. Advances in digital imaging equipment have allowed physicians to read scans remotely, which has meant that scans are now being read by English-speaking physicians anywhere in the world. Radiology services are particularly amenable to this arrangement, as they are highly knowledge-intensive and the physician does not have to be physically present to read the scan. Figure 2.6 provides an illustration of how unbundling the information and physical elements allows the scan

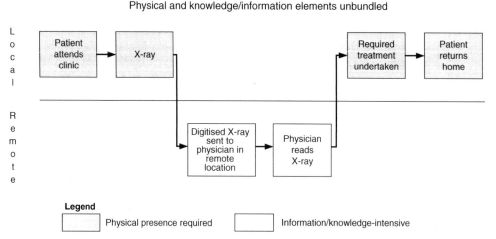

Figure 2.6   How ICTs drive outsourcing in radiology services

to be read remotely. Other potential candidates in the healthcare sector for global outsourcing include analysis of tissue samples, the reading of electro-cardiograms and the monitoring of intensive care units.

Globalisation and emerging economies

Over the last few years the external business environment has become increasingly global for many industries, with many organisations competing on a global basis.[18] The globalisation of trade has led organisations in developed nations in North America, Europe and Asia to expand the geographical scope of their business operations in terms of the markets they serve, and the locations for the creation of their products and services. At the same time, emerging economies such as India, China and Brazil have experienced economic growth and increased their positions in the global economy. Many emerging economies have growing markets with large populations and greater disposable incomes. These changes have presented organisations with significant opportunities. Organisations have been in a position to achieve greater economies of scale, share investments in research and development and marketing across their various markets and access lower-cost labour sources for both the manufacture of their products and the delivery of their services. Emerging economies such as India have proactively developed their competitiveness and encouraged large multi-national firms to locate many of their back-office services, such as IT and customer contact, to their shores. These countries have developed their attractiveness through investments in their telecommunications infrastructure, low corporation taxes, favourable business legislation, growing labour markets, competitive labour costs and a strong emphasis on education.[19]

Illustration 2.3 Economic arguments for and against global services outsourcing

Global services outsourcing has provoked much more debate and controversy than domestic outsourcing, as it has involved the transfer of jobs to foreign countries. This has led to a political backlash against global services outsourcing in the USA and Europe. States in the USA have enacted legislation to prevent parts of government contracts being transferred to offshore locations, which has led to accusations of protectionism from governments in favoured emerging economies. In addition, the outsourcing of services jobs in the developed economies has provoked a much stronger reaction from politicians and opinion-formers in the media than that associated with the global outsourcing of manufacturing jobs. Employees in services jobs are white-collar workers, often with university educations, which means they have been able to lobby politicians strongly and enjoy considerable media coverage.

Proponents of global outsourcing argue that it should be viewed as an important opportunity for a nation's businesses, consumers and company shareholders, citing an economic study carried out by the McKinsey Global Institute, which analysed the economic benefits of offshoring between the USA and India. This study estimated that for every dollar of spending that American companies transfer to India, $1.46 in new wealth is created. India receives 33 cents, through wages paid to local workers, profits earned by Indian outsourcing providers and their suppliers and additional taxes collected by the government. The US economy captures the remaining $1.13, primarily through cost savings to businesses, increased exports to India and repatriated earnings from US-owned offshore vendors.[a] Proponents of global services outsourcing propose that the following benefits can be obtained.

Cost savings. Companies can make considerable savings by offshoring service jobs, which leads to economic benefits for their home country of operation. Cost savings can be reinvested in higher-value-added jobs where companies are more productive than their offshore counterparts. Consumers in the home nation benefit through lower prices, which allows them to spend these price savings on additional products and services.

Flexibility. Companies can use global outsourcing to achieve flexibility in responding to changing market conditions. This is particularly pertinent in nations that have strict labour laws where companies are constrained in their ability to lay off workers and create new job opportunities. Companies in countries with strict labour laws, such as Germany, have had greater difficulty in adjusting their labour forces than American companies, which means they cannot react to changes in their product and service markets.

Additional revenue generation. Offshoring contributes to export growth for companies in emerging economies. Vendors in emerging economies need to buy products and services to run their operations. For example, a software development centre in India is likely to use Dell computers, Siemens telephones and Microsoft software, which benefits the US economy. It has been estimated that for every dollar spent by US companies in India, US exports to India increase by an additional five cents. These export figures for developed economies are likely to increase as vendors in emerging economies continue to grow.

Repatriated earnings. US companies have gained earnings through the growth of services providers in emerging economies. Many outsourcing vendors in India are wholly or partly owned by US companies. The growth of these vendors has allowed the parent companies to repatriate these earnings to the USA.

Move to higher-value-added activities. A potentially positive outcome of workers being displaced as a result of services outsourcing is that these workers can be redeployed into higher-value-added activities at higher labour rates in other parts of the economy. Although some displaced workers may not find new jobs quickly, proponents of global services outsourcing argue that many workers are likely to find new jobs and at higher labour rates than manufacturing jobs. A related benefit is that greater competition from global vendors can act as a stimulus for local services providers to achieve productivity improvements and higher levels of innovation.

Of course, many have challenged the view that offshore outsourcing creates mutual benefits for developed economies and emerging economies. The counter-arguments are normally based around the erosion of wage rates in developed economies, powerful corporate interests and difficulties with redeploying displaced workers.[b]

Wage erosion. Rather than allowing workers to move into higher-value-added jobs, opponents of global services outsourcing argue that it is eroding wage levels. The emergence of global labour markets for many services means that outsourcing is likely to place pressures on wage rates in developed economies. In addition, the standardisation of many outsourced processes and associated labour inputs is perceived as a further weapon to reduce the wage rates of workers. These pressures on wage levels reduce the spending power of consumers, which in turn reduces national income.

Shifting bargaining power. The shifting power of organisational stakeholders means that the interests of workers have been diluted. Many companies have shifted from a position of looking after the welfare of their workers to giving greater attention to other stakeholders, such as shareholders. Cost savings attained by companies from global services outsourcing are often driven by the need to deliver shareholder value at the expense of the welfare of the companies' workers. The advent of global labour markets for services has reduced the bargaining power of workers in relation to their employers. Global outsourcing allows organisations to access skilled labour in countries that offer few employment options and weaker regulatory environments than their home-country base. Some have argued that governments are now promoting corporate rather than national interests, and further diluting the power of unions to challenge the global services outsourcing phenomenon.

Redeployment difficulties. Opponents of global outsourcing have challenged the view that displaced workers can be redeployed into higher-value-added activities. Indeed, there is evidence to show that workers have considerable difficulties with finding new jobs and are often employed at lower wage levels. In a study of workers displaced by imports in the USA between 1979 and 1999, it was found that only 63.4 per cent of workers displaced across all sectors were re-employed, with an average weekly earnings *loss* of about 13 per cent. The study found that only 69 per cent of workers who lost their jobs in sectors other than manufacturing found new jobs within six months, with earnings losses of 4 per cent. Indeed, offshore services outsourcing poses significant challenges to policymakers in developed economies to enhance redeployment opportunities for displaced workers.

Notes:
[a] Farrell, D. and Agarwal, V. (2003). Offshoring and Beyond, *McKinsey Quarterly*, 4, 24–35.
[b] Levy, D. (2005). Offshoring in the New Political Economy, *Journal of Management Studies*, 42(3), 685–93.

Sources: Farrell, D. (2005). Offshoring: Value Creation through Economic Change, *Journal of Management Studies*, 42(3), 675–83; Levy (2005), see note *b* above.

Consumers demanding more for less

Consumers are more demanding as they become more knowledgeable on issues such as price, reliability and availability. Consumers are more mobile in terms of ease of access to alternative sources of supply as a result of increased competition in many markets and the advent of the Internet. With global access through the Internet to more products and services than ever before and with instant communications, typical constraints, such as time and distance, are rapidly disappearing. As a result, the loyalty of consumers to products and vendors is diminishing. Consequently, organisations are being forced to be more responsive to customer needs in a range of areas. Such changes are not only affecting commercial organisations but are also having major implications for public sector organisations. Consumers are increasingly demanding higher levels of service and responsiveness from public sector organisations. With the consumer demanding a more information-enriched and interactive relationship with commercial organisations, public sector organisations are having to respond with innovations in the way in which they interface with citizens in order to achieve greater accessibility and efficiency. In the past, many public sector organisations have been 'protected' from the harsh commercial reality of competition and an ever increasingly demanding citizen. However, in the future, the expectations of consumers will continue to rise with the increasing use of online trading, which allows business to be conducted at any time of the day.

The shareholder value model

Organisations have been under pressure to provide greater value for shareholders, and have been increasingly using outsourcing to reduce investments in capital assets to enhance shareholder value. Shareholders often react positively to outsourcing, since improved profit levels can be achieved with lower fixed investments. The shareholder value model has been extremely influential in driving this trend. Shareholder value is measured by the efficient use of capital invested in a company, and the costs of servicing it. The shareholder value concept increased in prominence in the 1980s through the widespread acceptance of the economic value-added (EVA) formula developed by the consulting firm Stern Stewart in the USA. EVA is defined as the after-tax cash flow generated by a business, less the cost of the capital required to generate that cash flow. When a company invests in new equipment it has to determine how much additional profit is required to pay for the investment. EVA can be improved through increasing profitability, lowering costs or deploying capital more effectively. As shareholders have used EVA to assess the company value, managers have increasingly used outsourcing as a means of improving this measure. For example, the economic benefits of outsourcing can be achieved by reducing costs in a process, by releasing fixed capital commitment in that process and/or by increasing profitability through outsourcing the process. Therefore, the logic of EVA involves outsourcing as many non-core processes as possible to increase profitability.

Corporate restructuring

Corporate restructuring has become an important strategy for organisations to improve performance. Since the 1980s, many organisations have used corporate restructuring programmes to refocus their operations, to remove cost and generate revenue.[20] Outsourcing is a common element of many corporate restructuring efforts. Restructuring often involves focusing on core areas that are critical to competitive advantage, and outsourcing areas that are resource-intensive and have little impact on competitive advantage. Back-office functions such as IT, HR and F&A have become targets for outsourcing as a result of corporate restructuring programmes. Many back-office function tasks are duplicated across different geographical locations. This situation has been further compounded as organisations have embarked upon mergers and acquisitions and taken over larger numbers of support staff. Outsourcing and shared services arrangements in particular have allowed organisations to consolidate and re-engineer business processes from geographically dispersed business units into single service centres. Developments in ICTs, business process methodologies, and vendors with an increasing range of capabilities have further driven this trend.

2.7 The arguments for services outsourcing

There are a number of compelling arguments for outsourcing. Outsourcing allows an organisation to concentrate on areas that drive competitive advantage, and outsource peripheral processes where it can leverage the specialist skills of vendors. External vendors are often highly specialised in the creation and delivery of services, allowing them to achieve lower costs than the outsourcing firm. Organisations can achieve considerable cost reductions through benefiting from vendor cost advantages based on economies of scale, experience and location. As well as reducing costs, organisations are increasingly relying on specialist vendors to transform process performance.

In the past, organisations attempted to control the majority of processes internally on the assumption that controlling supply eliminates the possibility of short-run service disruptions, or demand imbalances in its customer markets.[21] However, such a strategy is both inflexible and inherently fraught with risks. As a result of cost pressures, rapid changes in technology and increasingly sophisticated and demanding consumers, it is very difficult for organisations to control and excel at all the processes that create competitive advantage. Outsourcing can provide an organisation with greater flexibility, especially, for example, in the sourcing of services that include rapidly changing technologies. Such a strategy allows an organisation to shift the burden of risk and uncertainty on to vendors.

Many organisations are reluctant to outsource because they fear they may lose the capability for innovation in the future. However, significant opportunities exist in many supply markets to leverage the capabilities of specialist vendors. Rather than attempt to replicate the capabilities of vendors, it is often better to use outsourcing to fully exploit the vendors' investments, innovations and specialist capabilities. In addition, organisations can build relationships with vendors that deliver competitive advantage. Through outsourcing certain processes and then building idiosyncratic and valuable relationships with vendors, organisations can innovate and reduce transaction costs. For example, the client–vendor relationship may facilitate further learning and the cross-fertilisation of ideas that drive innovation.

Illustration 2.4 Specialisation and the vendor advantage

Vendors often enjoy considerable advantages over outsourcing organisations as a result of the gains from specialisation. Services providers such as IBM, Accenture and InfoSys possess economies of scale and scope through developing technology, products, personnel and client and vendor relationships.

These vendors can take on investment and development costs, whilst sharing the risks among many customers, and thereby reducing supply costs for all customers. Firms in a range of industries have been reducing costs by outsourcing processes to specialist vendors. Many banks in the financial services industry have outsourced high-volume transaction processing functions such as electronic payments and cheque processing to vendors with greater economies of scale in order to reduce the cost of each transaction. Modularisation and standardisation have also allowed vendors to further specialise, as large organisations have unbundled one business process from another and separated IT functions from business processes. Supply chain modularisation in the electronics industry has led to the unbundling of design, engineering and manufacturing processes for many manufacturers, and allowed contract manufacturers to aggregate manufacturing capacity and in turn reduce costs.

Vendors can develop capabilities as a result of complementarities in organisational design. Management practices in one outsourcing-related capability can strengthen capabilities in other areas. In IT development projects, developing capabilities in project management methods can strengthen technical capabilities and develop a better understanding of client requirements. For example, vendors in the Indian software industry have developed important client-specific capabilities through repeated interactions with clients across a range of projects over time in different geographical locations. Repeated interactions with clients have allowed vendors to acquire tacit knowledge of the client's business and operating procedures, and also to exploit this knowledge in projects for other clients. Vendors have further developed their project management capabilities through deliberate and persistent investments in infrastructure and systems that improve the firms' software development process. Internal IT functions in large diverse organisations are not in a position to compete with these capabilities. Although the IT function can develop its own internal IT capabilities, this can often conflict with optimising its core business processes.

In addition, the IT function is often viewed as a cost centre and not an area where the company should invest in developing internal capabilities. To further exacerbate the situation, the IT function cannot offer the salary levels to compete with external vendors, and companies find it extremely difficult to recruit skilled professionals for their internal IT departments. Career development opportunities for employees in specialist functions such as IT in large diverse organisations are often restricted to a single function. Vendors are also able to recruit and retain scarce information technology and business process experts who may prefer a more specialised and intensive knowledge environment. Specialist vendors offer opportunities to employees to develop their skills and knowledge through exposure to a wide variety of project and client environments.

Sources: Ethiraj, S., Kale, P., Krishnan, M. and Singh, J. (2005). Where Do Capabilities Come From and Why Do They Matter? A Study in the Software Industry, *Strategic Management Journal*, 26, 25–45; Shi, Y. (2007). Today's Solution and Tomorrow's Problem: The Business Process Outsourcing Risk and Management Puzzle, *California Management Review*, 49(3), 27–44.

2.8 The arguments against services outsourcing

Although the trend towards outsourcing has been growing rapidly, it is not without its pitfalls. Outsourcing can lead to the loss of critical skills and of the potential for innovation in the future – sometimes referred to as 'hollowing out'. In the long term, an organisation needs to maintain innovative capacity in a number of key processes in order to exploit new opportunities in its target customer markets. Where an organisation has outsourced too many critical processes, its ability to innovate may be severely diminished. These risks can become more pronounced when the objectives of the outsourcing company and the vendor are in conflict. For example, the client may decide to establish a short-term contract with a vendor to obtain the lowest price and keep the vendor in a weak position. However, this will seriously undermine any incentive for the vendor to pass on any benefits associated with the innovation to the client. Vendors can also become competitors in the future once they obtain the requisite knowledge and skills to deliver the entire service requirements of which the outsourced process is a significant element.

There is evidence to suggest that when organisations outsource to save costs, costs do not decrease as expected and, in some cases, increase. When organisations outsource with cost motives, there is normally an early anticipation of cash benefits and long-term cost savings. However, many organisations fail to account for future costs and in particular for those of managing the outsourcing arrangement. In addition, organisations often assume that vendors will improve performance in processes which have traditionally caused problems. However, it is erroneous to assume that once the process is outsourced the problem will disappear. Prior to outsourcing, it is more prudent to understand the causes of poor performance and why vendors can achieve higher levels of performance in the process.

Organisations can encounter significant risks when they use vendors for processes that they have performed internally in the past. Overdependency on a particular vendor can lead to the threat of opportunism from vendors. Opportunistic behaviour can lead to the vendor extracting more from the relationship by shirking on agreed requirements or withholding information on future price increases. Organisations often do not monitor changes in the supply market as the outsourcing arrangement develops. When an organisation chooses to outsource it may do so on the basis of the presence of competition among a number of vendors in the supply market. However, the balance of power may shift towards the supply market if there has been consolidation of a number of smaller vendors into a few large vendors. Many organisations fail to recognise that managing an external vendor requires a different set of skills from those associated with managing an internal department. Vendors in outsourcing markets are extremely adept at exploiting any naïveté on the part of the outsourcing organisation in areas such as contract negotiation and relationship management.

Outsourcing has significant organisational change implications, which are often ignored in favour of the need to reduce costs. The effective management of organisational change implications is crucial as employees view outsourcing as a denigration of their performance, which can often lead to industrial action. Outsourcing can involve the redeployment of staff within the outsourcing organisation or the transfer of staff to the vendor. Outsourcing has a negative impact upon the job security and loyalty of employees even when they retain their positions in the outsourcing organisation. The perspectives and responses of employees at all levels and positions can have a significant impact on the successful implementation of strategic change processes.

2.9 Influences on the mobility of service processes

There is much debate in both the academic literature and popular media on the types of occupations in developed economies at risk of outsourcing to foreign locations. Factors such as labour costs, the impact of ICTs, and low-skilled versus high-skilled occupations are introduced to explain the types of job at risk from global outsourcing. However, much of the debate in this area fails to explain fully which jobs are being impacted, and often makes sweeping simple generalisations. Some commentators have attempted to explain this phenomenon by ranking industries that are at greatest threat from global outsourcing. The distinction between low-skilled and high-skilled jobs has also been used as a means of classifying jobs being outsourced, the assumption being that lower-skilled jobs are at a higher risk than higher-skilled jobs. However, in reality, higher-skilled jobs such as research and development and management consultancy are increasingly being outsourced to foreign locations, whilst lower-skilled jobs such as hairdressing and cleaning are still being performed locally. In order to understand more fully the mobility of service jobs, it is necessary to understand both service design principles and regulatory and political and security and confidentiality influences. These influences are now considered.

Labour intensity

Service processes differ in labour intensity levels. An organisation with high labour intensity involves a relatively small amount of plant and equipment investment, and a considerably higher investment of labour time, effort and cost. Professional services such as management consultancy and software development are examples of high labour intensity businesses. At the other end of the spectrum, low labour intensive organisations are characterised by relatively low levels of labour cost relative to investments in equipment, and examples include hospitals and communications organisations. Although these organisations have a high number of employees, they also have a significant amount of expensive capital equipment, which increases the capital intensity level. Clearly, labour-intensive organisations place particular emphasis on attempting to reduce labour costs by outsourcing to locations with lower labour costs. However, there are other characteristics of the service that will influence this strategy.

Customer contact

The production of services processes differs from manufacturing processes in that many services are co-produced with the customer, i.e. production and consumption occur simultaneously. This has important implications for the mobility of service processes. An important construct for understanding this influence is that of customer contact. Services scholars have proposed a theory of customer contact to explain this phenomenon.[22] For example, Chase examined the distinction between high and low contact processes, and defined the level of customer contact as the ratio of time during which a customer is in direct contact with the service facility to the total time required for the creation of the service. Making this distinction allowed Chase to provide a classification of service systems, and provide guidelines on the design of service delivery systems. In particular, this has led to the distinction between back-office and front-office service processes, which is widely employed in global services outsourcing.

Back-office services consist of processes that require little or no contact with the customer, and these types of service are the focus of many organisations in their outsourcing efforts. The separation of the back-office process from customer contact means the process can be carried out in any location. In addition, organisations have sought to achieve efficiencies in back-office processes by adopting principles associated with mass production. This has involved standardising tasks and segmenting processes into clearly specified tasks to allow for limited spans of control and close supervision, which reduces both skill requirements and training time. These principles have allowed companies to transfer responsibility for such processes to vendors regardless of location.[23]

Front-office services consist of processes that are performed while the customer is present. Customers actively interact and are involved directly in the delivery of front-office services. Front-office processes are often viewed as a way in which organisations can differentiate themselves from competitors. Front-office personnel interact directly with the customer and can be a significant influence on the overall satisfaction and reputation of the organisation. Organisations place particular emphasis on both empowering and training staff to enhance the level of service delivered to customers. Consequently, front-office services have not been outsourced to the same extent as back-office service processes. However, organisations have used outsourcing to achieve cost reductions in some front-office processes. Many companies have used foreign customer contact centres to provide after-sales services such as help-desk support to customers.

Service customisation

Service customisation is closely related to customer contact. Services can be either highly customised or standardised. Services tend to be highly customised when there is a lot of overlap between production and consumption. Professional services such as management consultancy and software development are often highly customised services. Clearly, service customisation will impact upon the ability of a company to outsource the process. The high degree of overlap between production and consumption for some services will make global outsourcing difficult. In the medical field, physicians provide customised services and may have to modify the service provided as circumstances change. However, advances in ICTs have made the outsourcing of customised services possible in areas such as software development and research and development.

The need for physical presence

It has already been shown that the need for high customer contact can be a significant influence on the mobility of a service process. It has also been shown that ICTs can allow high customer contact processes to be outsourced to global vendors. However, the need for physical contact in the production and consumption of the service can be an absolute impediment to global outsourcing. Many services require physical contact, and therefore cannot be replaced by ICTs. Blinder has identified a number of service types that fit into this category including face-to-face contact services (child care), 'high touch' services (nursing), high levels of personal trust services (psychotherapy) and location-specific services (retailing).[24] These categories apply to many service sectors including the leisure and hospitality sectors, where the customer has to be physically present to consume the service.

Regulatory and political influences

The regulatory environment in which an organisation operates can either hinder or encourage global outsourcing. Some countries have been using existing legislation, or enacting new legislation, to prevent certain services from being transferred to foreign locations. A number of states in the USA have stipulated in government contracts that the work should be carried out locally rather than globally to protect local jobs. Governments in emerging economies have labelled such actions as protectionist. However, powerful lobby groups in certain service sectors can encourage governments to implement such measures. For example, in response to the outsourcing of healthcare and legal services in the USA, lobby groups in these sectors have been making efforts to thwart this trend through tactics such as stipulating that physicians and lawyers should be certified by state officials before being qualified to practise in certain states.[25] However, few sectors have such protection and in an era where public sector organisations are being forced to reduce costs, there will be pressures for governments to enact legislation that will allow certain services to be outsourced.

Security and confidentiality influences

Security and confidentiality issues are often impediments to the outsourcing of service processes. Companies may decide not to outsource certain human resource functions because of data protection concerns.[26] Although companies are increasingly outsourcing aspects of the human resource function, there is the potential for employee data to be compromised at foreign locations, and the disclosure of such data can lead to identity theft. There have been instances of employees in foreign call centres fraudulently accessing customer credit card details. Such compromises can lead to significant financial loss and damage to company reputation. Where organisations cannot guarantee both security and confidentiality, service processes will have to be performed locally. Confidentiality concerns in the healthcare sector in the USA have prevented some transcription services being outsourced to emerging economies, because the privacy concerns of hospitals and physicians cannot be overcome.

These factors that influence the mobility of service processes can be placed on a spectrum, as shown in Figure 2.7. When considering the mobility of service processes, it is important to consider the relationship between each of the factors. Although companies will focus efforts on outsourcing highly labour-intensive processes, the need for both high customer contact and customisation in the service delivery process will stymie such efforts. Some services such as hairdressing and taxi-driving are immune from the threat of offshoring because of the need for physical presence. However, the influence of some factors on the mobility of service processes is likely to evolve, and allow more services processes to be outsourced in the future. Rapid advances in ICTs will continue to make the remote development and customisation of services possible, as production and consumption are increasingly separated. Video-conferencing and project management approaches allow many aspects of software development to be carried out remotely. Moreover, regulatory and political pressures can change as governments change and in response to constraints on public sector spending.

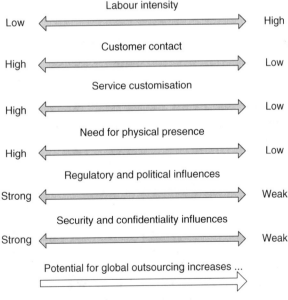

Figure 2.7   Influences on the mobility of service processes

Illustration 2.5 The mobility of information technology services in the global economy

The outsourcing of IT jobs to foreign locations has received considerable media attention in developed economies. IT jobs are viewed as being under threat because of the ability to deliver IT services digitally independent of location, and the increasing capabilities of lower-cost offshore locations. However, differentiating between different aspects of the software development process, and introducing the factors that influence service mobility, illustrates how some areas are more at risk than others. Routine labour-intensive and low-skilled tasks that require no physical contact and limited customisation for the client have been outsourced extensively. Examples include help-desk support for users and system testing. Other areas such as programming that require higher skill levels have also been extensively outsourced.

Programmers write, test and maintain the software that drives IT applications for the client. The project nature of the software development process allows the programming element to be separated from the client requirements analysis phase. Systems analysts determine the requirements, and derive the specifications for the IT application through working closely with the client. Programmers can then write and test the software remotely, and any queries can be resolved through email and telephone contact. Although programmers require a higher level of training than help-desk staff, the declining need for physical contact with the client means writing and testing software remotely is a straightforward area to outsource. In addition, as organisations increasingly transfer entire business processes to remote locations, the tasks associated with developing and maintaining the supporting IT infrastructure have also been transferred to remote vendors.

Although many IT jobs have been outsourced globally, there are many areas of IT that cannot be performed remotely. Network administration is one area that is not suitable for moving to foreign locations. Network administrators install, configure, maintain and administer the physical network infrastructure and operating systems on site in an organisation. The hands-on nature of these tasks, the increasing responsibilities in areas such as network security, and rapidly changing technologies require the need for physical presence in an organisation. In addition, the network administrator has to make frequent changes to the network to improve speed and deal with security issues. Specialised IT skills in the areas of project management and systems integration are other areas that cannot be performed remotely. Organisations that have outsourced IT functions require personnel that can manage contracts, build relationships with vendors, and co-ordinate different phases of development projects globally. These tasks require physical presence in the client site and also a high level of customisation, as client needs may change throughout the application development process. Confidentiality and security concerns have also proved to be strong impediments to the offshore outsourcing of some aspects of IT services. For example, organisations often employ security experts locally to protect confidential data and information systems from attack, and allow emergencies to be addressed quickly.

Sources: Shao, B. and David, J. (2007). The Impact of Offshore Outsourcing on IT Workers in Developed Countries, *Communications of the ACM*, 50(2), 89–94; Stack, M. and Downing, R. (2005). Another Look at Offshoring: Which Jobs are at Risk and Why? *Business Horizons*, 48, 513–23.

2.10 How service characteristics create outsourcing challenges

Labour cost comparisons between client and vendors are common elements of the outsourcing decision in both services and manufacturing. However, services outsourcing poses a number of challenges that are not present in manufacturing outsourcing. These challenges arise out of the differences between services and products as shown in Table 2.3. The distinctive characteristics of services increase the challenges of outsourcing in a number of areas.

In contrast to manufacturing processes where the outputs are tangible and the product specification is explicit, many service processes have intangible elements, which make service specification difficult and hard to articulate to vendors.[27] Intangible elements are difficult to standardise, making quality very dependent on the individual delivering the service. Language and cultural differences further exacerbate this problem in global services outsourcing, as it can lead to employees in vendors misinterpreting and failing to understand client requirements. For example, when a US financial services organisation outsourced the development of its loan processing information system to an offshore vendor, staff in the vendor misunderstood the term 'mortgage' as a result of language differences. Domestic vendors with the same culture and language can understand the explicit and implicit elements of clients' requirements. Where the service has a significant level of intangibility, the client has to expend considerable effort in drafting very detailed requirements for the foreign vendor in order to limit the potential for any misunderstandings.

In contrast to manufacturing where production and consumption can be separated, the customer is part of the service process, which means that careful attention has to be given to managing the interface between production and consumption. Although developments in ICTs and project management techniques have allowed companies to separate service consumption from production, outsourcing services such as software development requires considerable interaction between vendor and client staff in service production and consumption. Facilitating client and vendor

Table 2.3 The impact of product and service characteristics on outsourcing

Service characteristic	Impact on outsourcing	Product	Service
Intangibility	Expectations	Specifications are precise	Vague and imprecise service level agreements
	Predictability of demand	Dependent on the accuracy of forecasts for final customer demand	Vary with project scope
	Problem resolution	Formal process, clear responsibilities	Lack of established processes, and more subjectivity
	Cost	Pre-negotiated per unit and easy to determine in advance	Dependent on changing project scope and requirements
	Payment	Match receipts with purchase orders, verifiable	Bills submitted without tangible evidence
	Verification of contract completion	Physical evidence through delivery	Internal sign-off
Inseparability	Points of contact	Few points of contact; limited or no customer contact	Increased interaction both in a business-to-business and business-to-consumer context
	Physical separation of client and vendor facilities	Physical distance between client and vendor	Service created at point of use; tight coupling
Heterogeneity	Quality Consistency of output	Measurable, pre-specified Clear specifications, tight quality control	Subjective, user-dependent Services vary with the vendor, and broader specifications with a range of acceptable outcomes

Sources: Ellram, L., Tate, W. and Billington, C. (2007). Services Supply Management: The Next Frontier for Improved Organisational Performance, *California Management Review*, 49(4), 44–66; Ellram, L., Tate, W. and Billington, C. (2004). Understanding and Managing the Services Supply Chain, *Journal of Supply Chain Management*, 40(4), 17–32; Allen, S. and Chandrashekar, A. (2000). Outsourcing Services: The Contract is Just the Beginning, *Business Horizons*, 43(2), 25–34.

interaction in real-time and over a long distance is extremely challenging. Where the vendor is in a different time zone, the client has to employ project managers round-the-clock to manage the vendor, which is an additional cost over in-house sourcing or domestic outsourcing.

In contrast to manufacturing, the intangible nature of services makes it difficult to specify and measure performance objectively in services outsourcing, which creates a number of challenges. Where the client cannot specify and measure performance, there is the potential for opportunism, as the vendor might shirk on its responsibilities. Some clients have compounded this problem through inviting vendors to suggest performance measures. Often the vendor suggests performance measures that are biased in its favour, and also uses it as an opportunity to offer additional services that the client does not require.

Monitoring service quality is a further outsourcing challenge, which arises out of the heterogeneous nature of services. Many service processes are characterised by heterogeneity, as both the vendor and customer interact in the service delivery process, which creates the potential for variation in service quality.[28] The customer, the vendor and the surroundings are all sources of variation. Even in the case of a highly standardised service, maintaining a consistent quality of service to the customer is extremely challenging. Service quality problems with foreign vendors have received a lot of attention in the popular media, and some companies have become concerned about the impact upon their reputation and competitive position. It has been difficult for companies to assess the true impact of poor quality of service in areas such as call centre services. Poor service quality in customer contact services can alienate existing customers, and also hinder the company's attempts to attract new customers. Indeed, this has led some companies in developed economies, such as Aviva and Dell, to advertise that they use domestic call centres, as a result of poor perceptions among customers of foreign call centres.[29]

Service quality is relevant in a number of services outsourcing contexts including: (1) the vendor's responsiveness to client needs in an outsourced development project; (2) internal users of an IT system developed by an external vendor; and (3) customers of the client organisation receiving services such as technical support from vendor staff. Companies have been employing a number of instruments to measure service quality in outsourcing arrangements.[30] Many of these instruments measure service quality on the basis of the perceptions and expectations of the customer. Customer satisfaction depends on how the perception of service quality meets the expectations of the customer. Where there is a significant gap between the perceptions and expectations of the customer, the vendor will receive a lower service quality rating. The most prominent model is the SERVQUAL model, which has evolved from its application in the retail industry.[31] The SERVQUAL model was developed by Parasuraman,

Zeithaml and Berry, and included ten dimensions of service quality comprising reliability, responsiveness, competence, access, courtesy, communication, credibility, security, understanding the customer, and tangibles (such as physical facilities). The client can employ some of these dimensions to assess customer satisfaction levels with vendors, and internal employees' service quality ratings of IT systems developed by external vendors.

2.11 Summary implications

- There has been significant growth in the trading of business services. Organisations have been using services to complement core product offerings, and have diversified into services to achieve further growth. Using business process redesign techniques along with ICTs, organisations have been restructuring fragmented processes to improve process performance, and to deliver services to customers and internal employees.

- As well as outsourcing routine processes, organisations have been outsourcing more complex processes, as vendors have upgraded their initial capabilities in cost reduction to transforming process performance for clients. Organisations have been selecting a number of configurations to manage services outsourcing arrangements both locally and globally. Typical sourcing models for managing global services outsourcing arrangements include fee-for-service, joint venture, build–operate–transfer and captive.

- There are a number of drivers of services outsourcing including the business process perspective, developments in ICTs, globalisation and emerging economies, consumers demanding more for less, the shareholder value model and corporate restructuring programmes.

- The arguments for services outsourcing include focusing on areas that drive competitive advantage, reducing costs through vendor cost advantages, leveraging specialist vendor skills to improve performance, achieving flexibility and building relationships with vendors to drive innovation and reduce transaction costs. The arguments against services outsourcing include the loss of critical skills and potential innovation, cost increases, vendor opportunism and failure to consider the organisational change implications.

- Service design factors such as labour intensity, customer contact, service customisation and the need for physical contact are important influences on the mobility of services in the global economy. Regulatory and political influences and security and confidentiality also influence the mobility of services.

- Services outsourcing poses a number of challenges on account of the distinctive characteristics of services. The intangible nature of many services makes specifying requirements clearly to vendors difficult, and increases the difficulties of specifying and measuring performance levels objectively in services outsourcing. Careful attention has to be given to managing the interface between service production and consumption in many services processes, particularly where the vendor is located remotely from the client.

Notes and references

1 Sako, M. (2006). Outsourcing and Offshoring: Implications for Productivity of Business Services, *Oxford Review of Economic Policy*, 22(4), 499–512; Abramovsky, L., Griffith, R. and Sako, M. (2004). Offshoring of Business Services and its Impact on the UK Economy, Advanced Institute of Management Research Report.

2 Sawhney, M., Balasubramanian, S. and Krishnan, V. (2004). Creating Growth with Services, *Sloan Management Review*, 45(2), 34–43.

3 There are other classifications of global services outsourcing. Kedia and Lahiri have identified three types of outsourcing: tactical, strategic and transformation. These three types are based on the objectives of outsourcing ranging from cost reduction to significant changes in performance. See Kedia, B. and Lahiri, S. (2007). International Outsourcing of Services: Expanding the Research Agenda, *Journal of International Management*, 13, 22–37.

4 Metters, R. and Verma, R. (2008). History of Offshoring Knowledge Services, *Journal of Operations Management*, 26(2), 141–7.

5 For further information, see Robinson, M. and Kalakota, R. (2005). *Offshore Outsourcing: Business Models, ROI and Best Practices*, 2nd edn, Alpharetta, Ga.: Mivar Press.

6 Rottman, J. and Lacity, M. (2004). Proven Practices for IT Offshore Outsourcing, *Cutter Consortium*, 5(12), 1–27.

7 Youngdahl, W. and Ramaswamy, K. (2008). Offshoring Knowledge and Service Work: A Conceptual Model and Research Agenda, *Journal of Operations Management*, 26(2), 212–21.

8 Jagersma, P. and van Gorp, D. (2007). Redefining the Paradigm of Global Competition: Offshoring of Service Firms, *Business Strategy Series*, 8(1), 35–42; Vestring, T., Rouse, T. and Reinert, U. (2005). Hedge Your Offshoring Bets, *Sloan Management Review*, 46(3), 27–9.

9 Aron, R. and Singh, J. V. (2005). Getting Offshoring Right, *Harvard Business Review*, 83(12), 135–43.

10 Rottman, J. and Lacity, M. (2006). Proven Practices for Effectively Offshoring IT Work, *Sloan Management Review*, 47(3), 56–63.

11 Hammer, M. (2002). Process Management and the Future of Six Sigma, *Sloan Management Review*, 43(2), 26–32.

12 Davenport, T. (2005). The Coming Commoditization of Processes, *Harvard Business Review*, 83(6), 100–8.

13 Mani, D., Barua, A. and Whinston, A. (2006). Successfully Governing Business Process Outsourcing Relationships, *MIS Quarterly Executive*, 5(1), 15–29.

14 For a discussion on the impact of electronic commerce on outsourcing, see Kotabe, M., Mol, M. and Murray, J. (2008). Outsourcing, Performance, and the Role of E-Commerce: A Dynamic Perspective, *Industrial Marketing Management*, 37, 37–45.

15 Karmarkar, U. (2004). Will You Survive the Services Revolution? *Harvard Business Review*, 82(6), 101–7.

16 Evans, P. and Wurster, T. (1999a). Getting Real About Virtual Commerce, *Harvard Business Review*, 77(6), 85–94; Evans, P. and Wurster, T. (1999b). *Blown to Bits: How the New Economics of Information Transforms Strategy*, Boston: Harvard Business School Press.

17 See Youngdahl and Ramaswamy (2008) in note 7 above.

18 Useful references on globalisation include Stiglitz, J. (2002). *Globalisation and its Discontents*, London: Penguin; and Thompson, J. (2001). Globalisation: Its Defenders and Dissenters, *Business and Society Review*, 106(2), 170–9.

19 For a summary of emerging economies and specialist outsourcing services offered to clients, see Javalgi, R., Dixit, A. and Scherer, R. (2009). Outsourcing to Emerging Markets: Theoretical Perspectives and Policy Implications, *Journal of International Management*, 15, 156–68.

20 Bergh, D., Johnson, R. and Dewitt, R. (2008). Restructuring through Spin-off or Sell-off: Transforming Information Asymmetries into Financial Gain, *Strategic Management Journal*, 29, 133–48; Pettigrew, A., Whittington, R., Melin, L., Sanchez-Runde, C., van den Bosch, F. and Numagami, T. (2003), *Innovative Forms of Organizing*, London: Sage.

21 Shi, Y. (2007). Today's Solution and Tomorrow's Problem: The Business Process Outsourcing Risk and Management Puzzle, *California Management Review*, 49(3), 27–44.

22 References on key service classification models include Apte, U. and Mason, R. (1995). Global Disaggregation of Information-Intensive Services, *Management Science*, 41(7), 1250–62; Schmenner, R. (1986). How can Service Business Survive and Prosper? *Sloan Management Review*, 27(3), 21–32; Shostack, G. (1984). Designing Services that Deliver, *Harvard Business Review*, 62(1), 133–9; and Chase, R. (1981). The Customer Contact Approach to Services: Theoretical Bases and Practical Extensions, *Operations Research*, 21(4), 698–705.

23 See Youngdahl and Ramaswamy (2008) in note 7 above.

24 Blinder, A. (2006). Offshoring: The Next Industrial Revolution? *Foreign Affairs*, 85(2), 113–28.

25 Stack, M. and Downing, R. (2005). Another Look at Offshoring: Which Jobs are at Risk and Why? *Business Horizons*, 48, 513–23.

26 Shao, B. and David, J. (2007). The Impact of Offshore Outsourcing on IT Workers in Developed Countries, *Communications of the ACM*, 50(2), 89–94.

27 Stringfellow, A., Teagarden, M. and Nie, W. (2008). Invisible Costs in Offshoring Services Work, *Journal of Operations Management*, 26(2), 164–79.

28 Van Looy, B., Gemmel, P. and van Dierdonck, R. (2003). *Services Management: An Integrated Approach*, London: FT Prentice Hall.

29 For a discussion of this trend in the UK, see Winterman, D. (2007). Just Returning Your Call, *BBC News*, 14 February, http://news.bbc.co.uk/1/hi/magazine/6353491.stm; and Cave, A. (2007). Norwich Union Returns Call Centre Work to UK, *Daily Telegraph*, 29 January, www.telegraph.co.uk/finance/2803424/Norwich-Union-returns-call-centre-work-to-UK.html.

30 Allen, S. and Chandrashekar, A. (2000). Outsourcing Services: The Contract is Just the Beginning, *Business Horizons*, 43(2), 25–34.

31 For an overview of the SERVQUAL model, see Parasuraman, A., Zeithaml, V. and Berry, L. (1985). A Conceptual Model of Service Quality and Implications for Further Research, *Journal of Marketing*, 49, Fall, 45–50; and Parasuraman, A., Zeithaml, V. and Berry, L. (1988). Servqual: A Multiple-Item Scale for Measuring Consumer Perceptions of Service Quality, *Journal of Retailing*, 64, Spring, 12–40. For a critique of the SERVQUAL model, see Buttle, F. (1996). Servqual: Review, Critique, Research Agenda, *European Journal of Marketing*, 30(1), 8–32.

Recommended key reading

Blinder, A. (2006). Offshoring: The Next Industrial Revolution? *Foreign Affairs*, 85(2), 113–28. This paper discusses the effects of the offshoring of service jobs to emerging economies, and argues that the information age has expanded the scope of tradable services and changed the distinctions among labour skills. It is argued that offshoring will not lead to mass unemployment, but a shift towards personal services industries in developed economies.

Sako, M. (2006). Outsourcing and Offshoring: Implications for Productivity of Business Services, *Oxford Review of Economic Policy*, 22(4), 499–512. This paper reviews the implications of outsourcing and offshoring for the productivity of business services in the UK. It is shown how productivity is enhanced through specialisation, standardisation, process consolidation, and the shift towards higher value-added processes. It is argued that future productivity depends on two sources of productivity enhancement – greater standardisation, and capturing value from customised solutions.

Stack, M. and Downing, R. (2005). Another Look at Offshoring: Which Jobs are at Risk and Why? *Business Horizons*, 48, 513–23. This paper provides a framework for examining the types of healthcare and information technology jobs at risk from offshoring, and argues that the model can be applied to other industries to better understand jobs under threat from offshoring.

Youngdahl, W. and Ramaswamy, K. (2008). Offshoring Knowledge and Service Work: A Conceptual Model and Research Agenda, *Journal of Operations Management*, 26(2), 212–21. This paper presents a model that draws upon service operations literature to conceptualise the offshoring of knowledge and service work, and identifies the associated challenges.

Making the services outsourcing decision

3.1 Introduction

Outsourcing has become a critical strategic decision that allows organisations to develop and leverage the capabilities required to compete in today's global business environment. Leading firms have been adopting more sophisticated outsourcing strategies, and have been outsourcing core processes such as design, engineering, customer service and marketing. These organisations have been benefiting greatly from accessing the specialist capabilities of vendors in a range of business processes.[1] Leveraging the capabilities of more capable vendors allows organisations to outsource more critical business processes and enhance their own core capabilities that drive competitive advantage. However, many organisations are failing to capitalise on the opportunities offered by outsourcing, and often rush into outsourcing without fully understanding the complexities and risks. Selecting the most appropriate sourcing strategy encompasses a number of critical issues including the implications for competitive advantage, vendor capabilities, risks in the supply market and achieving a balance between the use of formal contracts and collaborative relationships.

This chapter presents a framework for identifying suitable outsourcing strategies for business processes.[2] Integrating transaction cost economics (TCE) and the resource-based view (RBV), the framework provides a mechanism for understanding which processes should be kept internal and which should be outsourced, based on both organisational capability and opportunism considerations. The chapter is structured as follows. An overview of TCE and the RBV is presented, along with a rationale for integrating both theories into outsourcing decision-making. An overview of the outsourcing methodology is provided, followed by the implications of the potential sourcing strategies and appropriate outsourcing relationships. Throughout this analysis, illustrations are provided of the sourcing strategies and outsourcing relationships in practice. Finally, summary implications are presented.

3.2 Transaction cost economics and the resource-based view

Two influential theories in the study of outsourcing have been TCE and the RBV. TCE specifies the conditions under which an organisation should perform a process internally within its boundaries, referred to as hierarchies, and the conditions suitable for outsourcing the process, referred to as markets.[3] Hierarchies involve performing processes inside the firm, using management authority to make and execute decisions. Markets involve relatively short-term, contracting relationships between independent clients and vendors. The needs of the client are non-specific and the process can therefore be sourced from a number of vendors. The logic of TCE is that a company should make the outsourcing decision on the basis of reducing production and transaction costs.

Production costs refer to the direct costs involved in creating the product or service and include labour and infrastructure costs. Production costs are likely to be lower with outsourcing as result of the vendor having economies of scale from serving a number of clients. Transaction costs include the costs of selecting vendors, negotiating prices, writing contracts and monitoring performance. Essentially, transaction costs, which are similar to co-ordination costs, involve the costs of monitoring, controlling and managing the outsourcing contract with vendors. Transaction costs are likely to be lower when performing a process internally, as organisations will find it less costly to co-ordinate, monitor, control and manage internal employees than external vendors. For example, organisations can implement a system with incentives and punishments to discourage employee opportunism, which includes shirking on their responsibilities. Alternatively, organisations are likely to encounter higher transaction costs when negotiating the contract and managing an outsourcing relationship with a vendor.

Another valuable theory for understanding the outsourcing decision is the RBV, which views the firm as a bundle of assets and resources which, if employed in distinctive ways, can create competitive advantage.[4] A major concern of the RBV is how an organisation's capabilities develop and affect its competitive position and performance. A capability with the potential to create competitive advantage must meet a number of important criteria, including *value*, *rarity*, *imitability* and *substitutability*. Capabilities are considered valuable if they allow an organisation to exploit opportunities and counter threats in the business environment. The rarity criterion is related to the number of competitors who possess a valuable resource. Clearly, where a number of competitors possess a valuable resource, then it is unlikely to be a source of competitive advantage. The imitability criterion is concerned with considering the ease with which competitors can replicate a valuable and rare resource possessed by an organisation. In effect, this analysis is concerned with determining the sustainability of the competitive advantage in the resource. Substitutability is concerned with whether or not a strategically equivalent capability exists to deliver the same output from a process. In other words, the more difficult it is for organisations to find substitute capabilities, the greater the strategic value of the capability.

The RBV is important to the study of outsourcing, as superior performance achieved in organisational processes relative to competitors would explain why such processes are performed internally. The outsourcing decision is influenced by the ability of an organisation to invest in developing a capability and sustaining a superior performance position in the capability relative to competitors. Processes in which the organisation lacks the necessary resources or capabilities internally can be outsourced. Organisations can access complementary capabilities from external providers where they can gain no advantage from performing such processes internally. Figure 3.1 shows how the key criteria of the RBV impact the outsourcing decision.

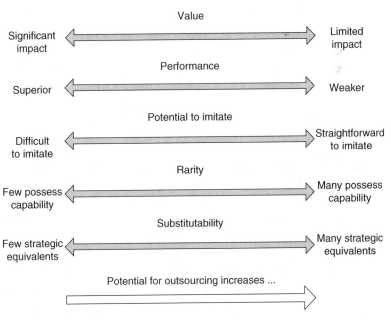

Figure 3.1   How capability attributes influence outsourcing

3.3 The logic of integrating transaction cost economics and the resource-based view

Although TCE and the RBV are focusing on two different issues – (1) the most efficient sourcing strategy, and (2) the search for competitive advantage – organisations have to deal with these two important issues when making outsourcing decisions. Practitioners have to assess their capabilities across a range of business areas as they are increasingly being confronted with constraints on resources. This means that they have to prioritise resource allocation in certain key business areas where they possess strengths and outsource less critical areas. Indeed, the trend towards specialisation in many business service markets has opened up opportunities for further outsourcing as specialist vendors chase demand through offering a wider range of capabilities in more critical business services. Organisations view outsourcing as a means of achieving performance improvements in many areas of the business. Specialist vendors are expected to deliver cost efficiencies whilst, at the same time, offering a higher level of value.

Of course, organisations can employ outsourcing as a means of achieving performance improvements in the areas of cost, service and quality. However, the potential for performance improvements has to be balanced against the prevailing conditions in the supply market. TCE provides a powerful theoretical lens to augment this analysis. Organisations have to consider factors that influence the potential for opportunism, such as the level of specific investments with the vendor, performance measurement difficulties and the inclusion of contractual safeguards to allow for uncertainty and changes in requirements. Possessing an understanding of these factors allows an organisation to adopt an appropriate outsourcing relationship, which reduces the risks of outsourcing whilst at the same time leveraging the specialist capabilities of vendors.

3.4 An overview of the outsourcing methodology

The principal proposition of the outsourcing methodology is that implementing a successful outsourcing strategy must involve an analysis of a number of dimensions including relative capability in the process, contribution of the process to competitive advantage and the potential for opportunism from outsourcing the process. Analysing each of these dimensions yields a number of sourcing strategies. The relationship between each of these dimensions and the sourcing strategies is shown in the matrix in Figure 3.2. The importance of considering these dimensions in outsourcing decisions is now discussed.

QUADRANT ONE

Most appropriate when:

Relative capability – possible to replicate and advance upon the superior performance position of competitors/vendors in the process;

Contribution to competitive advantage – superior performance in the process has a major impact upon competitive advantage; and

Opportunism potential – high potential for opportunism associated with outsourcing.

QUADRANT TWO

Most appropriate when:

Relative capability – sourcing organisation possesses a significant performance advantage over competitors/vendors which is difficult to replicate;

Contribution to competitive advantage – superior performance in the process has a major impact upon competitive advantage; and

Opportunism potential – high potential for opportunism associated with outsourcing the process.

Most appropriate when:

Relative capability – not possible to sustain superior performance position in the process.

Contribution to competitive advantage – process likely to diminish in importance in the future; and

Opportunism potential – possible to manage the potential for opportunism by adopting an appropriate outsourcing relationship.

QUADRANT THREE

Most appropriate when:

Relative capability – not possible to replicate the superior performance position of competitors/vendors in the process;

Contribution to competitive advantage – process likely to diminish in importance in the future; and

Opportunism potential – possible to manage the potential for opportunism associated with outsourcing by adopting an appropriate outsourcing relationship.

Most appropriate when:

Relative capability – not possible to replicate the superior performance position of competitors/vendors in the process;

Contribution to competitive advantage – process not a source of competitive advantage; and

Opportunism potential – possible to manage the potential for opportunism by adopting an appropriate outsourcing relationship.

QUADRANT FOUR

Most appropriate when:

Relative capability – sourcing organisation possesses a significant performance advantage over competitors/vendors in the process;

Contribution to competitive advantage – process not a source of competitive advantage; and

Opportunism potential – possible to manage the potential for opportunism by adopting an appropriate outsourcing relationship with a vendor or spinning it off as a separate business.

Most appropriate when:

Relative capability – sourcing organisation possesses a significant performance advantage over competitors/vendors which is difficult to replicate;

Contribution to competitive advantage – process not a source of competitive advantage; and

Opportunism potential – outsourcing not possible due to the lack of capable vendors and spin-off not feasible.

INVEST TO PERFORM INTERNALLY

OR

OUTSOURCE

PERFORM INTERNALLY & DEVELOP

OR

OUTSOURCE

OUTSOURCE

OUTSOURCE

OR

KEEP INTERNAL

Critical to competitive advantage

Not critical to competitive advantage

Contribution to competitive advantage

Relative capability position

Non-distinctive

Distinctive

Figure 3.2   The sourcing strategies

Contribution of the process to competitive advantage

Resource-based theorists argue that organisations will attain competitive advantage by building superior performance positions in processes that are valued by customers. Therefore, organisations should perform internally, and build capabilities in areas that deliver competitive advantage. For purposes of outsourcing, processes are either critical to competitive advantage or not critical to competitive advantage. Processes that are critical to competitive advantage have a major impact upon the ability of a company to achieve competitive advantage, either through the ability to achieve a lower cost position and/or create higher levels of differentiation than competitors. Adhering to the logic of the RBV, building a superior performance position in such a process that is difficult to replicate will lead to sustainable competitive advantage.

Alternatively, processes that are not critical to competitive advantage have a limited impact upon the ability of a company to achieve competitive advantage. Although these processes have to be performed well, and are necessary for serving the needs of customers, any performance improvements achieved in such processes are unlikely to be a source of competitive advantage as they are not key differentiators in the eyes of customers. The logic of the RBV is that such processes are of limited value, readily accessible in the supply market, easy for competitors or vendors to imitate, and provide no basis for competitive differentiation if performed internally.

Processes that are not critical to competitive advantage include those that have either a marginal or insignificant impact upon competitive advantage. Resource-based theorists argue that organisations should focus scarce

Table 3.1 Contribution to competitive advantage factors

Factor
Does achieving superior performance levels in the process enable an organisation to achieve a competitive advantage?
Will improving performance in the process allow an organisation to win more business or improve the chances of gaining more business?
Will investing additional resource in the process allow an organisation to achieve a competitive advantage?
Can important knowledge associated with the process be exploited in other parts of the organisation to enhance future performance?
Is it likely that senior management will commit additional internal resource to achieving superior performance levels in the process?

resource on processes that are valuable, rare and difficult to imitate. Although processes that have a marginal or insignificant impact upon competitive advantage are necessary for serving the needs of customers, they are not a means through which competitive advantage is created, and therefore are potential candidates for outsourcing. In addition, there are risks with focusing scarce resource on such processes, as this will divert resource from areas which are critical to competitive advantage, and where a company can build superior performance positions that are difficult to replicate. Processes that are critical to competitive advantage are limited in number and require considerable resource and management attention to maintain and develop strong performance positions. Table 3.1 outlines the key questions that should be considered when assessing the contribution of a process to competitive advantage.

Relative capability position in the process

A key issue in competitive strategy involves understanding why one firm differs in performance from another. Some firms gain advantage over others because they conduct certain processes in a superior manner relative to their competitors. Superior performance in the process is considered sustainable where it is difficult for competitors to replicate. Determining organisational performance in processes relative to competitors is a key concern for organisations in the outsourcing decision. Determining the relative capability position in a process involves identifying the performance disparity between the client and competitors and vendors. For outsourcing purposes, the client can possess either a distinctive capability position or a non-distinctive capability position in the process. The logic of the RBV is that organisations must perform internally processes that are valuable, rare and difficult to imitate, to gain sustainable competitive advantage. This logic is integrated into the relative capability position dimension.

Processes in which an organisation has a distinctive capability position should be performed internally, whilst processes with a non-distinctive capability position are potential candidates for outsourcing. Non-distinctive capability position processes include those in which an organisation has a lower or par performance position. Clearly, an organisation should outsource processes in which it has a weaker performance position. However, par performance processes are also potential outsourcing candidates, as they do not create competitive advantage and competitors or vendors can achieve similar levels of performance. If all an organisation can do is perform processes in the same way as competitors or vendors, the best performance it can achieve is competitive parity.[5] However, RB theorists argue that an organisation should perform internally processes in which it has a superior performance position that is difficult to replicate.

Determining relative capability position involves understanding both the type and source of advantage in the process.

> *Type of advantage.* This can be based on attributes such as lower costs, superior quality, service levels, time-to-market and reliability. Superior performance in a process can also include a combination of these attributes. There are a number of aspects to this analysis including cost analysis and benchmarking. Cost analysis involves comparing the costs of performing the process internally with the costs of sourcing the process from a vendor. An assessment of the relative cost position of the client in relation to both vendors and competitors in the process under scrutiny should be undertaken. The major drivers of cost associated with the process should be identified. For example, for capital-intensive processes, the major cost drivers are likely to be the cost of equipment and production volume. Alternatively, in highly labour-intensive manufacturing processes, the major driver of costs is labour rates. Benchmarking is another useful tool for assessing the organisation's capabilities in the process relative to potential vendors and competitors. Benchmarking also involves consideration of the cost position relative to competitors and vendors.
>
> *Source of advantage.* This is concerned with understanding how superior performance in the process is achieved. Examples of sources of advantage include scale economies, process experience, location and cross-functional linkages that create superior performance. Determining the type of advantage will have revealed valuable insights into the reasons for any disparity in performance identified. The analysis may have revealed that external vendors can provide the process at a much lower cost than internally within the client organisation. However, it is important to understand how this relative cost position is achieved. The superior cost performance of vendors may have been as a result of scale economies and greater experience in the process under scrutiny. These types of insight will inform the analysis of the sustainability of a superior performance position. This type of analysis can also assist in understanding how performance can be improved internally without having to outsource the process. Many organisations mistakenly rush into outsourcing without attempting to understand the underlying causes of poor performance.

Table 3.2 outlines the key questions that should be considered when assessing relative capability position in the process.

Table 3.2 Relative capability position factors

Factor
Is it difficult to understand how an organisation or its vendors/competitors achieve superior performance levels in the process?
Is it difficult for an organisation or a competitor to replicate the superior capability of any organisation in the process?
Is it difficult for vendors or competitors to replicate or advance upon superior levels of performance in the process?
Do resource constraints within an organisation impact upon the sourcing decision, for example, reductions in capital expenditure impede internal improvement or developing a capability in the process internally?

Potential for opportunism

This stage involves assessing the potential for opportunism from outsourcing the process. Opportunism is at the heart of transaction costs, and refers to the ability or willingness of organisations to pursue their own interests at the expense of other parties to the relationship by shirking on responsibilities or withholding information. There are a number of indicators of opportunism potential in outsourcing situations.

Asset specificity. This refers to the level of customisation associated with the outsourcing arrangement. Highly asset-specific investments represent costs that have little or no value outside the outsourcing arrangement. The presence of investments in assets specific to a particular relationship will create switching costs for the client. These costs can be in the form of physical asset specificity (level of product or service customisation), human asset specificity (level of specialised knowledge involved in the transaction) or site specificity (location). Asset specificity can be non-specific (highly standardised), idiosyncratic (highly customised to the organisation) or mixed (incorporating standardised and customised elements in the transaction). TCE asserts that the potential for opportunistic behaviour is greatest in an outsourcing situation when one or both parties have to make significant transaction-specific investments. For example, the vendor may use its specific investments in an outsourcing arrangement as bargaining power over the client when the contract is being renewed, as other vendors would have to commit the same investment to win the contract.

Uncertainty. This can occur both in the business environment and in the requirements of the client. The presence of uncertainty means that it is not possible to write complete contracts, and renegotiation and frequent amendments are required as circumstances change. Rapid advances in technology associated with the outsourced process can create high uncertainty and lead to frequent changes during the contract and at renegotiation.

Performance measurement. Difficulties with measuring the contribution and performance of the vendor can also create opportunism potential in an outsourcing arrangement, as the vendor might renege on its requirements. The presence of performance measurement difficulties means the client must expend additional resource on monitoring performance. For example, the contract can include clauses to allow third-party performance monitoring and benchmarks to assess performance. Differences in relation to the interpretation of performance can create difficulties in the relationship. Where effective performance measures have not been developed for the outsourced process, it will be difficult to determine whether the vendor has executed the process better than when it was performed in-house.

Process interdependencies. This refers to the interconnections between processes, business units and tasks. Complex interdependencies between business processes can also increase the potential for opportunism. The presence of interdependence means that the performance on one process is dependent upon the execution of other processes, which can have a negative impact upon performance. High levels of interdependencies between processes – either internally or with other outsourced processes – increase the need for co-ordination, joint problem-solving and mutual adjustment. Interfaces between processes performed by vendors and those performed internally can be complex to manage, and often require close co-operation to maintain the integrity of the interfaces.

Small number of vendors. This refers to the number of capable vendors the client has to meet its requirements. The presence of a limited number of vendors means that the client is in a weak position when negotiating the contract and will incur additional costs when switching to another vendor. Such conditions make the client vulnerable to opportunism during the contract, and at the time of contract renewal.

Table 3.3 outlines the key questions that should be considered when assessing the potential for opportunism when outsourcing a process.

There are a number of strategies that companies can adopt to deal with opportunism. Firstly, the high potential for opportunism may lead the client to retain the process internally. In certain circumstances, it may not be

Table 3.3 Opportunism potential factors

Factor
Is the approach to performing the process highly customised to the needs of the organisation?
In order to undertake the process, would the chosen vendor have to acquire highly specific knowledge of the operating procedures of the process and the organisation?
If the contract were to be terminated with the vendor, would there be considerable costs incurred in switching to another vendor or bringing the process back in-house?
Can the potential vendor undertake standardised routines in relation to delivery of the process?
Is it possible to establish clear written rules and procedures to enable the vendor to perform the process?
Is it difficult to predict current and future demand levels associated with the process?
Is it possible to establish clear performance levels for the process, for example, in terms of quantity, quality and timeliness of output?
Is it possible to negotiate a contract that clearly specifies the standards of performance required and the means of evaluation?
How critical are the results of the outsourced process to the execution of one or more internal processes?
How critical are the results of the outsourced process to the execution of one or more outsourced processes?
How many capable external vendors are available to provide the process?

possible to draft a sufficiently complete contract to deal with the potential for opportunism. However, in many circumstances it is possible to deal with the potential for opportunism by adopting an appropriate outsourcing relationship. In an outsourcing situation where there is a low level of investment in specific assets and relative certainty in requirements, a short-term outsourcing relationship can be adopted with the vendor. Alternatively, where the requirements of the client are highly specific and there is uncertainty surrounding the transaction, a relational outsourcing relationship is more appropriate. Relational contracting involves more than a formal contract and includes social mechanisms that promote flexibility, information exchange and joint problem-solving. Finally, a potential sourcing strategy involves reducing the complexity of the process by redesigning it into a number of more non-specific processes that can be provided by more than one vendor. This in turn will reduce the level of uncertainty in the transaction. Moreover, it is possible that these more standard outsourced processes share some of the characteristics of a short-term market contract. A further strategy for reducing opportunism involves transferring the process to a vendor with which the client already has a relational contracting arrangement. In fact, the outsourcing of such a process may be part of a wider strategy of the client, further strengthening a relational contracting arrangement with one of its key vendors.

3.5 The sourcing strategies

Quadrant One

This quadrant includes critical processes where competitors or vendors are more capable than the client. In this case, the client has to consider how performance in the process can be improved. There are a number of potential sourcing strategies for improving performance.

Invest to perform internally

This option involves investing the necessary resources to address the performance disparity in this process. The selection of this option will be influenced by the significance of the disparity in performance. Where the disparity is not significant, there is the potential to invest resources to perform the process internally. Furthermore, the client may have to consider this option on account of the high potential for opportunism as indicated by the lack of capable vendors. However, the client should ensure that it is in a position to replicate and advance upon a superior performance position held by one or more of its competitors. There are a number of situations where this option may be desirable:

- In a case where the technologies associated with the process are in the early stages of development and offer potential for future growth, investing in this area may be the most appropriate option.
- Analysis of the process may reveal that the disparity in performance is in an area such as quality or productivity, which can be addressed through an improvement initiative. An effective benchmarking exercise may assist in determining what actions need to be taken in order to improve performance. In addition, the potential for opportunism associated with outsourcing such a process to a vendor may force the client to improve the process and keep it internal as outlined in Illustration 3.1.

Illustration 3.1 Process improvement at an insurance company

This illustration focuses on a company that offers a range of insurance products. A major concern for the company over a number of years had been the area of claims processing. The company had been experiencing considerable growth in demand for its services, whilst internal systems could not cope with the increasing volume of claims. A senior management team investigated the feasibility of outsourcing this area to address the issue. This involved an investigation both of their existing systems in claims processing and of the capabilities of external vendors. The investigation revealed that the company had under-invested in the necessary technology, and was managing the increased workload through increasing staff numbers and the introduction of excessive overtime. The investigation also revealed that management in the claims processing department were spending much of their time fire-fighting ongoing operational problems, which prevented them from effectively managing the department. There was a lack of proper management and reporting structures and inadequate training programmes were in place.

In relation to the analysis of external vendors, senior management identified and carried out some initial analysis of a number of potential vendors. These vendors had a lower cost base and could provide higher levels of service than the insurance company could attain internally, primarily through achieving greater economies of scale and investing more resource in technology. A more in-depth analysis of one of these vendors with the necessary scale was carried out, which involved undertaking a benchmarking exercise. This vendor had the capability to deliver much quicker turnround times for processing claims than the insurance company could achieve internally. Initially, this seemed an ideal vendor to select as an outsourcing provider for claims processing. However, analysis of the insurance company's internal claims processes had revealed that there were complex interdependencies in the form of unwieldy reporting structures and process duplications that would prevent the company from transferring the relevant processes to this vendor. In particular, the current structures made it extremely difficult to establish clear requirements and linkages with other internal processes such as policy administration. Senior management in the insurance company were also concerned that it did not have the volume of business relative to other clients of this vendor, which would have increased the potential for opportunism in the outsourcing relationship.

Therefore, senior management decided to radically redesign the existing claims processing structure internally, which involved establishing clear interfaces between claims processing and policy administration. This involved redefining current work roles and drawing up key performance indicators including productivity rates, quality of work and turnround times. Additional investment was allocated to its information technology infrastructure. In particular, the company wanted to expand the functionality of its website so that a lot of claims processing information could be entered online. Establishing clear interfaces between claims processing and policy administration would also enable the company to outsource the processing element in the future if it found a suitable vendor.

- The presence of internal constraints such as workforce resistance and the threat of industrial reaction may force the organisation to improve the process internally rather than opt for the outsourcing option.

A further option for investing to perform a process internally involves acquiring an organisation that possesses superior performance in the process. This may be considered when it is not possible to achieve the required performance levels internally and there is a high level of risk associated with using an external vendor. Pursuing an acquisition strategy has a number of advantages. An acquisition can serve as a rapid, low-cost route into a new service area through the accessing of existing knowledge on both technology and the market. However, the merits of the acquisition option must be weighed against the limitations. Acquisition is an option open only to large organisations. Acquisition can be costly in terms of the financial costs involved in making the acquisition. Again, the costs of ownership must be considered – the risks associated with managing and developing too many processes internally. Finally, acquisition may not be possible because of legal constraints and local ownership rules.

Outsource

Where the capabilities of the organisation lag considerably behind the capabilities of competitors, it may be difficult to justify a substantial investment of resources to match or advance upon external capabilities. This option is likely if it is both difficult and costly for the client to replicate a superior performance position. Consider a mobile telephone network operator that previously designed and delivered customer service processes for all its insurance services internally. The same company considered customer service to be an important process and a source of competitive advantage. However, through an extensive analysis of its internal capabilities it determined that it no longer possessed the skills and resources necessary to match the performance levels achieved by competitors. Even though perceived as an important process and a source of competitive advantage, it had no other choice than to source customer service processes for a number of its services from a specialist vendor.

The importance of the process in the future will influence the choice of this option. Although a process has added value in the past or is currently adding value, changes in the business environment such as new technology or changes in customers' preferences may render the process less valuable in the future. Organisations often outsource a process which is likely to diminish in importance in order to focus resource and effort on processes that have the potential to be a source of competitive differentiation in the future. Of course, the potential for opportunism has to be manageable if the organisation is considering outsourcing such a process. For example, the client may decide to partially outsource the process whilst maintaining internal capacity. Partially outsourcing a process to a vendor can allow the client to assess its own internal performance in the process, and stimulate the improvement of internal performance as outlined in Illustration 3.2.

Illustration 3.2 How outsourcing improves internal performance

This illustration focuses on a power generating company and the refurbishment of its network. The upgrading of the network had become a major issue for the company because of its vulnerability to power cuts in times of adverse weather conditions. The ageing nature of the network meant that customers, particularly in rural areas, experienced frequent power cuts, which placed considerable strains on the company. In addition, the company was receiving a significant amount of adverse publicity in the media as a result of these difficulties. A critical process associated with the refurbishment programme involved replacing and upgrading overhead lines. Although the company had an existing cohort of internal staff in this area, it did not have sufficient internal capacity to undertake the full refurbishment of the network. One option was to recruit and train additional staff to meet the additional demand. However, the company was concerned about internal productivity levels in this area, and at the same time, the company was under pressure from the industry regulator to demonstrate clearly that it was efficient in all areas performed internally within the business.

The company considered undertaking a benchmarking exercise in this area with other utilities to address the productivity issue. However, previous experiences with benchmarking in other areas had revealed inconsistent results due to comparison difficulties such as differences in overhead allocations. Therefore, the company decided that the only means of determining a true measure of productivity in this area was to partially outsource this area through seeking tenders from a number of independent contractors. It was not possible for the company to outsource the entire process because of the need to have permanent staff to provide 24/7 emergency cover throughout the year. There were a number of advantages associated with partially outsourcing this process. When the company employed the external contractor in this area they obtained a true reflection of the productivity of internal staff, which was found to be 15–20 per cent poorer than that of contractor staff. The company was careful to mix both internal staff and contractor personnel in the same projects, which had the effect of stimulating internal improvement. The lack of internal capacity to refurbish the network meant that the company could bring in external contractors with little employee resistance. This strategy also proved to be a flexible way of dealing with internal capacity constraints as the company established short-term contracts with the contractors.

Quadrant Two

Processes that are critical to competitive advantage in which the client has a strong performance position are located in this quadrant. There are a number of potential sourcing strategies in this case.

Perform internally and develop

This sourcing strategy involves performing the process internally and further developing future capability. The significance of the disparity in performance in the process should be considered. Where the organisation has built up a significant performance advantage through experience over time, it may be difficult for other companies to replicate such a capability. Such a capability may be difficult to copy because other companies cannot understand the relationship between the resources and capabilities controlled by the company that possesses the capability – referred to as causal ambiguity.[6] In addition, the superior performance position in the process may be based upon a long and complex learning process. Consider a company with a strong quality position in a particular process. Such a capability has been developed over a long period of time through the many interactions of people within the company that are either directly or indirectly responsible for the quality of the process. Therefore, it is extremely difficult for a competitor to quickly replicate such a strong position.

Clearly, keeping a process internal is most appropriate when the organisation is in a strong position to sustain its performance advantage over time. In many instances with this scenario, it may not be possible to outsource such a process because of a lack of vendors in the supply market that can meet the performance levels required in the process. However, even in the case of a number of vendors having the potential to offer the process, the organisation may still decide to perform the process internally because of the impact upon its competitive position, as outlined in Illustration 3.3.

Illustration 3.3 Protecting and building knowledge through insourcing

This illustration relates to the outsourcing decision for a design process in an electronics company that designs and manufactures products for the telecommunications industry. These products included a number of important components that are important drivers in the functionality and cost of its final products. The company had been under considerable pressure to achieve advances in the design of these components as a result of increasing customer demand, and a high level of competition in the market-place. These developments were placing considerable pressures on design resource in the company. Senior management believed that a more focused approach should be taken to allocating design resource in areas that would deliver long-term value for the company.

In one component portfolio under scrutiny, vendors were becoming more competent in design, and were actively encouraging their customers to allow them to design as well as manufacture these components. In fact, some of the competitors of the company had already outsourced some of the design for components. The company had carried out extensive analysis of its own capabilities in this design process relative to those of its vendors and competitors. The analysis revealed that it was marginally more capable than many of its competitors and vendors. However, the analysis had also revealed that two of its direct competitors had been recently investing in this area. Consequently, the company had to make a decision on whether to rely more heavily on vendors or invest in this area in order to build upon its current capabilities.

In this instance, the company decided to retain this design process internally and allocate additional resource to build upon its current position. By divesting its capability in this area, the company believed it would potentially lose a source of competitive differentiation both currently and in the future. Although the company was aware of vendor capabilities it believed it would lose important knowledge in the design process, which had been built up over time through complex interactions with other business functions. In addition, the learning and knowledge accumulated in the design process could be exploited in the design of other components. The company believed that additional investment would further strengthen its capability. As part of this strategy, the company placed considerable emphasis on better accessing the capabilities of vendors in this design portfolio.

Outsource

Ideally, an organisation would wish to have superior performance in as many critical processes as possible. However, it is only possible to possess superior performance positions in a limited number of processes because of the resources required to maintain such a position. In certain instances, any superior performance position currently held by an organisation is not sustainable and can be quickly replicated by competitors. For example, many advantages attained from innovations in high-technology industries are typically very short-lived since competitors can rapidly replicate or advance upon any such innovations. Also, it may be more prudent to focus on other processes in which the organisation possesses a stronger performance position and that are more critical to success in the future. Increasingly, many organisations are recognising that competitive advantage can be achieved in the process of specifying and integrating external services and other purchases, rather than in assembly and production of the goods themselves. Companies such as Dell and Cisco Systems in high-technology industries have been pursuing similar arrangements with their vendors. These companies outsource services such as product design and logistics to specialist vendors. Also, the majority of manufacturing is outsourced whilst maintaining control over final assembly, test and customisation of the end product to customer requirements. Dell believes that many of these processes create little value for the end customer and can be more readily sourced from the supply market.[7] Instead, Dell has pursued a strategy of 'virtual integration' that has involved sourcing the relevant technologies from the supply market and developing strong collaborative relationships with its most important vendors.

The sourcing options in both quadrants 1 and 2 present significant challenges for organisations, as they involve processes that are critical to competitive advantage. It is extremely difficult for both cultural and historical reasons to outsource processes that are regarded as critical to competitive advantage. The logic of the outsourcing framework is that organisations can have either a distinctive or non-distinctive capability position in the process. A key consideration in this stage of the analysis involves understanding the sustainability of the superior performance position in the process – possessed either by the client or by competitors and vendors. Understanding the sustainability of the performance advantage will provide a sound indication of the difficulties of attempting to replicate or surpass superior performance levels in the process. Table 3.4 outlines a number of factors that provide valuable insights into the potential for replicating a superior performance position in a process.

Quadrant Three

In this quadrant, there are competitors or vendors who are more capable than the client in a process which is not critical to competitive advantage. Where possible, such processes that are not critical to competitive advantage should be outsourced. This quadrant can include the many routine processes performed by the client. Such processes can often be readily sourced in the supply market and therefore cannot be a source of competitive advantage. Many companies fail to appreciate the opportunity costs of investing in processes that are not critical to business success. In addition, as a result of cultural and historical issues, there may be a prevailing view that everything can be performed in-house.

The central premise of the RBV is that organisations should 'stick to their knitting', with the decision to perform processes internally being based

Table 3.4 Indicators of difficulties of replicating a superior performance position

Indicator	Description
Causal ambiguity	It is not possible to understand the actions necessary for performing a process. Such a capability may be difficult to replicate, as other organisations cannot understand the relationship between the resources and capabilities controlled by the company that possesses the capability. Essentially, organisations are unable to understand what the capability is, and how to create it.
Unique historical conditions	The development of a capability by an organisation may have been as a result of certain unique historical conditions. The ability of an organisation to develop and exploit a capability can depend upon being in the 'right place at the right time'. Over time or under different conditions, organisations that do not possess the capability face a significant cost disadvantage in obtaining and developing such a capability.
Social complexity	A capability may be difficult to imitate because it is composed of socially complex phenomena that other organisations find hard to systematically manage and influence. The culture of an organisation is a significant determinant of its ability to respond to changes in the external environment. Although the value of such a capability is well known to other organisations, it can be extremely difficult to create in the short term.
Path-dependent	Developing a superior performance position in a process can involve a long and complex learning process. When there is no shortcut or straightforward means of developing a strong performance position in a process, it is referred to as path-dependent.

Note: For causal ambiguity, see Reed, R. and DeFillippi, R. J. (1990). Causal Ambiguity, Barriers to Imitation, and Sustainable Competitive Advantage, *Academy of Management Review*, 15(1), 88–102; and Lippman, S. and Rumelt, R. (1982). Uncertain Imitability: An Analysis of Inter-firm Differences in Efficiency under Competition, *Bell Journal of Economics*, 13, 418–38. For unique historical conditions, see Barney, J. B. (1991). Firm Resources and Sustained Competitive Advantage, *Journal of Management*, 17(1), 99–120. For social complexity, see Reed and DeFillippi (1990) above. For capabilities based on path dependence, see Arthur, W. (1989). Competing Technologies, Increasing Returns, and Lock-in by Historical Events, *Economic Journal*, 99, 116–31.

upon capability considerations. Since an organisation has a basic area of competence, gradually accumulated through experience, this becomes the source of advantage as well as the competitive constraint.[8] Over-extending the scope of its processes into diverse areas not only damages the strength of its competence, but also increases the costs of performing such a diverse range of processes internally because of the lack of experience and expertise in these areas. Attempting to perform too many processes in-house inevitably leads to a situation where no process is given sufficient attention to create superior performance. Also, such an attitude may be reinforced by a culture that has failed to appreciate the capabilities of external vendors that can perform the same processes more competently.

Potential ways of externalising processes located in this quadrant include selling it off to a specialist organisation or outsourcing it to a vendor. Where an organisation decides to outsource the process, the potential for opportunism from the vendor will influence the nature of the outsourcing relationship. In the case of non-specific requirements associated with the outsourced process, the client can adopt a more market-based contract with the vendor. In the case of less routine or standardised processes, the client will adopt a more collaborative relationship with the vendor in order to reduce the potential for opportunism. A further strategy may involve redesigning the process prior to outsourcing in order to reduce the level of specificity in requirements, as outlined in Illustration 3.4.

Illustration 3.4 Reducing opportunism potential via process redesign

This illustration focuses on a manufacturing company and human resource (HR) services outsourcing. As the company was under pressure to reduce costs from its customers, outsourcing back-office services such as HR, information technology and finance and accounting was viewed by senior management as a way of reducing costs. The company focused on a bundle of HR services including payroll processing, benefits management, training administration and selected recruitment services. Although internal functions delivered high levels of performance in these services, labour costs were a significant element of overall costs. Initial evaluation of a number of vendors in emerging economies including India had revealed that a number of vendors could offer significant labour cost savings. However, further in-depth analysis of these vendors had revealed that only two of them had the capacity and specialist skills to deliver the full bundle of HR services. At this stage a number of managers argued that processes should be retained internally because of a lack of capable vendors. However, this was not an option, on account of increasing pressures for cost savings in back-office services.

Management embarked upon an outsourcing strategy, which involved retaining some specialist services internally and redesigning the supporting business processes prior to outsourcing. Redesign involved mapping out clearly the interfaces and interdependencies between the supporting processes for each service. Further analysis of the vendor market was carried out to identify the standard services offered by a range of vendors. The principal objective of the outsourcing strategy involved increasing the number of vendors capable of delivering the services, which would reduce the potential for opportunism in the event of vendor failure.

Once the redesign process was completed, a vendor in India was selected. The company established an agreement with the offshore vendor which would allow it to transfer the processes to another vendor or back internally in the event of vendor failure. Although the initial vendor agreement included a one-year contract renegotiated annually, the company was considering giving additional business and committing to a longer contract if the vendor met both cost and performance targets. However, because of the constant pressures for cost reductions the company considered a short-term contract to be the most appropriate strategy in the early phases of the relationship.

Quadrant Four

In this quadrant, the client is more competent than competitors and vendors in a process that is not critical to competitive advantage. There are a number of potential sourcing strategies.

Outsource

Although the client has a strong performance position, the process is not central to competitive advantage. Ideally, the organisation should consider externalising such a process, and focusing resources on building capabilities in processes that are more critical to the competitive position of the organisation. However, conditions in the supply market will influence the type of sourcing strategy chosen. The presence of a vendor with similar capabilities in the process may allow the client to establish a vendor development initiative, through the transfer of employees and equipment to this vendor. However, externalising the process through such an arrangement may not be appropriate because of the high potential for opportunism. In this case, another potential outsourcing strategy option involves exploiting the capability in this area by creating a spin-off business, which specialises in this area of operation and creates additional revenue streams. Organisations have spun off processes such as human resource and information technology into separate businesses to concentrate further on their core business, or as an alternative to outsourcing the function to an independent vendor. The spin-off arrangement can be an attractive alternative to straightforward outsourcing as the staff transferred will have an intimate knowledge of requirements, and the parent will still have significant influence over the spin-off business. Although the spin-off operation will generate sales from the parent company, its success depends on sales it generates from new customers. Therefore, the spin-off must have a viable service portfolio to attract new customers, and possess the necessary commercial and marketing skills required to develop the spin-off.

Keep internal

In certain circumstances it may not be possible for an organisation to outsource a process that is not critical to competitive advantage, and in which it has a strong competitive position. Although spinning off the process into a separate business offers a viable sourcing strategy in the case of a lack of capable vendors in the supply market, in some cases this may not be appropriate. The organisation may have to retain the process internally either because it does not possess the skills to develop the area into a separate business or because there is not a viable product to attract a significant amount of external customers. A potential option for retaining control of the process internally, whilst at the same time reducing costs, is to establish a captive facility in a foreign location where there is a sufficiently skilled and lower-cost labour pool. However, as is the case with the outsourcing decision there may be internal constraints such as work-force resistance to moving the process to another location – either locally or globally.

3.6 The outsourcing relationship

In the case of processes deemed suitable for outsourcing, the client will adopt an appropriate outsourcing relationship, which will be influenced primarily by the potential for vendor opportunism. Factors that influence opportunism include issues such as complex process interdependencies, performance measurement difficulties, uncertainty in requirements and high vendor dependency. These factors will influence the choice among the following generic outsourcing relationships available to the client.

Illustration 3.5 Fundamentals of contracting

Formal contracts are recognised as an essential element of successful outsourcing arrangements. An effective contract is an important mechanism for achieving flexibility, dealing with performance problems, encouraging performance improvements and acting as a safety net in the event of a deteriorating outsourcing relationship.[a] There are a number of important characteristics of effective contracts:[b]

- *Precise* – cost and performance requirements should be established, and clearly specified by the client.
- *Complete* – a more complete and detailed contract will limit the potential for opportunism from the vendor, and will limit the likelihood of costly renegotiations.
- *Incentive-based* – mechanisms should be incorporated into the contract allowing the vendor to share any cost savings or profits generated

---

in the outsourcing arrangement. Incentive contracts are often employed to encourage performance improvements in areas such as cost reduction and service levels. The contract should include mechanisms that ensure the vendor shares any savings that are realised from performance improvements.

- *Balanced* – a contract should be balanced, protecting the interests of both the client and vendor. Attempts at employing clauses to obtain benefits for only one party will be corrosive, with both parties losing.

A further characteristic of effective contracts is the inclusion of mechanisms to create outsourcing flexibility. There are a number of methods of incorporating flexibility into contracts:[c]

- *Price flexibility* – allows prices to be renegotiated as circumstances change during the contract. Incorporating price flexibility means that all future contingencies do not have to be fully considered at the outset, as the client and vendor are aware that prices can be adjusted to reflect changes in circumstances.
- *Renegotiation* – mechanisms are incorporated into the contract that allow for renegotiation based upon changes in the business environment. The contract may include specific clauses under which renegotiation should occur including fixed calendar dates, or changes in economic indices. Renegotiation often involves more than price, and can also include the terms of contract.
- *Contract length* – shorter contracts can be employed to achieve flexibility. At the end of the contract period a new contract can be negotiated that reflects the current circumstances both internally and externally.
- *Early termination* – a clause may be incorporated into the contract setting out the conditions under which the contract may be terminated. The omission of such a clause can result in penalties in the event of the contract being terminated prematurely.

It is often not possible, however, to use formal contracts as the only mechanism for achieving outsourcing flexibility, primarily because of the problem of incomplete contracting.[d] In many cases it is not possible to design a complete contract which accounts for all future contingencies and dynamics of the business environment. Moreover, rigid adherence to the contract can be detrimental to a development of the outsourcing relationship, and lead to outsourcing failure. Therefore, relational contracts that foster collaboration are often used to compensate for any gaps in formal contracts. Relational mechanisms such as a joint problem-solving culture can be used to improve any deficiencies in vendor service levels. For example, in the management of quality it is much better for the client to assist the vendor in improvement efforts rather than impose penalties on the vendor as set out in the contract. Such an approach allows the relationship to develop over the longer term as the individuals at the client–vendor interface build up an understanding, and adapt to each other's requirements.

Notes:

[a] For useful recommendations on effective contracting, see Saunders, C., Gebelt, M. and Hu, Q. (1997). Achieving Success in Information Systems Outsourcing, *California Management Review*, 39(2), 63–79; and Lacity, M. and Hirschheim, R. (1993). The Information Systems Outsourcing Bandwagon, *Sloan Management Review*, 35(1), 73–86.

[b] Barthélemy, J. (2003). The Seven Deadly Sins of Outsourcing, *Academy of Management Executive*, 17(2), 87–98.

[c] Harris, A., Giunipero, L. C. and Hult, G. (1998). Impact of Organisational and Contract Flexibility on Outsourcing Contracts, *Industrial Marketing Management*, 27, 373–84.

[d] Richmond, W., Seidmann, A. and Whinston, A. (1992). Incomplete Contracting Issues in Information Systems Development Outsourcing, *Decision Support Systems*, 8(5), 459–77.

Non-specific contracting

In this case, the process can be readily sourced from a number of vendors in the supply market. The supply market for the process is extremely competitive with a high level of rivalry between vendors aggressively competing for business from clients who share similar sourcing requirements. The outsourcing arrangement is driven primarily by the contract. It is based on the classical market contracting arrangement associated with TCE, which includes relatively short-term, bargaining relationships between independent clients and vendors. The primary objective of this outsourcing relationship is to achieve cost reductions. Non-specific contracting is appropriate in a transactional outsourcing arrangement where the outsourced process is not critical to competitive advantage, has limited interdependencies with other processes and has low complexity. There are clearly defined service level agreements, and client requirements are relatively stable throughout the contract. The needs of the client are non-specific, which enables the vendor to achieve economies of scale on production costs. In addition, selecting a vendor in a location with lower labour costs will deliver further cost savings.

Recurrent contracting

In many cases, the needs of the client can be quite specific. In this case, recurrent contracting is an appropriate outsourcing relationship, which involves repeated exchanges of assets with moderate levels of asset transaction-specific investments.[9] The low potential for opportunism is indicated by the presence of a number of capable vendors in the supply market. Contracts can be employed in which future contingencies are specified and the impacts of unforeseeable events are limited by incorporating provisions for third-party arbitration to resolve disputes. Recurrent contracting can allow the client to establish a contractual arrangement, which allows it to switch to other competing vendors that have become more capable, for example, as a result of changes in technology. Although the client may employ more asset-specific investments to co-ordinate complex and non-standard processes with the vendor, excessive dependence on a single vendor is avoided, and the client can incorporate a number of mechanisms that allow it to switch to another vendor in the event of contract termination.

Relational contracting

This outsourcing relationship involves adopting a longer-term collaborative relationship. This approach is appropriate in the case of a process which is critical to competitive advantage and for which there is high potential for opportunism, indicated by the small number of vendors, and the inability to fully specify or control all elements of the process. Adopting this approach allows the client to establish and build a mutually advantageous relationship with the vendor. In relational contracting, the enforcement of obligations, promises and expectations occurs through social processes that promote norms of flexibility, solidarity and information exchange.[10] The focus in a relational contracting arrangement is moving beyond a contractual mindset and developing a trust-based and mutually beneficial relationship.[11] Relational contracting is appropriate where the client and vendor are attempting to achieve a rapid, sustainable, step-change improvement in organisational and process performance – sometimes referred to as transformational outsourcing.[12] Illustration 3.6 presents an example of relational contracting in logistics outsourcing.

Illustration 3.6 Relational contracting in logistics services outsourcing

This illustration focuses on an electronics company that outsourced logistics services and adopted a relational contracting arrangement with the vendor. An increasing emphasis on cost reduction and time-to-market on its product portfolio was driven by considerable growth in demand and increasing competition. The company had invested considerable resource in logistics, as it had a considerable impact upon costs and lead times, and was regarded as critical to competitive advantage. However, senior management believed they could achieve performance improvements by outsourcing logistics processes to external vendors. A number of external vendors were identified who could provide a higher level of service at a lower cost globally. The company could not replicate these capabilities, as these vendors were exploiting volume discounts through serving the needs of a number of customers. Outsourcing would also allow supply management to become involved in more value-adding type processes such as new product development.

As part of the outsourcing strategy, management at corporate level evaluated a number of global logistics vendors. This analysis revealed a number of potential vendors that would provide higher levels of service to its manufacturing sites globally. The company selected one of the world's largest distributors of electronic components to customers in North America, Europe and Asia. The logistics company had developed a range of capabilities to become an integral part of the supply chain, providing support and delivering services and products which impacted every part of the manufacturing cycle from R&D right up to the point of manufacture. The electronics company established a relational contracting arrangement with the logistics services provider. This involved the adoption of a longer-term collaborative relationship with the vendor. Taking this approach allowed the company to establish and build a mutually advantageous relationship with the vendor.

The company at corporate level established an alliance with this logistics vendor for the supply of logistics services to all its sites globally. Implementing this arrangement involved the company in outsourcing many logistics processes including inventory management, quality inspection and expediting activities. In effect, the logistics vendor would act as the interface between the company and each component vendor, which involved maintaining and managing an on-site store of items. The company had to make relationship-specific investments in a number of areas, including integrated order management and delivery systems, and interorganisational information systems, which had created a high level of asset specificity. Although there were a number of other potential logistics vendors to switch to if the arrangement failed, there would have been considerable cost incurred in doing so.

Table 3.5 outlines the relationship between the transaction cost variables and the outsourcing relationships.

There are a number of common factors in managing outsourcing relationships in local and global outsourcing contexts including measuring vendor performance, dealing with uncertainty and managing process interdependencies. However, managing global services outsourcing arrangements is more complex and an additional set of factors has to be considered. In particular, location factors such as culture, language and time zone differences will influence the selection of an outsourcing relationship and sourcing model, and these factors will increase the transaction costs of outsourcing. Table 3.6 provides a summary of how location factors impact transaction costs in global services outsourcing. Organisations have been adopting a range of sourcing models to reduce the transaction costs of global outsourcing, and leverage the value that global locations offer. Fee-for-service models are appropriate for clearly specified services where there are short-term internal capacity constraints, whilst joint ventures with vendors have been employed to reduce risk and share the resource burden involved in services with highly specific requirements. In addition, the client can retain

Table 3.5 Transaction cost variables and the outsourcing relationships

Transaction cost variable	Non-specific contracting	Recurrent contracting	Relational contracting
Asset specificity	Low asset specificity indicated by standard requirements; clearly established rules and procedures for performing the process; and clients who share similar requirements.	Medium levels of asset specificity indicated by presence of some specific and idiosyncratic requirements.	High asset specificity indicated by highly specific requirements for performing the process.
Uncertainty	Relatively stable requirements unlikely to change during the contract.	Moderate levels of uncertainty indicated by uncertainty in internal and external business environment. Contracts can be employed to limit the impacts of uncertainty.	High levels of uncertainty indicated by inability to specify all the future contingencies associated with the process in the contract.
Performance measurement	Straightforward to specify clear performance levels and monitor vendor performance.	Difficulties with specifying performance levels for some elements of the process.	Not possible to specify performance levels for all elements of the process.
Complex interdependencies	Clearly defined and understood interfaces between the outsourced process and other processes.	Additional co-ordination costs associated with managing inter-dependencies between the outsourced processes and other processes.	Highly specific nature of client requirements often leads to highly complex process interdependencies. Collaborative mechanisms, as well as complex contracts, employed to manage interdependencies.
Number of vendors	Extremely competitive supply market with a high number of capable vendors available.	Competitive supply market with capable vendors available. Overdependence on a single vendor is avoided.	Few capable vendors available.

Note: For a discussion on these contracting arrangements, see Ring, P. S. and van de Ven, A. H. (1992). Structuring Cooperative Relationships between Organisations, *Strategic Management Journal*, 13, 483–98.

Table 3.6 How location factors impact transaction costs

Category	Impact on transaction costs
Culture and language differences	Culture and language differences impact a number of areas. • Incomplete understanding of client requirements, particularly if the client requires a highly customised service and there are complex interdependencies with other processes. • Difficulties with understanding and delivering on required service performance levels. • Changes in client requirements during the contract will take longer to introduce. In order to address these issues, additional resource has to be committed both in specifying clearly the requirements in the contract and monitoring performance throughout the contract.
Time zone differences	Time zone differences between client and vendor locations increase the costs of managing the outsourcing relationship. For example, the client has to employ project managers around the clock to co-ordinate and manage the vendor. Transaction costs associated with time zone differences will further increase in the case of customised services and complex process interdependencies.
Geopolitical	Geopolitical risk in the form of government instability, conflict and terrorism creates uncertainty and impacts continuity and quality of service.
Unstable infrastructure	Unstable infrastructure associated with service delivery, such as telecommunications, can hinder service provision and performance.
Ineffective legal system	Countries with under-developed and ineffective legal systems can lead to difficulties in dealing with disputes and enforcing contracts.
Other legal	Inflexible labour legislation, changes in tax laws, export restrictions and difficulties in obtaining visas are examples of other legal issues that can impact transaction costs.
Security and privacy	Additional mechanisms have to be incorporated into the contract to pre-empt and deal with any breaches in security and privacy.
Labour	High labour turnover, skills levels and experience can adversely impact service quality and increase uncertainty. The client has to commit additional resource to monitoring and managing these issues.

ownership of the process by selecting the captive model, which not only allows the accessing of highly skilled labour at a lower cost, but also provides the opportunity to establish a sales presence for services in the foreign location and adjacent markets. These issues are explored more fully in Chapter 4, which provides a detailed outline of the issues involved in selecting the location and sourcing model in global services outsourcing arrangements.

Illustration 3.7 Critical aspects of transaction cost economics and the resource-based view in outsourcing decisions

Although TCE and the RBV are powerful theoretical frameworks for understanding the outsourcing decision, each theory has limitations. The logic of TCE has been critiqued in a number of areas. A frequent criticism of the transaction cost perspective is an over-emphasis on opportunism as the primary determinant for making the outsourcing decision. TCE fails to recognise that opportunism can also be present in hierarchical internal sourcing arrangements. Some organisations can exercise more control over external vendors than internal employees, particularly when the goals of the organisation and internal employees are not aligned. Organisations often have to outsource processes in the face of high opportunism as a result of internal resource constraints or the need to rapidly develop a capability in a process. For instance, in rapidly changing high-technology industries, organisations have to access particular capabilities quickly, and do not have the resource to acquire another organisation with the capability. A further criticism of TCE is the simplistic nature of the hierarchy–markets continuum and the inadequate focus on other forms of sourcing arrangements. Organisations in many industries have been employing a range of complex and collaborative relationships that involve high levels of asset specificity in order to pre-empt the threat of opportunism from vendors.

The influence of uncertainty on the need for performing processes internally has also been challenged, and academic studies in this area have been inconclusive. Some studies have found that uncertainty can lead to more outsourcing, whilst others have found that uncertainty can lead to more processes being performed internally. A further limitation of TCE is using the single transaction as the unit of analysis when determining the opportunism potential of a vendor in an outsourcing arrangement. TCE does not consider an organisation's existing set of relationships with the vendor. Organisations often have existing relationships with vendors, which can influence the decision to outsource more processes to these same vendors. Another limitation of the transaction cost perspective is that it cannot fully explain differing levels of outsourcing in the same industry. The transaction cost perspective assumes that organisations confronted with the same transaction attributes (such as asset specificity, uncertainty, vendor numbers etc.) will perform internally and outsource similar processes. However, if one considers industries such as the automotive industry, it can be seen that Japanese companies such as Toyota and Western car-makers such as Ford have different levels of outsourcing, even though the transaction attributes are similar. Additional factors such as the experience and capability in managing vendors have to be considered to explain more fully differing levels of outsourcing.

The RBV evolved as a critique of the transaction cost perspective, with some arguing that it is a more appropriate theory for understanding the outsourcing decision. Rather than viewing outsourcing from an opportunism perspective, viewing the organisation as a bundle of valuable strategic capabilities links outsourcing with competitive advantage. In addition, the RBV views collaboration as a means of accessing complementary capabilities, in the face of resource constraints, rather than as a means of avoiding opportunism. However, the RBV is not without its limitations as a theoretical framework for understanding the outsourcing decision. Some of these difficulties stem from an often-cited criticism of the RBV – it does not sufficiently address 'how' resources and capabilities are more likely to lead to sustainable competitive advantage. Organisations often encounter difficulties in determining which processes are critical to competitive advantage when applying the RBV. Defining cause–effect relationships between processes and competitive advantage can be difficult, as there are many factors that create competitive advantage including strategic planning, information technology, culture, human resource strategy etc. In addition, many exemplars of superior resources in the RBV literature do not lend themselves to application in the outsourcing decision. Organisations focus on the business process as the unit of analysis when making the outsourcing decision, which makes it difficult to understand the linkages between business processes and potential strategic resources such as brand names, in-house knowledge and the employment of skilled personnel.

The RBV has a 'black-and-white' approach to defining capabilities as being strategic or non-strategic. Again, this logic may be difficult to apply in an outsourcing context, and may create internal disagreements between business functions on which areas are core and which non-core. This problem is further exacerbated as a result of the linkages between core and non-core processes. Outsourcing non-core processes may affect performance in core internal processes, for example as a result of the formal and informal co-ordinating mechanisms between these processes. The logic of the RBV is that only strategic capabilities matter, and non-strategic capabilities should be outsourced. However, organisations perform many non-strategic capabilities internally for a number of reasons. It may not be possible to split non-strategic capabilities from strategic capabilities. In addition, non-strategic capabilities have the potential to become more critical in the future and, therefore, serve as a pathway to developing strategic capabilities.

Although TCE and the RBV are valuable complements for understanding the outsourcing decision, each theory should be applied with caution as a result of contradictory prescriptions in some instances. In TCE, the prescription in relation to the outsourcing decision is influenced primarily by the potential for opportunism. Whilst in the RBV, the prescription in relation to

	Q1 **Contradictory**	Q2 **Complementary**
Superior resource position	RBV - Perform internally TCE - Outsource	RBV & TCE - Perform internally
Q3 **Complementary**	Q4 **Contradictory**
Weaker resource position	RBV & TCE - Outsource	RBV - Outsource TCE - Perform internally

Low   High

Potential for opportunism

Figure 3.3   Complementary and contradictory prescriptions of transaction cost economics and the resource-based view in outsourcing decisions

the outsourcing decision is influenced by the capability of an organisation to develop a sustainable advantage in the resource. Considering the lower and upper limits of each theory – potential for opportunism (TCE) and resource position (RBV) – illustrates both the complementary and contradictory prescriptions of the two theories in outsourcing decisions, as shown in Figure 3.3. Quadrants 2 and 3 illustrate how the theories are complementary, i.e. 'Perform internally' in the case of a superior resource position and high opportunism potential, whilst 'Outsource' in the case of a weaker resource position and low opportunism potential. Quadrants 1 and 4 illustrate how the two theories can be contradictory. In the case of a superior resource position and low potential for opportunism in Quadrant 1, the RBV prescribes the 'Perform internally' option, whilst TCE prescribes 'Outsource'. In the case of a weaker resource position and higher potential for opportunism in Quadrant 4, RBV prescribes 'Outsource', whilst TCE prescribes 'Perform internally'.

Sources: McIvor, R. (2009). How the Transaction Cost Theories and Resource-based Theories of the Firm Inform Outsourcing Evaluation, *Journal of Operations Management*, 27, 45–63; Hodgson, G. (2004). Opportunism is not the Only Reason Why Firms Exist: Why an Explanatory Emphasis on Opportunism may Mislead Management Strategy, *Industrial and Corporate Change*, 13(2), 401–18; Leiblein, M. and Miller, D. (2003). An Empirical Examination of Transaction- and Firm-level Influences on the Vertical Boundaries of the Firm, *Strategic Management Journal*, 24, 839–59; Ghoshal, S. and Moran, P. (1996). Bad for Practice: A Critique of the Transaction Cost Theory, *Academy of Management Review*, 21, 13–47.

3.7 Summary implications

• Outsourcing is only one of a number of strategies for improving
process performance. Prior to outsourcing, organisations must understand the causes of poor performance and why vendors can deliver
performance improvements. This involves addressing the following
issues. Can the process be improved through an internal improvement initiative? How much resource is required to improve internal
performance? Why can the client not achieve the performance levels
attained by vendors in the process? If outsourcing is necessary, how
long will it take the vendor to achieve the required performance levels
in the process? Can partially outsourcing the process stimulate internal
performance improvement?

• Organisations often outsource processes without fully understanding the nature of the process and linkages with other parts of the business, which, for example, can lead to poorly specified requirements in
the contract. Understanding the process and linkages involves addressing
the following issues. Are there complex interdependencies between the
outsourced process and other internal processes? How can the client better
understand and reduce the complexities of internal processes? If outsourcing is necessary, how can processes be better understood to derive clearer
requirements specifications for vendors? Is it possible to reduce the level of
asset specificity by removing idiosyncratic requirements from the process?

• Many organisations rush into outsourcing without understanding the potential for vendor opportunism. Understanding opportunism
involves addressing the following issues. How many capable vendors are
there available to perform this process? How difficult is it to establish
performance measures for vendor performance in providing the process? Are future changes associated with the process difficult to assess?
How readily can the process be transferred to another vendor in the
event of vendor failure?

• There are a number of potential outsourcing relationship options,
including non-specific contracting, recurrent contracting and relational
contracting. Drafting a robust contract in outsourcing arrangements is
an important mechanism for dealing with opportunism. However, the
management of the relationship with the vendor becomes an essential
complement in dealing with gaps in the contract, particularly in the case
of complex outsourced processes, and involves considering the following issues. What contractual safeguards can be employed to reduce the
potential for opportunism? How can the contract be drafted to encourage

vendor performance improvement in the process? What collaborative practices can be developed between the client and vendor to deal with unforeseen process changes?

Notes and references

1 Gottfredson, M., Puryear, R. and Phillips, S. (2005). Strategic Sourcing: From Periphery to the Core, *Harvard Business Review*, 83(2), 132–9.

2 The analysis presented in this chapter has evolved from research concerned with analysing both the theoretical and practical influences on outsourcing in a range of organisations. This research sought to develop and apply the principles associated with the RBV and TCE in a range of practical settings. The objective of this work was to develop a practical methodology that could be applied in a range of organisational settings. The initial phase of the research involved analysing the literature on TCE and the RBV in the area of outsourcing decision-making. Research was then carried out, using interviews with practitioners and analyses of documentary evidence, to understand how organisations approached the outsourcing process, which facilitated the development of an outsourcing methodology. Original cases were developed from the software, electronics, financial services and utility industries as part of the research.

3 Oliver Williamson developed TCE, and key references include Williamson, O. E. (1985). *The Economic Institutions of Capitalism: Firms, Markets and Relational Contracting*, New York: Free Press; and Williamson, O. E. (1975). *Markets and Hierarchies*, New York: Free Press. The concept of transaction costs was discussed as far back as 1937 by Ronald Coase. See Coase, R. (1937). The Nature of the Firm, *Economica*, 4, 386–405.

4 Key sources on the resource-based view include Peteraf, M. A. (1993). The Cornerstones of Competitive Advantage: A Resource-Based View, *Strategic Management Journal*, 14, 179–91; and Barney, J. B. (1991). Firm Resources and Sustained Competitive Advantage, *Journal of Management*, 17(1), 99–120.

5 See Barney (1991) in note 4 above.

6 Reed, R. and DeFillippi, R. (1990). Causal Ambiguity, Barriers to Imitation, and Sustainable Competitive Advantage, *Academy of Management Review*, 15(1), 88–102.

7 Dedrick, J. and Kraemer, K. L. (2005). The Impacts of IT on Firm and Industry Structure: The Personal Computer Industry, *California Management Review*, 47(3), 122–42.

8 Madhok, A. (2002). Reassessing the Fundamentals and Beyond: Ronald Coase, the Transaction Cost and Resource-Based Theories of the Firm and Institutional Structure of Production, *Strategic Management Journal*, 23, 535–50.

9 See Williamson (1985) in note 3 above.

10 Poppo, L. and Zenger, T. (2002). Do Formal Contracts and Relational Governance Function as Substitutes or Complements? *Strategic Management Journal*, 23, 707–25.

11 For further reading on relational contracting, see Baker, G., Gibbons, R. and Murphy, K. (2002). Relational Contracts and the Theory of the Firm, *Quarterly Journal of Economics*, 117, 39–84.

12 For useful references on transformational outsourcing, see Linder, J. (2004). Outsourcing as a Strategy for Driving Transformation, *Strategy and Leadership*, 32(6), 26–31; and Mazzawi, E. (2002). Transformational Outsourcing, *Business Strategy Review*, 13(3), 39–43.

Recommended key reading

Bahli, B. and Rivard, S. (2005). Validating Measures of Information Technology Outsourcing Risk Factors, *Omega*, 33, 175–87. This paper provides an analysis of how transaction cost economics can be used to explain risk factors in information technology outsourcing.

Barney, J. B. (1999). How a Firm's Capabilities Affect Boundary Decisions, *Sloan Management Review*, 40(3), 137–45. This paper provides a critique of transaction cost economics, and argues that an organisation's set of capabilities is a necessity for understanding the outsourcing decision. Practical examples are introduced to illustrate the analysis.

Boardman, A. and Hewitt, E. (2004). Problems with Contracting Out Government Services: Lessons from Orderly Services at SCGH, *Industrial and Corporate Change*, 13(6), 917–29. This paper provides an excellent illustration of the explanatory power of transaction cost economics in a services outsourcing situation in an Australian hospital. Transaction cost variables are introduced to illustrate outsourcing failure, and how the hospital brought the services back in-house to reduce cost and improve quality.

Jacobides, M. G. and Winter, S. G. (2005). The Co-evolution of Capabilities and Transaction Costs: Explaining the Institutional Structure of Production, *Strategic Management Journal*, 26, 395–413. This paper proposes that TCE and the RBV are necessary for explaining the boundary of the firm – the outsourcing decision. The dynamics of TCE and the RBV are illustrated with examples from the mortgage banking industry in the USA, and the Swiss watch-making industry.

Ring, P. S. and van de Ven, A. H. (1992). Structuring Cooperative Relationships between Organisations, *Strategic Management Journal*, 13, 483–98. This paper discusses a range of collaborative relationships that are not fully considered in the markets and hierarchies continuum associated with TCE. Particular emphasis is placed on relational and recurrent contracting, and the role of trust and risk in relationships.

Location and sourcing model choice in global services outsourcing

4.1 Introduction

The conventional view of location choice is that it involves a comparison of the relative advantages of a number of locations, with labour costs being the dominant criterion. Outsourcing can be a very attractive option, with labour cost differentials between developed economies and emerging economies as high as 60 per cent. Senior executives transfer IT and HR tasks and processes to lower-cost locations, and expect cost savings to mirror closely those of the perceived labour differentials. However, some executives have been disappointed with the savings, and seen labour costs and labour turnover rise in some locations. These experiences are primarily driven by insufficient analysis, and a lack of understanding of the dynamics of the location decision. The attractiveness of some locations in terms of labour costs can diminish as increasing demand for services drives up the cost of labour and leads to skills shortages. In addition, some companies in the USA and UK have chosen India as their preferred location for services outsourcing, following the lead of competitors, rather than understanding the underlying factors that influence its attractiveness both currently and in the future.

The emphasis on costs means that insufficient emphasis is placed on factors such as language, culture and geographical differences. These factors have proved to be significant barriers to managing global services operations effectively. Cultural and geographic distance hinders communication and the development of trust between the client and vendor. Language and cultural differences can lead to employees in vendors misinterpreting or failing to understand client requirements, which in turn affects service quality. Failure to understand language, culture and geographic distance can increase the transaction costs of managing foreign operations and offset any gains from labour cost savings.

The over-emphasis on efficiency concerns is also evidence of the lack of a formal strategy for global outsourcing, which means that organisations are not achieving the potential benefits it offers and increasing the associated risks.[1] Organisations are often unaware of the sourcing models available for different types of services. It is possible to maintain control over critical service processes through ownership models, whilst at the same time outsourcing standard processes via purely contractual models. In addition, the rush towards offshore outsourcing for services blinds companies to the benefits of selectively outsourcing certain processes to domestic vendors. Companies can use local vendors for customer contact processes that require local knowledge and cultural closeness; this is not possible through remote offshore call centres. Moreover, companies are transferring services to foreign nearshore locations that are geographically and culturally close, rather than to remote offshore locations.

This chapter provides a structured approach for understanding the issues involved in selecting the location and sourcing model in the global services outsourcing decision. There are a number of important interrelated dimensions to this process. Once an organisation has decided to outsource a service, making the location decision involves consideration of a range of factors including culture, language, geographic distance, infrastructure, political risk, legal matters, government policy and labour issues. Part of this analysis involves selecting a location distance from among domestic, nearshore and offshore options. The most important factors in the choice among these options are culture, language and geographic location, including time zone and travel distance. The characteristics of the service will influence the relative importance of these factors. Where frequent and intensive face-to-face meetings are required in creating and delivering the service, the offshore option may be totally unsuitable owing to geographic distance barriers.

Selection of an appropriate sourcing model is closely linked with the location choice. Several sourcing models are available, including the captive, joint venture, build–operate–transfer and fee-for-service arrangements. This choice is driven primarily by the characteristics of the service process and includes process interdependencies, performance measurement, risk and knowledge intensity. There are a number of strategies for disaggregating service processes prior to outsourcing including codification, standardisation and modularisation. These issues are discussed more fully in the following sections.

4.2 Location choice

The location decision will normally begin with a shortlist of locations, and then an assessment of the relative attractiveness of each location with regard to a number of factors. This will involve rating each location along the factors both objectively and subjectively. Factors such as labour and infrastructure costs can be assessed objectively, whilst culture and perception of risk are more subjective in nature. Moreover, it is likely that analysis of factors such as labour and infrastructure costs may lead a company to considering additional cities in the same country, as a result of wide variations in these costs across the country. As well as rating the factors, weightings will be applied to reflect their relative importance. Where the primary objective is to access low-cost labour to deliver the service, this factor will receive the highest weighting. Alternatively, where a company is searching for a location to establish a joint venture with a local vendor to serve its local customers, labour cost, infrastructure cost and security are likely to receive the highest weightings. The next step involves multiplying the weightings by the rating score for each factor to determine an overall score for each potential location. After considerable debate and discussion among management, the location with the highest overall score will be chosen from the shortlist of locations. Table 4.1 provides a summary of the factors relevant to location choice, which are now discussed in detail.[2]

Culture

Managing cultural differences is one of the most challenging aspects of global outsourcing arrangements. The culture of a country is influenced by lifestyle, language, value systems, beliefs and behaviour. In a business context, culture affects the way in which employees interact with managers, perceive the importance of group harmony, respond to gender issues and manage quality-of-life issues. For example, in face-to-face meetings the language and behaviour of different individuals vary and their mutual understanding of one another's culture will influence the effectiveness and efficiency of communication between them.[3] It is often the case in global outsourcing arrangements that the patterns of thought and behaviour in employees in foreign vendors may be entirely incomprehensible and alien to employees in the client organisation.[4] Culture is also an influence on organisational structures and decision-making approaches. Establishing collaborative relationships between clients and vendors with contrasting organisational structures is extremely challenging.

Some of the underlying dimensions of culture allow us to understand the impact of different cultures on global services outsourcing.

Power distance. This refers to how society deals with inequalities in power that exist between individuals, and has implications for the way in

Table 4.1 Summary of location factors

Factor	Summary
Infrastructure	Cost and reliability of telecommunications and electricity infrastructure
	Scale and quality of transportation networks
	Property rental and purchase costs
Political risk	Political stability
	Potential for conflict with other nations
	Level of bureaucracy
	Potential for changes in legislation that impact trade
	Inflation and currency rate fluctuations
Legal matters	Data privacy and security protection
	Intellectual property (IP) protection
	Procedures for dealing with contractual disputes
Culture	Compatibility with prevailing culture
	Cultural distance indicators including lifestyle, language, value systems, beliefs and behaviour
Geographic distance	Travel distance indicated by factors such as travel time and flight frequency
	Time zone differences
Language	Impact of culture on language
	Impact of accents and dialects on speech intelligibility
Government policy	Presence of incentives for foreign investment
	Taxation burden
	Employment and social regulation
	Attitudes to corruption
	Government policy on investment in infrastructure, education and skills development
Labour issues	Relative labour rates
	Labour turnover
	Factors influencing labour rates and labour turnover including skills shortages etc.
	General labour quality including factors such as education levels, skills levels, technical expertise and previous experience etc.
	Future trends in labour quality

which organisations are structured. High power distance is synonymous with hierarchical organisation structures, with autocratic leadership and less employee participation in decision-making. In low power distance organisations, managers and employees are more equal and work together to achieve organisational objectives. The USA is regarded as a country with low power distance, whilst countries such as India, with strong hierarchical relationships reinforced by the bureaucratic traditions of its colonial past, have a high power distance.

Individualism versus collectivism. This refers to the extent to which individuals function primarily as individuals or as members of a group. In the case of individualism, individuals view themselves as individuals and tend to focus on their own personal objectives, with little attachment to a group. Countries such as the USA, UK and Australia are individualistic societies, where competition for resources is prevalent and those who compete best achieve the greatest financial rewards. In the case of collectivism, the relationship between individuals in the group and the goals of the group are more important than those of the individual. Countries such as China and South Korea exhibit these characteristics, and business is conducted in a group context and the views of each individual are considered.

Communication style. Communication styles differ among cultures. Communication in Western cultures is direct and the listener does not have to know much about the context or speaker to interpret it – this is sometimes referred to as 'low context', where there is emphasis on spoken words.[5] This contrasts with other cultures, such as Japan and India, where the meaning is embedded in the way in which the message is presented – sometimes referred to as 'high context', where there is emphasis on non-verbal messages. Communication is less explicit and relies upon interpreting subtle nuances and certain meanings, often only possible through face-to-face contact.

Geographic distance

Although ICTs have reduced the need for physical presence for many service processes, geographic distance is still a critical aspect of the location choice, and can be a barrier to using remote vendors. There are two aspects to geographic distance in the context of services.

Travel distance. The nature of some services still requires face-to-face communication. Although the creation and delivery of some services only requires communication media such as electronic mail, more complex services, involving complex and in-depth interaction, require face-to-face communication – sometimes referred to as 'richness'.[6] Communication richness is high when individuals in either the client or vendor have complex queries that may have no definitive correct answer. In this instance, it is not possible to outsource such services to geographically remote locations because of the large travel distance required for face-to-face communication.

Time zone differences. A difference in time zone between the client and vendor has both positive and negative influences on geographic distance. On the one hand, a client can exploit a time zone difference from the vendor to produce and deliver services around the clock, thus speeding up development and enhancing customer service – sometimes referred to as 'follow-the-sun' development. Alternatively, time zone differences can create additional co-ordination costs, arising from delayed communications and misunderstandings of requirements, which can offset labour cost savings. Examples of co-ordination costs in this context include the additional resource required for managing the vendor around the clock, and any delays as a result of communication difficulties. Time zones can be a major inhibitor to outsourcing relationships that require intensive and instant communication between the client and the vendor.

The difference in hours between time zones will influence co-ordination costs for the client in managing the vendor. Where the difference is less than eight hours, synchronous communication is possible because of the overlap in working days, which means that feedback on issues can be given within the working day. However, where the difference is greater than eight hours, synchronous communication is impossible, which means feedback has to be scheduled for the next working day. In joint development projects such as research and development where there is a high level of dependency between individuals in executing tasks, significant time zone differences can slow down development times. For example, when an individual in one time zone queries a certain aspect of the project with an individual in another time zone, it can take a day to resolve, and thereby create project delays. In order to alleviate these difficulties, the client may incur additional co-ordination costs by employing staff on different shifts that overlap with the vendor or encourage the off-shore vendor to employ staff on shifts to mirror client working hours.

Language

Differences in language can act as a barrier to effective communication in outsourcing arrangements. Speaking a common language is important for communication-intensive services such as a technical support help-desk. India has become an attractive location for US and UK telephone customer support services because of the availability of a highly educated, English-speaking work-force. However, difficulties can still arise even where the same language is being spoken. The use of expressions related to culture in conversation can lead to misunderstandings. Speech intelligibility hindered by a strong accent and speaking too quickly also represents a barrier to communication between individuals. Some US companies have had to relocate customer help-desks from India back to the USA, as a result of strong accents creating communication problems and having a detrimental impact on service quality. Accents have an influence on how people identify with one another. Studies have shown that it is easier to establish a rapport with a person who is regarded as being similar, than with one who is perceived as different.[7] In addition, individuals with foreign accents can be regarded as less competent and credible than those with similar accents. The use of additional communication media such as email can reduce communication difficulties associated with conversation.

How culture, language and geographic distance affect the location distance choice

Culture, language and geographic distance have become important influences on location distance choice, i.e. the choice among domestic, nearshore and offshore options. There is an assumption that developments in ICTs have eliminated the difficulties of co-ordinating service work with vendors in remote locations. However, distance still matters and the characteristics of some services mean that culture, language and geographic distance are significant barriers to using vendors in remote locations. Studies on distributed software development have shown that distance creates difficulties in areas of communication, control, supervision, co-ordination, creating social bonds and building trust.[8] Rather than using offshore locations, companies have begun to opt for either domestic or nearshore locations for certain services in order to reduce culture, language and geographic barriers. Table 4.2 shows the relationship between these factors and the domestic, nearshore and offshore location options.

The nearshore option has increased in prominence, as it has allowed companies to reduce the barriers associated with distance, while achieving the benefits of lower labour costs. A nearshore location is relatively close in terms of distance and offers a number of benefits including a similar culture, language and time zone to that of the client. German firms have been outsourcing IT service work to vendors in Hungary and the Czech Republic, primarily because of similarities in language, culture and time

Table 4.2 The relationship between culture, language and geographic distance and the location distance option

	Domestic	Nearshore	Offshore
Culture	Same culture required.	Similar cultural characteristics in areas such as language, way of life, values, beliefs, or approach to doing business.	Different cultural characteristics. Possible to train employees on the culture of client.
Language	Same language required. Complexity of service makes it difficult for non-native speaker to deliver service without impacting service quality.	Share language similarities. For example, US companies expect vendor to adopt English as business language.	Different language, but employees of vendor speak native language of client.
Travel distance	Physically close, making it easy for client and vendor to meet face to face frequently.	Physically close making it easy for client and vendor to meet face to face.	Physically remote. Possible to communicate and co-ordinate work through communication media such as email and video conferencing.
Time zone	Same time zone required. Continuous interaction between client and vendor.	Some overlap between time zones.	Distant time zones with no overlap in many cases.

Sources: Carmel, E. and Abbott, P. (2007). Why 'Nearshore' Means that Distance Matters, *Communications of the ACM*, 50(10), 40–6; and Carmel, E. (2006). Building Your Information Systems from the Other Side of the World: How InfoSys Manages Time Zone Differences, *MIS Quarterly Executive*, 5(1), 43–53.

zone. The nearshore location has been increasing in prominence for a number of reasons. Companies have difficulties with managing vendors in remote offshore locations, and also experience poor service quality as a result of language and cultural differences. As companies outsource more complex services, the transaction costs of managing offshore vendors have increased considerably. In addition, proactive vendors in nearshore locations have emphasised the advantages that proximity offers over their competitors in offshore locations.

Infrastructure

The quality and cost of infrastructure is an important determinant of location choice. The nature of the service operation will determine the type of infrastructural requirements. The location of IT-intensive services such as software development will be influenced by the cost, quality and availability of telecommunications networks. Telecommunications and network services are also important requirements for call centres. Countries that have established themselves as attractive locations for these services have invested considerable resource in upgrading telecommunications networks and services and reducing the cost of using them. The reliability and cost of energy provision is another important consideration, particularly for services that require large amounts of energy. The scale and quality of transportation networks are elements that can also enhance the attractiveness of a location.

Political risk

Political risk refers to political factors that can negatively affect the attractiveness of a location, and includes factors such as political instability, conflict between nations, excessive bureaucracy, protectionism and changes in legislation that affect trade. Political risk is likely to be higher in developing countries where governments are unstable. However, political risk is also present in developed economies and can be a significant influence on the location decision. Governments often stipulate that contracts for public sector services have to be executed domestically, which prevents an organisation selecting vendors in lower-cost locations performing the work. Political risk can be at the macro or micro level.[9] Macro political risk impacts all companies in the location in the same way and includes factors such as general government legislation and political strife. Micro political risk affects certain parts of the economy of the country and includes factors such as regulation and taxes targeted at specific industry sectors. Table 4.3 presents an overview of the sources and impacts of political risk.

Legal factors

Although globalisation has led to similar rules for the trade between many countries, legal systems differ from country to country. Legal systems often favour home-country nationals, enacting laws to promote the interests of local business and the economy.[10] Commercial and private law are particularly relevant to the location decision. Commercial law includes business transactions, whilst private law regulates relationships between persons and organisations, including contracts, and liabilities that may arise as a result of negligent behaviour. National laws and regulations influence the

Table 4.3 Sources and impacts of political risk

Sources of political risk	Impacts of political risk
Political philosophies that are changing or in competition with each other	Seizure of assets with or without compensation
Changing economic conditions	Restriction of operating freedom in areas such as recruitment policies etc.
Social unrest	Cancellation or revision of contracts
Armed conflict or terrorism	Damage to property and/or personnel through terrorism or social unrest
Rising nationalism	
Vested interests of local business groups	Financial restrictions including ability to repatriate profits
Competing religious groups	Increased taxes and other financial penalties
Newly formed international alliances	

Source: Adapted from Rugman, A., Collinson, S. and Hodgetts, R. (2006). *International Business*, 4th edn, Harlow: FT Prentice Hall.

attractiveness of a country, and therefore have a significant impact upon an organisation's location choice.

Important legal issues in outsourcing arrangements include data privacy and security, the protection of intellectual property (IP) and procedures for dealing with dispute resolution. Data privacy laws differ considerably from country to country. In the European Union (EU), the Data Protection Directive has placed very stringent privacy standards on companies exporting data on EU citizens around the world.[11] Such legislation can create difficulties for EU companies when outsourcing processes with customer or employee data to countries that have no formal data protection laws. Similarly, IP is another complex issue in foreign locations. When the client hands over software code and systems designs to vendors in business process outsourcing arrangements, they run the risk of competitors accessing such applications.

Although the World Trade Organisation (WTO) has attempted to standardise the way in which IP is protected across member countries, organisations have to invest considerable time in researching the trade laws of potential offshore locations. In the event of disputes, enforcement of contracts in offshore locations can be extremely difficult and time-consuming, as some US companies have found with India. Litigation in the Indian legal system is frequently a fifteen-year process and Indian courts will not enforce legal judgements or awards made in the USA.[12] In addition, enforcing arbitration in a third country has been used as the standard clause for dealing with disputes between the client and the vendor.

Government policy

Government policy can be a significant influence in enhancing the attractiveness of a location, and is particularly relevant when the outsourcing company is deciding to establish a subsidiary operation rather than use a local vendor. The host government can influence everything from taxation rates through to employment law. Economies have been competing for international investment, through offering incentives and having favourable policies to encourage companies to locate their operations. These incentives and policies encompass a range of areas. Large firms often play off one government against another, as they compete against one another for foreign investment by offering the best incentives packages. Another important policy used to enhance the attractiveness of a location is favourable taxation rates. Ireland used low corporation tax rates through the 1990s and beyond to encourage large US firms to set up captive centres, particularly in the area of financial services and software development.

Employment and social regulation are also important levers used by governments to enhance their attractiveness. Some countries have enacted employment laws to hamper the functioning of trade unions and to reduce employee rights in areas such as rights to redundancy payments and periods of notice required for termination of employment. In addition, some countries have introduced legislation to prevent employees from frequently changing jobs, thus reducing the potential for high labour turnover and the associated increases in labour costs. A government's attitude towards corruption is a particularly important consideration when considering location to developing economies. Another consideration is government policy on investment in infrastructure, education and general skills development. Outsourcing firms often view a location as attractive where the regulatory burden is low and where there is a generally favourable environment for business.

Labour issues

There are a number of aspects to the labour dimension including labour costs and labour quality and experience. Lower labour costs have been the dominant motive for many companies in their global outsourcing strategies. Where service processes are highly labour-intensive, companies have had to relocate parts of their service operations to reduce labour costs and remain competitive. Labour costs for various locations can be easily compared quantitatively. However, there are a number of important influences on labour costs that have to be considered. The dynamics of the labour pool in the location should be considered, which include labour availability and labour inflation trends. As some foreign locations become increasingly popular outsourcing destinations, the influx of captive centres and increasing demand on local vendors from firms in developed economies have led to increased labour costs and skills shortages in certain areas. Trends in labour costs and labour turnover rates can be reliable indicators of both current and future skills shortages in certain areas.

Labour quality is another aspect of labour issues and includes factors such as education levels, skill levels, technical expertise and previous job experience. As companies outsource more complex services, education and skills have increased in prominence. For customer contact services, important aspects of labour quality include the ability to understand the language and dialect of the customers of the outsourcing organisation. For more complex processes such as research and development and financial analytics, the education level and analytical skills aspects of labour quality become more important. Again, as with labour costs, the dynamics of labour quality should be considered. The future supply and demand in the target location for young professionals and middle managers with the required skills should be estimated. For example, gathering data from colleges and universities will assist in estimating the number of graduates in the required disciplines both currently and in the future. Incentives for training and the provision of university education, ranging from the undergraduate to the PhD level, are also influences on the future supply of labour quality.

Illustration 4.1 Leveraging the innovation potential of a location

As organisations move beyond cost motives alone and outsource more strategically important services such as research and development, the innovation potential of a location becomes an important consideration. An organisation can take advantage of captive models not only to exploit cost differentials but also to leverage the innovation potential of a location and transfer it to the organisation's home location and captive facilities in other locations. Much of the innovation literature tends to emphasise the importance of internal capabilities and processes for developing and commercialising innovations. Porter and Stern argue that the external environment is as important for exploiting innovations, and have developed a useful framework for understanding the national innovation potential in the location decision. Using the term *national innovation capacity* to assess the ability of a nation to produce a series of commercially viable innovations, they propose a framework that includes three important indicators of national innovation capacity. These indicators, explained in the following paragraphs, are of particular relevance to the location decision.

Common innovation infrastructure. This comprises factors that foster innovation in a nation and includes the human and financial investments devoted to scientific and technological advances, public policies on innovation and the level of technological sophistication. The number of employed scientists and engineers, overall expenditure on R&D activities, percentage share of GDP spent on higher education, intellectual property protection mechanisms and the openness of the economy to international trade are measures of common innovation infrastructure.

Cluster-specific environment. The majority of innovation and commercialisation of new technologies occurs in clusters, which are geographic concentrations of interconnected companies and other organisations in a particular field. Porter and Stern employed indirect measures to assess this element, including the share of national R&D investments by the private sector as a measure of the overall private R&D environment. The relative concentration of patenting activity across a number of technological areas was used as another measure. An important feature of the cluster-specific environment is the flexibility and capacity to transform ideas into reality. Local companies, suppliers and other institutions can be involved in the innovation process and the complementary relationships involved in innovation are more likely where the participants are located nearby.

Quality of linkages. The relationship between the common innovation infrastructure and the cluster-specific environment is mutually reinforcing. Porter and Stern use the term *institutions for collaboration* to describe the presence of formal and informal organisations and networks in a nation. Universities were found to be the most important institution linking a nation's innovation infrastructure with clusters.

Understanding the innovation potential in a potential location has important implications for competitive advantage. Rather than viewing the location decision solely on factors such as tax rates, government incentives and labour rates, analysing a location in terms of special relationships and access to institutions means that the location choice can be used to build capabilities that are difficult to replicate. Porter and Stern provide recommendations on how companies can leverage innovation in the location decision. Clearly, companies should locate in a nation with a favourable track record in innovation and strong clusters in the relevant field. Companies should establish mechanisms for exploiting the strengths of the location, which means actively participating in industry associations, fostering relationships with universities and understanding the needs of local sophisticated customers. Companies should engage in activities that strengthen the local innovation capacity and make the nation more conducive to future innovation. This may involve encouraging further investment and policies that strengthen the national innovation infrastructure and clusters through lobbying government and industry associations.

Source: Porter, M. E. and Stern, S. (2001). Innovation: Location Matters, *Sloan Management Review*, Summer, 28–36.

4.3 Sourcing model choice

As well as having potential locations to consider, there are a number of sourcing models available to manage the arrangement, as shown in Figure 4.1. The selection of location and of a sourcing model are closely linked, and involve a number of common factors including culture, data security, IP protection and government policy. Where data security and IP protection are weak in a country, a sourcing model with a high level of control may be more appropriate than sourcing the service from a local vendor. Such an arrangement may also allow the company to exploit the full benefits of lower labour costs, rather than using a vendor where the benefits are shared. Sourcing model selection can influence the location distance decision. For example, a nearshore location may be more suitable for a service where the

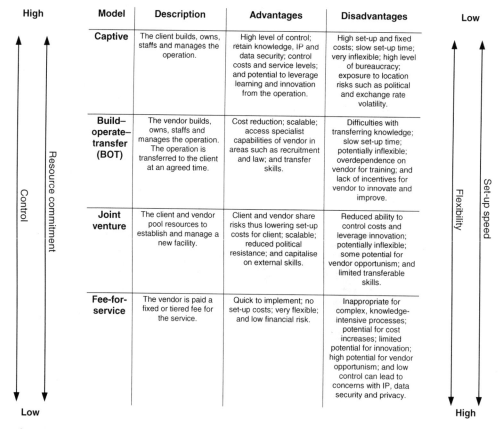

	Model	Description	Advantages	Disadvantages	
High / Low	**Captive**	The client builds, owns, staffs and manages the operation.	High level of control; retain knowledge, IP and data security; control costs and service levels; and potential to leverage learning and innovation from the operation.	High set-up and fixed costs; slow set-up time; very inflexible; high level of bureaucracy; exposure to location risks such as political and exchange rate volatility.	Low / High
	Build–operate–transfer (BOT)	The vendor builds, owns, staffs and manages the operation. The operation is transferred to the client at an agreed time.	Cost reduction; scalable; access specialist capabilities of vendor in areas such as recruitment and law; and transfer skills.	Difficulties with transferring knowledge; slow set-up time; potentially inflexible; overdependence on vendor for training; and lack of incentives for vendor to innovate and improve.	
	Joint venture	The client and vendor pool resources to establish and manage a new facility.	Client and vendor share risks thus lowering set-up costs for client; scalable; reduced political resistance; and capitalise on external skills.	Reduced ability to control costs and leverage innovation; potentially inflexible; some potential for vendor opportunism; and limited transferable skills.	
	Fee-for-service	The vendor is paid a fixed or tiered fee for the service.	Quick to implement; no set-up costs; very flexible; and low financial risk.	Inappropriate for complex, knowledge-intensive processes; potential for cost increases; limited potential for innovation; high potential for vendor opportunism; and low control can lead to concerns with IP, data security and privacy.	

Control — Resource commitment (left axis); Flexibility — Set-up speed (right axis)

Figure 4.1   Summary of sourcing models

risks associated with culture and language differences in the offshore location cannot be mitigated via any sourcing model.

Selection of the sourcing model is influenced by the specific requirements of the outsourcing organisation. Key considerations include the level of control, flexibility, set-up speed and resource commitment associated with each sourcing model (Figure 4.1). Closely related to these considerations are the attributes of the outsourced service. An overview of the sourcing models available is now presented. This is followed by an outline of how the service attributes influence the choice of sourcing model.

Captive model

With the captive model the client builds, owns, staffs and operates the facility in the foreign location. This model offers a number of advantages. The most important of these is control. It allows the client to obtain the advantages of control, co-ordination and internal communication whilst, at the same time, reducing labour costs. Many large firms in the financial services, consulting, software development and pharmaceutical industries have established captive facilities to carry out complex and highly knowledge-intensive work in low-cost locations. Goldman Sachs established a captive centre in Bangalore in 2004 to provide technology and analytical research support to its global operations.[13] The centre includes software designers and highly skilled analysts who produce modelling and other data that appear in research reports.

Knowledge can be retained and generated through transferring practices and processes from the client's home operations to the foreign captive centre and back again, through employee transfers and rotating managers. Culture can be an important influence on selection of the captive model. The captive model allows the firm to maintain control of the service by using an arrangement that is closely aligned with its internal culture. The captive model is often used to establish shared services arrangements in foreign locations, as it allows the firm to have more control in areas such as service quality, intellectual property rights and data confidentiality. Organisations prefer to hold ownership and control of shared services within the firm as opposed to entering into a contractual arrangement with an independent vendor.[14]

The captive model has a number of disadvantages. The major one is the costs associated with owning, establishing and running the facility. Organisations can under-estimate the investment required in start-up capital and management time in recruiting labour.[15] Setting up a captive facility takes much longer than sourcing services from a vendor, and there is no opportunity to leverage the scale and experience of a specialist vendor. Captive models are more expensive to manage, particularly if the firm does not have the necessary experience and scale to attain the full benefits. Although the captive model offers more control, there are still significant challenges with managing location issues such as culture and language differences.

The build–operate–transfer model

In the build–operate–transfer (BOT) model, the vendor builds, owns, staffs and operates the facility on behalf of the client. There are three phases in the BOT model:[16]

- *Build.* The vendor provides a complete solution for establishing the operation in the location, which involves dealing with administrative and legal issues, facility management, utilities, hardware and software, communications and office supplies. Professional support staff and operating licences are also provided to run functions such as call centres.
- *Operate.* The vendor provides a range of operations management services including human resource management, language and accent training, accounting, payroll processing, legal, facilities and security.
- *Transfer.* The client has the option of transferring the operation in-house from the vendor. The contract will include clauses stating that the client can buy the entire operation after a fixed period of time.

The BOT model has been prevalent in a number of industries including automotive, pharmaceuticals, aerospace, civil engineering and telecommunications. Tensilica, a semiconductor intellectual property company, expanded its engineering team by establishing a team of engineers in India via the BOT model.[17] During the 'build–operate' phase of the arrangement it paid eInfochips, the vendor, a fixed monthly fee based on the number of engineers provided. The 'transfer' phase occurred at the discretion of Tensilica, during the 18–24 month time-frame for a pre-negotiated transfer fee.

The BOT model offers a number of advantages to the client. The logic of the BOT model is that the client can establish an operation whilst maintaining a level of control not available through a contractual arrangement with an independent vendor. The client can also access the required capacity much more quickly than through an in-house effort such as the captive model. Establishing an operation in a foreign location requires considerable knowledge of the country, culture and recruitment practices. The model can also help the client bypass legal barriers, as it is easier for the vendor to establish the facility in its own country. The vendor can offer specialist knowledge in areas such as construction, utilities and recruitment.

However, there are a number of limitations with the BOT model. Vendors may be reluctant to get involved in an arrangement where they have to commit resource to establishing and running a facility, only to have to transfer it to the client at a later stage. There is little or no incentive for the vendor to innovate or drive service improvement. Culture and language differences can create difficulties in transferring knowledge. The client may not want to get involved in an arrangement where they have to pay the vendor a fee for running the facility, but gain little experience in establishing and running the facility.[18]

Joint venture

The joint venture model involves the client and vendor pooling their resources to create a new facility to deliver a service for a set time period. The client and vendor share ownership in the facility. This model is often chosen as an alternative to the captive model when the client is prepared to sacrifice some control in return for the vendor taking more of the risk. An often-cited example of the joint venture model in services is the arrangement between TRW, a supplier in the automotive industry, and the Indian company Satyam Computer Services Ltd.[19] The venture provided enterprise resource planning (ERP), supply chain management and e-business services to TRW, and also offered the same services to other customers. Joint ventures have management and organisational freedom to develop a culture different from the parent companies. The principal benefit of the joint venture is that both the client and vendor share the risk and resource commitment in the arrangement. However, the major limitation is the costs and inflexibility associated with ownership.

Fee-for-service model

In this model the client signs a contract with the vendor which has facilities and staff located in the foreign location. The contract is normally fixed-price or tiered based on the time and materials incurred by the vendor in delivering the service. The fee-for-service model is most appropriate for processes with clear business rules that are standard, and where there are limited interdependencies with other business processes. The client assigns clear responsibility to the vendor for delivering the service, and the relationship with the vendor is normally arm's-length. The key advantage of this arrangement is that it offers the lowest risk and highest level of flexibility to the client. The client can transfer work to foreign locations relatively quickly and alter the volume of work to match fluctuating demand. In addition, the client can use this arrangement as a stepping-stone in creating a more collaborative relationship with the vendor that requires greater trust and commitment. The downsides of the fee-for-service model are the potential for vendor opportunism and the lack of commitment from the vendor.

Illustration 4.2 Theoretical perspectives on global services outsourcing

Kedia and Mukherjee have developed an analytical framework to explain the global outsourcing phenomenon.[a] Using a number of theories from the strategy and international business literature they argue that organisations employ global outsourcing to achieve three types of advantage: disintegration advantages, location-specific resourcing advantages and externalisation advantages.

Disintegration advantages

Disintegration involves outsourcing non-core processes and focusing on internal core processes that create value for the organisation and customers. The theoretical basis for this advantage is based on the theories of core competence and modularity. Organisations use outsourcing to focus on their core competencies to outperform the competition in the same industries, whilst outsourcing non-core processes that have standard requirements across different industries.[b] Outsourcing non-core processes has allowed organisations to design specialised modular structures, and substitute the services of external vendors for under-performing internal functions.[c] There are three benefits of disintegrating processes: (1) it reduces the co-ordinating costs associated with hierarchical sourcing, i.e. internal sourcing; (2) it allows organisations to focus on their core capabilities; and (3) it creates modular structures to create flexibility and speed, and increase responsiveness.

Location-specific resourcing advantages

There are two types of advantage associated with location-specific resourcing: country-level and human-capital-specific advantages.

> *Country-level advantages.* Location has been an important consideration in the international business literature, particularly in foreign direct investment (FDI) decisions. This literature has been dominated by the work of Dunning[d] and the eclectic paradigm, which bases the location decision on infrastructure, country risk factors and government policy. Research in this area has identified a range of country-specific advantages including lower labour rates, labour productivity, transportation costs, tariff barriers, taxation structures and the political and legal environment.

Human-capital-specific advantages. Organisations can benefit greatly from labour arbitrage, and access the lower costs of human capital in emerging economies. However, in the long run the advantage of cost-related labour arbitrage can decline, and organisations have to move into higher value-added processes and achieve the benefits of knowledge arbitrage. Organisations can use global outsourcing to achieve the benefits of knowledge arbitrage by accessing higher qualified employees, and at lower labour rates than domestically. Although time zone is a location factor, organisations can use the benefits of time zone differences to work around the clock, and increase employee productivity and the speed of work.

Externalisation advantages

Transaction cost economics can explain the transaction costs associated with sourcing services from vendors in foreign countries.[e] Costs such as those of searching for vendors, bargaining and negotiating, designing contracts and monitoring performance are amplified in comparison with domestic sourcing. However, as well as reducing transaction costs, organisations can develop informal mechanisms such as mutual trust, co-operation and shared values with the vendor to create value – relationship capital-based advantages. Social exchange theory explains this phenomenon. Social exchange occurs where there is mutual dependence and high levels of trust between the client and vendor.[f] Some authors have argued that trust-based relationships can be a source of competitive advantage.[g] Relationship capital-based advantages create two further externalisation advantages.

Co-specialisation. This involves leveraging the specialised resources and capabilities of vendors. The resource-based view explains this advantage.[h] By utilising physical, human or organisational resources and capabilities, organisations can exploit environmental opportunities, outperform competitors and minimise threats. Therefore, some scholars argue, organisations can use the global outsourcing of non-core processes to access the specialist capabilities of foreign vendors to transform process performance.

Organisational learning. Socially embedded relationships in global outsourcing can create experience and learning for the client and vendor.[i] The importance of organisational learning is widely acknowledged in strategic alliance, joint venture and interorganisational relationship literatures.

Notes:

[a] Kedia, B. and Mukherjee, D. (2009). Understanding Offshoring: A Research Framework Based on Disintegration, Location and Externalisation Advantages, *Journal of World Business*, 44, 250–61.

[b] Jacobides, M. and Winter, S. (2005). The Co-evolution of Capabilities and Transaction Costs: Explaining the Institutional Structure of Production, *Strategic Management Journal*, 26, 395–413.

[c] Afuah, A. (2001). Dynamic Boundaries of the Firm: Are Firms Better Off Being Vertically Integrated in the Face of Technological Change? *Academy of Management Journal*, 44, 1211–28.

^{d} Dunning, J. (1988). *Explaining International Production*, London: Unwin Hyman.

^{e} Williamson, O. (1991). Comparative Economic Organisation: The Analysis of Discrete Structural Alternatives, *Administrative Science Quarterly*, 36, 269–96.

^{f} Blau, P. (1964). *Exchange and Power in Social Life*, New York: Wiley; Zaheer. A., McEviley, B. and Perrone, V. (1998). Does Trust Matter? Exploring the Effects of Inter-organisational and Inter-personal Trust on Performance, *Organisation Science*, 9, 141–59.

^{g} Barney, J. and Hansen, M. (1994). Trustworthiness is a Source of Competitive Advantage, *Strategic Management Journal*, 15, 175–90.

^{h} Barney, J. (1991). Firm Resources and Sustained Competitive Advantage, *Journal of Management*, 17, 99–120.

^{i} Kedia, B. and Lahiri, S. (2007). International Outsourcing of Services: A Partnership Model, *Journal of International Management*, 13, 22–37.

4.4 How service attributes influence sourcing model choice

There are a number of attributes of a service process that are important influences on sourcing model choice.

Process interdependencies

Process interdependencies refer to the interconnections between tasks, business units or functions.[20] Process interdependencies impact upon performance, as the performance of one task depends upon the completion of other tasks in the process. Interdependencies can also be between internal and external parts of an organisation. For example, one outsourced process may have a direct or indirect link with another process that is performed internally, whilst another outsourced process may have a direct or indirect link with yet other outsourced processes. The presence of high levels of interdependence increases the need for a sourcing model with a high level of control and co-ordination. Using the concepts of sequential, pooled and reciprocal interdependence allows us to explain how process interdependencies are relevant to sourcing model choice.[21]

Sequential interdependence. This involves a process where the task of one individual is 'handed off' to the next one. This type of interdependence is straightforward to outsource, as responsibility for such tasks can be clearly explained and transferred to vendors. For example, a process with long, standardised steps such as expenses management can be outsourced via the fee-for-service model.

Pooled interdependence. This involves a service where individuals work concurrently and integrate the output of each task at the end. The development of a software application provides an illustration. Initially, there will be agreement on the modules involved in developing the full application and who is responsible for each. Each member will then develop their module and come together at the end to integrate the modules in the final application. This service requires a sourcing model with a high level of control as a result of the interdependencies between tasks, and the need for co-ordination and management.

Reciprocal interdependence. This involves a service where individuals work concurrently on tasks while at the same time communicating constantly and amending their work in response to the changes of others. An example is the development of a new service involving complex interactions between functions such as marketing and research and development across the organisation. This service requires a sourcing model with a high level of control and mechanisms to ensure knowledge-sharing, as it involves frequent and intensive interaction and relies on individuals with tacit knowledge.

Performance measurement

As with domestic outsourcing arrangements, difficulties with specifying and assessing performance levels associated with processes can increase the risks of outsourcing. Performance measurement difficulties increase the potential for the vendor to renege on their requirements. Aron and Singh have argued that only by drawing up effective metrics and continuously measuring employee performance can an organisation successfully transfer processes to global vendors.[22] Establishing metrics allows the client to monitor vendor performance along a number of important dimensions including cost, quality and speed of deployment of new systems. However, the nature of some services makes performance measurement difficult. When insurance companies underwrite insurance policies, it is difficult to measure how well employees have performed the task since the events from which policy buyers are protecting themselves may never occur. Where an insurance company outsources this process to an independent vendor, it will have to inspect samples to ensure that the output meets its standards, which is difficult and expensive. In this case, it may be more prudent to retain the process locally or use a captive model to ensure greater internal control over quality levels.

Risk

Risk is an important factor in sourcing model choice, and the greater the risk the greater the need for control. Risk can be influenced by the industry context or characteristics of the service. There are a number of potential risks including the following.[23]

> *Intellectual property risk.* In some contexts, the creation of a service involves the development of IP. Where this IP is valuable and important to competitive advantage, the client has to ensure that the sourcing model and contract protect its IP rights. The client will have to incorporate additional control mechanisms to ensure that employees cannot disclose any valuable information to competitors.

> *Confidentiality risk.* Where the vendor is handling data that is confidential or sensitive, controls should be put in place to prevent intentional or accidental exposure. This is particularly important in the financial services sector where institutions hold confidential and sensitive information on their customers.

> *Compliance and regulatory risk.* This arises when outsourcing a service prevents the client from complying with a compliance or regulatory framework. For example, where the vendor fails to deliver the required services in the agreed time-frame, it may lead to the client failing to comply with legal requirements and thus be at risk of legal action.

> *Reputation risk.* There are a number of sources of reputation risk including the vendor failing to deliver the specified services to the customers of the client and the negative publicity surrounding the transfer of service jobs to foreign locations. The client may incorporate additional controls into both the contract and management of the arrangement in order to mitigate these risks.

Knowledge intensity

Many service processes involve judgement that is accumulated through integrating specialised knowledge, professional expertise and experience in a particular area. A process composed of extensive specialised knowledge and experience will be extremely difficult to transfer to offshore vendors. The characteristics of a process are a reliable indicator of the level of knowledge intensity. Well-structured processes with clearly defined outcomes that can be undertaken systematically through applying specific rules are likely to have low levels of knowledge intensity. Examples include standard production processes and transaction-oriented business processes. The tasks associated with these processes can be easily represented in words or numbers, and easily codified. The knowledge associated with the process can be easily documented in procedural manuals and databases. Therefore, it is possible for experts to transfer the knowledge to employees in offshore vendors through mechanisms such as training, process documentation and manuals.

In contrast, processes with a high level of knowledge intensity have the following characteristics:[24]

- People-intensive tasks that require insight and analysis based on skills, experience and judgement. The outcomes and recommendations of the process depend upon judgement rather than predefined rules.
- Processes are performed on the basis of skills, domain-specific knowledge and intellectual capability.
- The process is normally complex and unstructured. The tasks involved require interpretation, analytical skills, reasoning and judgement.
- The process requires professional and highly qualified staff educated to undergraduate degree level or above.
- The context of the process is dynamic and *ad hoc*. Tasks in the process may change rapidly and require *ad hoc* decision-making.
- The process may have a creative element that requires inspiration and complex modelling coupled with decision-making.

Organisations from a range of sectors are increasingly outsourcing highly knowledge-intensive processes such as those shown in Table 4.4. However, where the knowledge associated with a process is unstructured and based predominantly upon judgement and experience, it is more difficult to transfer the process to a vendor than to transfer one based upon more structured knowledge. Such a process may be based upon knowledge that is dispersed across people, processes and locations in an organisation. For example, research and development is often based upon the many detailed understandings of the linkages between customer requirements, system requirements and component specifications. Such a process is unique to the company and has been developed through numerous interactions across a number of functions. Therefore, when an organisation decides to outsource this process it is often via the captive model.

Illustration 4.3 Legal services offshoring

Organisations have been increasingly offshoring legal services to independent vendors, or establishing captive centres in emerging economies such as India and the Philippines. The motives for legal services offshoring are similar to those for offshoring other business services. The dominant motive is cost savings, followed by similar legal systems, English language capabilities and access to highly skilled labour. The similarities in the legal systems of the USA and the UK and India allow lawyers in India to understand and interpret US and UK laws more easily. Moreover, India can provide labour with good written English skills, and has over 250 universities with around 400 law schools. US companies have been at the forefront in legal services offshoring. In 2001, GE Plastics was one of the first companies to set up a captive centre in India for part of its legal department, which involved US staff interviewing and supervising Indian employees when establishing the captive centre. Employees in the captive centre drafted outsourcing agreements and confidentiality contracts, allowing GE to save an estimated $2 million in legal fees over a two-year period.

DuPont has also achieved considerable benefits from legal services offshoring. DuPont has offshored legal services to the Philippines where lawyers work twenty-four hours a day in three shifts, seven days a week preparing evidence in forthcoming legal cases, and working with employees in DuPont's US operations.[a] Lawyers are assisting legal projects such as monitoring old contracts and licensing agreements, and managing documentary evidence for product liability cases. Processing of legal documents can be a very tedious, labour-intensive process that involves reading, analysing and annotating digital images of memos, payroll and medical records, and other evidence used in DuPont legal cases. DuPont has been using offshore outsourcing to reduce processing time, and making savings of between 40 and 60 per cent on legal document processing.

The term unbundling can also be used in the context of legal services offshoring. Organisations have been unbundling legal services in a way that allows them to outsource non-core services to specialist law firms, whilst retaining certain core services internally. Non-core legal services include legal transcription, document conversion, legal data entry, legal coding and indexing, and core services include legal opinion, judgments and critical client communications. Moreover, these core services require that the vendor is registered in the country of jurisdiction. The level of complexity can also be used to differentiate between low and high value-added legal services. Low value-added services include transcriptions, document processing and legal data entry, and high value-added services, legal research and patent-related analysis.

Legal services offshoring is predicted to continue to grow, with countries like India set to benefit as organisations in developed economies set up captive centres or use independent vendors. It will continue to be attractive as emerging economies maintain their labour cost advantage, and also as independent vendors develop their capabilities in higher value-added tasks. Law associations in some US states have introduced regulations to limit the potential offshoring. However, there are still challenges to law firms in developed economies that have traditionally made much of their revenue on administrative tasks such as document processing that do not require the involvement of a lawyer. Although these law firms will continue to provide high value-added work to local clients, the growth in offshore legal services outsourcing will put pressures on their margins for lower value-added work.

Note:
[a] This phenomenon is sometimes referred to as the *24-hour knowledge factory*, which represents a globally distributed work environment where members of a global team work on a project round the clock, and each team member works the normal workday hours in his or her time zone. See Seshasai, S. and Gupta, A. (2007). The Role of Information Resources in Enabling the 24-Hour Knowledge Factory, *Information Resources Management Journal*, 20(4), 105–27.

Sources: Gupta, A., Gantz, D., Sreecharana, D. and Kreyling, J. (2008). Evolving Relationship between Law, Offshoring of Professional Services, Intellectual Property, and International Organisations, *Information Resources Management Journal*, 21(2), 103–26; Jain, A. (2006). The Emerging India Legal Offshoring Opportunity, *Financial Times*, 16 April.

Table 4.4 Sample of knowledge-intensive processes

Sectors	Knowledge-intensive processes
Financial services	Analysis of equities and derivatives, credit research, insurance research and mergers and acquisitions due diligence analysis.
Legal services	Casework analysis, intellectual property research and patent application.
Pharmaceuticals	Clinical trials, drug discovery, medical diagnostics and clinical research.
Research and development	Product design, prototype development, simulation and product testing.
Market research	Market segmentation analysis, competitive intelligence, data mining of websites and customer preferences and customer satisfaction survey analysis.

The level of knowledge intensity and the impact of a process on competitive advantage are closely linked. Such processes often have a considerable impact on competitive advantage, and transferring responsibility for such processes to vendors can lead to the relinquishing of important knowledge. Organisations can establish a process spectrum ranging from low knowledge intensity and a limited impact on competitive advantage to high knowledge intensity and a significant impact on competitive advantage. Figure 4.2 outlines such a spectrum for financial services processes. This spectrum shows examples of low knowledge intensity processes that are primarily rule-based, to high knowledge intensity processes that are based on judgement, experience and intellectual capability.

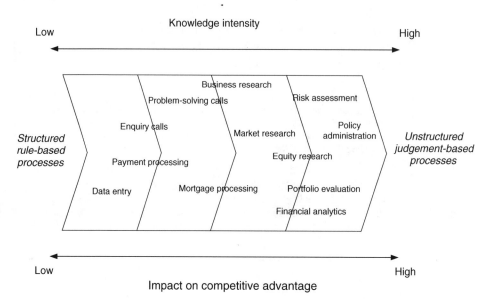

Figure 4.2   Knowledge intensity spectrum for financial services
(*Sources:* Currie, W., Michell, V. and Abanishe, O. (2008). Knowledge
Process Outsourcing in Financial Services: The Vendor Perspective, *European
Management Journal*, 26, 94–104; Sen, F. and Shiel, M. (2006). From
Business Process Outsourcing to Knowledge Process Outsourcing: Some
Issues, *Human Systems Management*, 25, 145–55.)

4.5 Strategies for disaggregating services

Organisations can influence some of the factors that affect the selection of
sourcing model prior to outsourcing. Developments in information technology and business process redesign techniques have made it possible to
reduce complex interdependencies and the level of knowledge intensity in
the service process. There are a number of mechanisms for disaggregating service processes prior to outsourcing, and these include codification,
standardisation and modularisation.[25]

Codification

Codification refers to the extent to which tasks associated with a process
can be described completely in a set of written instructions. Codifying
a service process involves capturing, coding specialist knowledge, specifying clear roles and operating procedures so that the knowledge can
be easily transferred to vendors. Codifying service processes allows an

organisation to establish clear boundaries between processes that are performed internally and those that are outsourced. For example, a financial services organisation can have the customer loan application service performed offshore if it has established clear rules on customer eligibility for loans and procedures for dealing with exceptional cases. Developments in information technology make it possible to codify tasks associated with complex service processes. Process modelling approaches such as flow charts, data flow diagrams and goal-based models have helped to create a process grammar to represent complex processes in software development.

As organisations develop greater levels of maturity and experience in many such processes, the potential for codifiability increases. The increasing use of offshore vendors for such services is evidence of this trend. However, it can be extremely difficult to codify processes that are highly knowledge-intensive, that require judgement and extensive experience. Contrast the occupation of an insurance underwriter with that of a heart surgeon. The process and acceptance criteria for an underwriter can be completely structured and documented, with clearly defined outcomes, whereas for the heart surgeon it is extremely difficult to document the steps involved in surgery and to derive predefined rules for every situation that may arise.

Standardisation

Standardisation refers to the extent to which the tasks in a process can be executed using a set of consistent and repeatable steps. For example, fast-food outlets such as Burger King and McDonald's use standard processes for serving customers. Establishing clear steps for processing a customer order means the process will be carried out in the same way regardless of location. Global services outsourcing has been made possible by the standardisation of business processes such as data entry, accounting and information technology support.[26] Alternatively, the lack of standardisation arising from, for example, the absence of procedures for dealing with customer problems makes outsourcing difficult. The differences between the ways in which organisations define processes mean it is difficult to define their requirements clearly for vendors. However, organisations are employing information technology to standardise many business processes to facilitate greater levels of outsourcing. The use of customer relationship management software by dispersed sales teams allows consistent information delivery and usage by all members of sales teams.

Modularisation

Modularising service processes is an important mechanism for reducing complex interdependencies between internal and external processes.[27] Modularisation involves breaking large and complex business processes into component modules and activities so that organisations and vendors can specialise in certain activities.[28] Modularising processes involves creating a high degree of independence of processes, which involves the design of process *architecture, interfaces* and *standards. Architecture* specifies which processes are part of the overall system and the functionality they perform. *Interfaces* specify how the process modules are integrated, and how they communicate with each other. *Standards* test conformity to the interface specifications, and measure performance with other modules in the system. Many companies have been applying modular design principles to services processes in order to access the lower production costs associated with many foreign locations. The constructs of co-ordination costs, transaction costs and production costs illustrate how modularisation drives outsourcing.[29]

Co-ordination costs increase when there is a need to manage complex interdependencies among processes. Modularisation reduces co-ordination costs through standard interfaces and performance specifications and thus limits the need for management intervention in co-ordinating the dependencies among processes.

Transaction costs increase when there is the potential for opportunism from the vendor, driven primarily by the presence of asset specificity in the relationship. Modularisation reduces transaction costs through the design of standard interfaces, which allow processes to be integrated without creating dependencies between the client and vendor. In a situation where the vendor behaves opportunistically, the client can readily switch to another vendor.

Production costs are the costs incurred in creating the process and include labour and infrastructure costs. The reduction of co-ordination and transaction costs through modularisation in turn reduces production costs. Reducing co-ordination and transaction costs increases the attractiveness of using external vendors with lower production costs. Vendors can reduce production costs by offering standard processes to a range of clients and achieving the benefits of scale economies and specialisation. In addition, production costs are further reduced through the use of vendors in lower-cost foreign locations.

Modularisation has been an important driver of global software development outsourcing. The increasingly modular design of software development has reduced the development and co-ordination costs for software development projects. As well as vendors in offshore locations enjoying significant labour cost advantages, software vendors in developed economies have been establishing subsidiaries to access these labour cost advantages. Modularising the software development process has reduced the difficulties of synchronising, communicating, travelling, monitoring, providing feedback and enforcing software development contracts. Advances in technologies for managing and co-ordinating development teams across geographic distances have allowed firms to modularise the software development process.

Illustration 4.4 The limits of modularity in equity analysis in financial services outsourcing

Financial services have been impacted by the outsourcing phenomenon. This has largely been driven by the modularisation of processes by organisations, low wage locations and developments in information technology. However, some financial services processes such as equity analysis have proved difficult to outsource. Equity analysts analyse companies in order to offer advice and investment recommendations to institutional investors. Data are collected and analysed from both primary company sources and secondary sources. Research reports on each company containing trading ideas are written and presented to both external clients and internal stock traders in their own organisation. Part of this process involves supporting and working closely with stock traders in the sales department of the bank. The equity analysis process involves continuous interactions with a number of internal and external contacts, as shown in Figure 4.3.

One might think that equity analysis would be a prime target for outsourcing, as it is a major cost for financial services organisations, largely as a result of the high salaries paid to analysts. However, a study carried out on equity analysis in a number of Western financial institutions revealed that although some technical analysis and data collection had been offshored, equity analysis had largely been unaffected. One reason was that financial institutions regarded research activities such as equity analysis as core competences, and an important source of competitive advantage. However, other reasons were linked to the lack of modularity in the equity analysis process. The study found that the equity research analysis process is deeply embedded in Western financial institutions, which makes offshore outsourcing difficult. The study found a number of important reasons for this 'embeddedness' including the presence of tacit knowledge, high interdependencies among tasks and the need for internal and external face-to-face contact and cultural proximity. Analysts have to interpret a range of signals, including share price

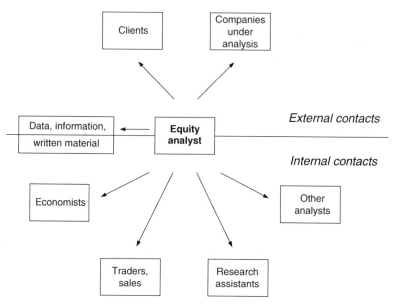

Figure 4.3   Contacts in equity analysis

movements, market rumours and the general mood in the stock market. Tacit
knowledge in the form of judgements and experience is required for understanding current and future events in the company and the relevant industry.
Qualitative information and knowledge are more widely employed in this
analysis than codified knowledge and information. In effect, equity analysts
are paid to know more than 'the market' does.

The need for frequent and intensive information and knowledge exchange
between departments and individuals, both internally and externally, also
limits the possibility of relocating parts of the process offshore. Face-to-face
contact with traders, other analysts and sales people allows equity analysts to
generate trading ideas. Equity analysts are often located within the trading
room of banks and have continuous communication with traders. In addition, there are frequent interactions among equity analysts in the same bank
to test ideas and react to changes in the market. When the share price of a
firm falls, analysts and traders have to schedule face-to-face meetings at short
notice in order to interpret the causes and generate trading options. Face-
to-face contact with analysts is also demanded by clients who require further explanations and interpretations of the analysis provided in the reports.
Cultural proximity is important; it involves understanding local regulations,
interpretation of accounting regulations, and language. For example, equity
analysts have to maintain face-to-face contact with the firms as well as with
investors, which confines them to the same nation or region as the firms they

> are analysing. Again, this process involves frequent exchanges of tacit know-ledge, which makes offshoring extremely difficult.
>
> *Source:* Grote, M. H. and Taube, F. A. (2007). When Outsourcing is not an Option: International Relocation of Investment Bank Research, *Journal of International Management*, 13, 57–77.

Developments in information technology have had a major impact upon service disaggregation by facilitating codification, standardisation and modularisation as shown in Table 4.5. Radiology provides a useful illustration of the impact of information technology on service disaggregation. IT drives codification through the high-resolution digitisation of scans and the transfer of scans for review to remote locations. In the case of standardisation, diagnostic software can screen radiology images for any unusual patterns. Modularisation is facilitated by workflow systems which enable image review and communication of results between a physician and a radiologist on a real-time basis and regardless of physical location.

4.6 Summary implications

- Location and sourcing model choice is a complex decision in global services outsourcing. Rather than being motivated by cost concerns, organisations should select the optimal location and sourcing model based upon current and long-term strategic business objectives.
- Influences on the location decision in global services outsourcing include culture, language and geographic distance, infrastructure, political risk, legal matters, government policy and labour issues. Culture, language, and geographic distance, including time zone and travel distance, are important influences on the choice among the domestic, nearshore and offshore location options.
- Location and sourcing model selection are closely linked, involving a number of common factors including culture, data security, IP protection and government policy. There are a number of sourcing models available for global services outsourcing including the captive, build–operate–transfer, joint venture and fee-for-service arrangements.
- The level of control, flexibility, set-up speed and resource commitment are important considerations in sourcing model selection. Attributes of the service process, including process interdependencies, performance measurement, the level of risk and knowledge intensity, also influence sourcing model selection.

Table 4.5 Impact of information technology on disaggregating service processes

	Codification	Standardisation	Modularisation
Description	Use of codes, models and languages to capture process.	Facilitates communication, handoff and benchmarking of processes.	Disaggregate complex cross-functional processes, whilst understanding and managing interdependencies.
Impact of information technology	IT facilitates recording and retrieval of process information through process modelling approaches such as flowcharts and data flow diagrams.	IT acts as a repository to store and access process information.	IT provides mechanism to transfer and access process knowledge.
How IT disaggregates service processes	Codification allows processes to be captured and transferred across organisations regardless of location.	Standardisation allows the establishment of clear handoffs for process both within and across organisations.	Modularisation allows the transfer and co-ordination of processes across organisational boundaries, and the re-integration of the processes inside the organisation.
Example	Software requirements definition involves non-codifiable knowledge. This contrasts with programming which has explicit requirements.	A help-desk employee can be trained to follow a standard process for dealing with customer queries, whereas a lawyer has to follow a different process for each case.	Multiple technical writers can write separate chapters for a user manual, whereas the work of an equity analyst cannot be modularised.

Source: Adapted from Mithas, S. and Whitaker, J. (2007). Is the World Flat or Spiky? Information Intensity, Skills, and Global Service Disaggregation, *Information Systems Research*, 18(3), 237–59.

- Developments in information technology and business process redesign techniques have made it possible to disaggregate service processes via codification, standardisation and modularisation prior to outsourcing.

Notes and references

1 Aron, R. and Singh, J. V. (2005). Getting Offshoring Right, *Harvard Business Review*, 83(12), 135–43; Gereffi, G., Humphrey, J. and Sturgeon, T. (2005). The Governance of Global Value Chains, *Review of International Political Economy*, 12(1), 78–104; Vestring, T., Rouse, T. and Reinert, U. (2005). Hedge Your Offshoring Bets, *Sloan Management Review*, 46(3), 27–9.

2 There are a number of models and classification schemes for location selection. A useful reference for further reading is www.atkearney.com/index.php/ Publications/offshoring-for-long-term-advantage.html. This reference provides an overview of A. T. Kearney's location attractiveness index, and how it has been used to rate the attractiveness of a number of locations for global outsourcing.

3 Rugman, A., Collinson, S. and Hodgetts, R. (2006). *International Business*, 4th edn, Harlow: FT Prentice Hall; Shenkar, O. (2001). Cultural Distance Revisited: Towards a More Rigorous Conceptualisation and Measurement of Cultural Differences, *Journal of International Business Studies*, 32, 519–35.

4 Rao, M. (2004). Key Issues for Global IT Sourcing: Country and Individual Factors, *Information Systems Management*, 21(3), 16–21.

5 Edward Hall was the first to make the distinction between *low context* and *high context* cultures in his seminal text: Hall, E. (1976). *Beyond Culture*, New York: Doubleday.

6 Stringfellow, A., Teagarden, M. and Nie, W. (2008). Invisible Costs in Offshoring Services Work, *Journal of Operations Management*, 26(2), 164–79.

7 See Stringfellow *et al.* (2008) in note 6 above.

8 Carmel, E. and Tija, P. (2005). *Offshoring Information Technology: Sourcing and Outsourcing to a Global Workforce*, Cambridge: Cambridge University Press.

9 See Rugman *et al.* (2006) in note 3 above.

10 Cavusgil, S., Knight, G. and Riesenberger, J. (2008). *International Business: Strategy, Management, and the New Realities*, Upper Saddle River, N.J.: Pearson.

11 See Rao (2004) in note 4 above.

12 Rottman, J. and Lacity, M. (2004). Proven Practices for IT Offshore Outsourcing, *Cutter Consortium*, 5(12), 1–27.

13 Lampel, J. and Bhalla, A. (2008). Embracing Realism and Recognising Choice in IT Offshoring Initiatives, *Business Horizons*, 51(5), 429–40.

14 Robinson, M. and Kalakota, R. (2005). *Offshore Outsourcing: Business Models, ROI and Best Practices*, 2nd edn, Alpharetta, Ga.: Mivar Press.

15 Howie, D. (2007). *Building a Successful Captive Services Centre in the Financial Services Sector*, London: TPI Research Report, www.tpi.net/pdf/ papers/BuildingSuccessfulCaptiveCenters.pdf.

16 See Robinson and Kalakota (2005) in note 14 above.

17 Dixit, A. (2007). Build Operate Transfer: Tensilica's Experience in Offshoring Engineering to India, cited in Metters, R. and Verma, R. (2008). History of Offshoring Knowledge Services, *Journal of Operations Management*, 26(2), 141–7.

18 See Lampel and Bhalla (2008) in note 13 above.

19 See Rottman and Lacity (2004) in note 12 above.

20 Bahli, B. and Rivard, S. (2005). Validating Measures of Information Technology Outsourcing Risk Factors, *Omega*, 33, 175–87.

21 See Stringfellow *et al.* (2008) in note 6 above.

22 See Aron and Singh (2005) in note 1 above.

23 Currie, W., Michell, V. and Abanishe, O. (2008). Knowledge Process Outsourcing in Financial Services: The Vendor Perspective, *European Management Journal*, 26, 94–104.

24 Bannerjee, I., Narendran, J. and Priyadarshini, R. (2007). *Knowledge Process Offshoring (KPO): A Balanced View of an Emerging Market*, London: TPI Research Report, www.tpi.net/pdf/researchreports/KPO_ResearchReport_july07.pdf; and see Currie *et al.* (2008) in note 23 above.

25 Mithas, S. and Whitaker, J. (2007). Is the World Flat or Spiky? Information Intensity, Skills, and Global Service Disaggregation, *Information Systems Research*, 18(3), 237–59.

26 Drezner, D. (2004). The Outsourcing Bogeyman, *Foreign Affairs*, 83(3), 22–35; Hall (1976) in note 5 above.

27 See Mithas and Whitaker (2007) in note 25 above.

28 For additional reading on modularisation, see Baldwin, C. and Clark, K. (1997). Managing in the Age of Modularity, *Harvard Business Review*, 75(5), 84–93; Schilling, M. and Steensma, K. (2001). The Use of Modular Organisational Forms: An Industry Level Analysis, *Academy of Management Journal*, 44(6), 1149–68; and Schilling, M. (2000). Towards a General Modular Systems Theory and its Application to Inter-firm Product Modularity, *Academy of Management Review*, 25(2), 312–34.

29 Tanriverdi, H., Konana, P. and Ge, L. (2007). The Choice of Sourcing Mechanisms for Business Processes, *Information Systems Research*, 18(3), 280–99.

Recommended key reading

Carmel, E. and Abbott, P. (2007). Why 'Nearshore' Means that Distance Matters, *Communications of the ACM*, 50(10), 40–6. This paper provides an excellent overview of the motives of companies for pursuing the nearshore location option for information technology services.

Currie, W., Michell, V. and Abanishe, O. (2008). Knowledge Process Outsourcing in Financial Services: The Vendor Perspective, *European Management Journal*, 26, 94–104. This paper examines knowledge process outsourcing, and finds that vendors are gradually offering more complex, knowledge-intensive services to clients. However, vendors face challenges including winning client confidence and reducing risks for clients.

Doh, J. (2005). Offshore Outsourcing: Implications for International Business and Strategic Management Theory and Practice, *Journal of Management Studies*, 42, 695–705. This paper reviews a number of international business and strategic management theories, and their relevance to the global outsourcing phenomenon.

Gereffi, G., Humphrey, J. and Sturgeon, T. (2005). The Governance of Global Value Chains, *Review of International Political Economy*, 12(1), 78–104. This paper presents a framework that explains governance patterns in global value chains. It identifies three key variables – the complexity of transactions, the ability to codify transactions and the capabilities in the supply base. The framework identifies five types of global value chain governance – hierarchy, captive, relational, modular and market.

Mithas, S. and Whitaker, J. (2007). Is the World Flat or Spiky? Information Intensity, Skills, and Global Service Disaggregation, *Information Systems Research*, 18(3), 237–59. This paper proposes a theory of service disaggregation, and argues that high information intensity makes an occupation more likely to be disaggregated because the activities in these occupations can be codified, standardised and modularised.

Sako, M. (2009). Globalisation of Knowledge-intensive Professional Services, *Communications of the ACM*, 52(7), 31–3. This paper uses the constructs of decomposition, iteration and disaggregation to explore the impacts of global outsourcing on legal services.

Managing global services outsourcing arrangements

5.1 Introduction

Organisations are often drawn to global services outsourcing to avail of the potential labour cost savings. However, organisations fail to take account of the transaction costs involved in managing global services arrangements. Transaction costs are difficult to measure objectively, and are much higher than those associated with domestic outsourcing as a result of differences in culture, language and time zone and of geographic distance. Cultural differences can lead to communication difficulties between client and vendor personnel, which can adversely impact service quality levels. In addition, where the vendor is in a different time zone, the client will have to employ project managers in different shift patterns to manage the vendor, which is an additional cost over domestic outsourcing. These transaction costs can offset any gains from savings on labour costs, and also lead to service quality problems.

An area where the global services outsourcing phenomenon has had a significant impact has been that of software development. Many software development projects now involve teams of people from the client and vendor working together, speaking a variety of languages, and separated by time and geographic distance. Although global software development can deliver reduced development times as a result of 'follow-the-sun' working, and of access to a highly skilled and lower cost labour pool, it presents significant challenges. The lack of face-to-face interaction between client and vendor personnel separated by geographic distance can lead to breakdowns in communication and misunderstandings in client requirements. In addition, culture and geographic distance increase the challenges of fostering collaboration and a team ethos in global software development projects.

This chapter focuses on the area of software development to illustrate the issues involved in managing global services outsourcing arrangements. Software development is one of the most challenging areas of global outsourcing, and provides an illustration of the complexity of managing such arrangements. In addition, this is a well-developed area in practice where companies have been adopting innovative and novel practices to obtain the potential benefits and mitigate the risks. The chapter is structured as follows. An overview of the software development process is presented, along with the risks involved in managing these arrangements in a global context. This is followed by an overview of the key issues involved in effectively managing global software development outsourcing projects. Throughout this analysis, illustrations of practices adopted by clients and vendors to manage the challenges of global software development outsourcing are introduced. Finally, summary implications from the analysis are presented.

5.2 Software development outsourcing

Software development involves producing information technology (IT) applications for organisations. Traditionally, in many organisations software development was performed by systems analysts and programmers internally in an IT department, taking input from users of the application inside the organisation. Users from functions such as human resources, operations, finance and marketing worked closely with systems analysts to develop applications to meet their requirements. In some cases, this involved implementing off-the-shelf applications from vendors, with little need for adaptation. However, in many cases users required a highly customised application, which involved frequent and intensive interaction between users and systems analysts to elicit user requirements for the application. The trend towards outsourcing has meant that the software development process is now being performed by both local and global software vendors, who work with IT personnel and users from various functions in the client organisation. There are a number of stages in software development outsourcing, as shown in Figure 5.1.

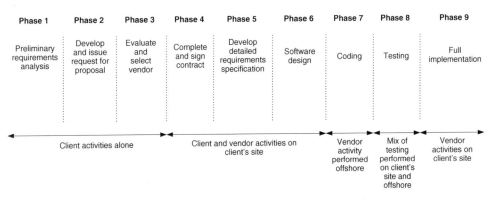

Figure 5.1   Software development outsourcing phases

The preliminary requirements phase involves users and systems analysts in the client determining preliminary system requirements, which is used to develop the request for the proposal (RFP). Vendors are then invited to submit tenders. The next phase involves selecting the most suitable vendor that meets client requirements. The client and vendor selected will agree on the most appropriate contract and negotiate the terms and conditions. In the detailed requirements analysis phase, systems analysts in both the client and vendor work together on the client's site to determine detailed requirements specifications. This involves vendor business analysts gaining an understanding of the client's business and the needs of users for the new application.

In the software design phase, the vendor business analysts develop a detailed specification of what the system will do, and how it will perform its functions. This is normally done on the client's site in consultation with client business analysts. The system then will be developed and coded by programmers in the vendor's offshore site. Communication will occur between the programmers offshore and vendor business analysts located on the client's site. Testing the system for errors and whether it meets user requirements will be completed both by programmers offshore and client and vendor staff located on the client's site. Finally, the implementation phase involves both the client and vendor installing the system and training users at the client's site.

Global software development outsourcing poses a number of challenges for the client. The requirements analysis phase provides an illustration. This phase involves users and systems analysts in both the client and vendor working closely to define application requirements on the client's site. These requirements are then sent to staff in the vendor's offshore site, where the code is written, and then sent back to the onsite vendor team for delivery to the client. The requirements may also change during the testing phase. However, requirements analysis is extremely challenging in a global context for a number of reasons:[1]

- The craft nature of software development relies on personal interaction between developers, rather than purely on the exchange of documentation.
- Software development involves high levels of ambiguity and uncertainty, as the client often cannot fully specify its requirements. This leads to inconsistencies and differences in interpretation of requirements.
- Users in the client organisation have different and changing interests and needs, which make it difficult for systems analysts to interpret and

analyse requirements. The effects of misinterpreting requirements can adversely impact later phases of software development, leading to poor quality and dissatisfied users.

The challenges of global software development outsourcing are not exclusive to the requirements analysis phase. Project management is an important aspect of software development, and involves estimating the time schedule and resource allocation involved in each phase of development. Even when organisations decide to develop software applications internally, the development effort often significantly exceeds the initial estimate. This becomes even more challenging in the context of global development projects, where the project requires varied levels of communication, co-ordination and management, and where some phases of the development process are done on the client's site and some offshore.[2] Normally, 70–80 per cent of the development effort is done offshore, and the other 20–30 per cent is done at the client's site. However, this onshore–offshore mix can change over time depending upon peaks and troughs in the workload and changing client requirements.[3] Therefore, many projects are characterised by cost overruns. In addition, the lack of skills and experience, high project complexity and poor requirements specification and design can lead to further project delays and poor quality.[4] The risks of offshore software development are influenced by other factors such as the lack of top management commitment in the client, inadequate user involvement and language and cultural barriers in project communications. These risks are summarised in Table 5.1.

5.3 Strategies for managing global software development outsourcing projects

Organisations have been pursuing a number of strategies to manage global software development projects effectively. There are a number of pre-contractual strategies that clients can pursue prior to outsourcing including having a formal global outsourcing strategy, effectively selecting vendors and selecting and designing an appropriate contract. In addition, there are a number of post-contractual strategies for managing the development project. These include establishing effective client–vendor interfaces, employing appropriate communication media, knowledge management, managing culture and managing time zone differences. These strategies are now discussed.

Table 5.1 Risk factors in offshore software development outsourcing

Risk factor	Description
Lack of top management commitment	Without top management support, projects face difficulties in securing the necessary resource and co-operation across the client organisation.
Requirements communication difficulties	Reduced face-to-face contact and informal communications between the client and vendor can lead to misunderstandings of requirements. Often assumptions have to be made in the case of very detailed requirements.
Language barriers	Lead to project delays and conflicts. Language misunderstandings occur due to cultural differences. It takes more time to communicate in offshore development projects.
Inadequate user involvement	Many development projects fail to involve users, which can lead to quality problems and project delays.
Lack of client expertise on offshore outsourcing	Many clients do not have the expertise to monitor offshore work and integrate new technology into their existing business. Offshore software development requires specialised expertise, often not available in the client organisation.
Failure to manage end-user expectations	Expectations must be managed to ensure that the system is consistent with user perceptions. This is extremely challenging in an offshore context, as users are not in direct contact with system developers.
Poor change controls	Requirements changes lead to delays and overruns when not managed properly. Even when changes are documented and justified, delays can occur due to questions and clarifications from offshore developers. If modifications are not managed well, contract disputes can arise.
Lack of business knowledge in vendor	Offshore staff do not have sufficient understanding of the client's business context, which can cause project delays and quality problems. Understanding the workflow and operations of the client is an important factor in effective software development.

Table 5.1 (*cont.*)

Risk factor	Description
Lack of technical expertise in vendor	Offshore vendors can over-sell their technical skills. The level of technical sophistication in a location may differ significantly from that of the client's home location. In addition, the vendor's most competent staff may be over-committed in other client projects.

Sources: Iacavou, C. and Nakatsu, R. (2008). A Risk Profile of Offshore Outsourced Development Projects, *Communications of the ACM*, 51(6), 89–94; Sakthivel, S. (2007). Managing Risk in Offshore Systems Development, *Communications of the ACM*, 50(4), 69–75; Qu, Z. and Brocklehurst, M. (2003). What Will it Take for China to Become a Competitive Force in Offshore Outsourcing, *Journal of Information Technology*, 18, 53–67.

5.4 Pre-contractual strategies

Formal strategy

As with any outsourcing initiative an organisation should have a formal strategy which focuses on maximising the benefits and mitigating the risks. There are a number of important aspects of a formal strategy for software development outsourcing.

Select the right project. Software applications with well-established technologies, standard business processes and relatively stable client requirements are suitable for global outsourcing. In addition, where there are clearly defined interfaces between system design, coding and testing phases, there are likely to be lower risks in managing the project with the foreign vendor. Applications important to the competitive advantage of the client and requiring untried technologies are unsuitable for offshoring.[5] Many offshore vendors do not possess the capabilities to develop these applications, because of a lack of investment in research and development and a lack of skills in the latest technologies. Strategically important applications require innovation and experimentation involving new technologies and users. Separating developers and users through significant geographical and time differences diminishes the potential for innovation.

Vendor strategy. There are a range of options available to the client when selecting and managing vendors. There are a number of location options when selecting a vendor, including local, nearshore and off-shore. For example, the client may decide to select a nearshore vendor because of a lack of experience of managing offshore vendors, and the need for cultural and geographical closeness in the development process. The client may select an offshore vendor for part of the project in order to encourage its local vendors to improve cost and performance. In addition, the client may select a number of offshore vendors for similar projects both to create competition between the vendors and to mitigate risk if one vendor fails. Selecting an appropriate sourcing model is another mechanism for mitigating risks. Establishing a captive arrangement eliminates the potential for opportunism when dealing with an independent vendor. The captive arrangement enables the client to have standardised and compatible development processes, intellectual property rights protection, better team cohesion and greater control.

Manage the people issues. Employing global software vendors inevitably leads to changes for IT staff and users of software applications in the client organisation. Prior to outsourcing, the client should have a plan in place to deal with these issues. This will include arrangements for dealing with possible redundancies, retraining and redeploying affected staff to other parts of the organisation. In the face of job losses, the client will have to reassure and motivate employees who remain in the organisation. The client should ensure that important knowledge is not lost through either redundancies or redeployment. There are also organisational change implications for employees remaining in the IT department. Different work patterns will have to be implemented in order to manage vendors in different time zones. The attitudes and needs of internal users of software applications will have to be considered. Internal users must be made aware of and educated on the cultural differences involved in working with global vendors rather than local vendors during the testing and implementation phases of the development project.

Develop vendor management capabilities. Managing offshore software vendors requires a different set of skills to those needed in managing local vendors. Firstly, the client must have a plan for developing the skill levels of its project managers and business analysts. This can be accomplished through training. Experimenting with small offshore development projects is a valuable mechanism for developing experience levels, and also for assessing the capabilities of offshore vendors. Recruiting new staff with experience of managing offshore vendors is another important aspect of developing vendor management capabilities. The client should ensure that they have adequate qualified staff for each phase of the development process. Developing vendor management capabilities requires support from top management and the allocation of sufficient resource. Therefore, it is important that global outsourcing is not viewed by top management solely as a strategy for reducing labour costs.

Vendor selection

Organisations must have a vendor selection approach which enables them to achieve the objectives of the outsourcing strategy. Vendor selection has become increasingly important as organisations outsource larger-scale software development projects, and develop more collaborative and longer-term relationships with vendors in foreign locations. Vendor selection can be extremely time-consuming and resource-intensive, as it involves in-depth analysis of potential vendors and, in some cases, site visits. Even when selecting vendors for short-term fee-for-service arrangements, the analysis extends to more factors than price alone. Factors such as service quality and responsiveness of the vendor have become increasingly prominent in vendor selection. In addition, the criticality and complexity of the software application will influence the level of attention that should be given to the vendor selection process. In the case of critical projects, vendor selection is a strategic decision that will involve active participation from senior management. There are a number of aspects to vendor selection.

Preliminary requirements analysis

Preliminary requirements analysis is the starting point for vendor selection and involves determining what is required from the vendor. This involves obtaining an overview of application requirements in order to establish the skills and resources required from the vendor. The objectives of the offshore outsourcing strategy will also assist in this phase. At the most basic level, these will include a specification of the software application the vendor should provide to the client. Once the client has decided what is required from the vendor, it can then determine the criteria it wishes to employ to evaluate potential vendors. Clearly, the complexity of requirements and the financial value of the contract will influence the criteria used for evaluation. In the case of highly complex development projects that require close collaboration with the vendor, criteria such as top management compatibility between the client and vendor, cultural alignment and the strategic direction of the vendor are important considerations. Although criteria such as top management compatibility and cultural alignment are highly subjective, they are important determinants of the success of outsourcing relationships.

Develop and issue request for proposal (RFP)

An RFP is a detailed specification of client requirements including skills required, language skills, IP protection, infrastructure and quality certifications etc. This provides vendors with an opportunity to prepare a bid for the contract. The client can contact a number of vendors and make a request for information on the services the vendor provides. This is normally done via a questionnaire that elicits information on vendor size, location, infrastructure, technical skills, pricing structures, industry know-how, references from other clients, internal processes, quality certifications and client base. The client should have an understanding of the types of vendor available in the foreign location. Once the information has been collected, each vendor will be compared against the required criteria. This will provide an opportunity to remove any vendors that are totally unsuitable.

Evaluation

This involves evaluating the vendors that submitted a tender for the development project. The outsourcing strategy will fail if the vendor lacks the depth and breadth of service capability, or cannot provide the full range of services required by the client. Therefore, significant attention will be given to evaluating vendors, particularly in the case of complex, high-value contracts where the client requires business improvement capabilities. This will involve a thorough review of vendors, usually involving visits to vendor facilities, interviews, presentations and information-sharing. This interaction will occur at both the operational and strategic levels.

Top management from the client and vendor must be involved in communicating the expectations of each party in the outsourcing arrangement. Interaction at the operational level is also important in the evaluation phase. The success of the relationship will be largely determined at the operational level where it is managed on a day-to-day basis. In effect, this analysis is concerned with evaluating the potential fit between the client's and vendor's management philosophies and commitment to the same values over time.

An important consideration in the context of large-scale software development projects is a long-term focus. As well as considering the current performance and capability of a vendor, the future direction and capabilities of a vendor should be assessed. The attitudes and culture of the vendor will provide a sound indication of its aspirations for the future. Financial standing will also be a sound indicator of the ability of the vendor to deliver the required capabilities over the long term. The commitment of the vendor to its areas of strength should also be considered through an analysis of its current commitments and future strategy.

Of course, it is possible that the client is familiar with a vendor through previous offshore outsourcing initiatives. In this case, the level of evaluation will be influenced by the client's prior experience with the vendor and the historical performance of the vendor. In many cases, the client will feel more comfortable with outsourcing further projects to a vendor with which it already has done business.[6] In fact, in-depth knowledge of the vendor's capabilities and performance may have created the initial impetus for outsourcing additional projects to the vendor. However, the client will still have to give careful consideration to the selection decision.

Selection

In the final selection decision, each vendor will be evaluated against its ability to meet the criteria identified. If the client cannot select a suitable vendor that meets the criteria, this will have significant implications for the outsourcing strategy. In fact, the failure to select a vendor may force the organisation to abandon outsourcing and continue to develop the application internally or use a domestic vendor. Therefore, it is important that the client should identify a number of suitable vendors at a very early stage of the global outsourcing strategy to avoid this scenario.

Contracting

Effective contracts in an offshore context share many of the attributes of contracts with local vendors. Cost and performance requirements should be specified as precisely as possible. Loosely defined performance levels and unspecified non-performance clauses are likely to lead to future difficulties in the outsourcing arrangement. Incentives should be incorporated into the contract to encourage the vendor to meet or exceed performance requirements. Clients' requirements can differ for each software development project, which means that different contract clauses on service levels, resolution of performance disputes and termination are required. Clients often start with a standard contract and customise it to meet the specific needs of each software development outsourcing project. The contract should be as complete as possible, avoiding the need for costly contract renegotiations. Differences in legal systems, as well as geographical, time zone and culture differences between countries increase the challenges of drafting

Table 5.2 Key elements of global contracts

Elements
• Definition of work schedule including time zones, holiday schedules at nearshore and offshore locations.
• Distribution of resources between the client's site and vendor at various phases of the development project.
• Skill levels of nearshore and offshore staff and mechanisms for dealing with staff turnover.
• Stipulations for handling sub-contracted work.
• Payment terms including currencies, payment schedules and payment frequency.
• Contract penalties and bonuses.
• Stipulations for resolution of disputes.
• Jurisdiction for resolution of disputes (often a third country of arbitration rather than vendor's country).
• Data security and confidentiality.
• Intellectual property rights protection.

Source: Adapted from Ranganathan, C. and Balaji, S. (2007). Critical Capabilities for Offshore Outsourcing of Information Systems, *MIS Quarterly Executive*, 6(3), 147–61.

complete contracts in an offshore context. Table 5.2 shows key aspects of global software development project contracts.

The two most prominent types of contract in software development outsourcing are *fixed-price* and *time-and-materials*.[7] In fixed-price contracts, the client pays a pre-negotiated, fixed price for the complete development project, which is linked to clearly defined deliverables. Under this contract, most of the risk is borne by the vendor. The vendor has to have extensive skills to estimate the time and resource required to complete the development project. The fixed-price contract provides the vendor with an incentive to staff projects with their most productive people in order to increase their margins.[8] However, a limitation for the client is that vendors may sacrifice quality to meet over-ambitious deadlines. Fixed-price contracts are only suitable for projects where client needs can be clearly specified.

Under the time-and-materials contract, the vendor contracts out its services, whilst the client is responsible for monitoring progress, and thereby incurring the costs of any overruns. The time-and-materials contract is employed when the requirements and implementation schedule are difficult to specify at the beginning of the contract. Clearly, the overall costs are higher in time-and-materials contracts as there is an onus on the client to actively manage the vendor to ensure quality is maintained and costs do not increase. For example, the vendor may place new employees on a contract as the client is subsidising the employee's learning curve.[9] Clients can pre-empt such actions by stipulating in the contract the minimum years of employee experience and requesting to see the curricula vitae of vendor employees.

As organisations have become more experienced with global outsourcing arrangements, they have been employing strategies to mitigate the risks of ineffective contracts. Companies have been forming contract design teams with legal, functional and information systems experts to develop and negotiate global contracts.[10] Specialist legal expertise has been introduced to include detailed dispute resolution mechanisms and stipulations to reflect the global nature of software development projects. Rather than relying solely on the contract, some companies have been employing other approaches to protect intellectual property (IP) in software development projects. Some clients have been splitting project development among a number of vendors, and thus distributing the IP. Through separating elements of the project, each vendor is unable to understand the important IP associated with the entire project.

5.5 Post-contractual strategies

Establish effective client–vendor interfaces

Clients and vendors have been establishing interface structures to ensure effective communication between the personnel involved in global software development projects. These structures are designed to create clear lines of communication and co-ordination, and clear interfaces between client and vendor teams. One structure employed is known as the funnel design, as shown in Figure 5.2. In this structure, communication from users of the application and technical staff in the client is funnelled through the client project managers to the vendor's on-site engagement manager. The skills and experience of the vendor's engagement manager are critical to ensuring the effectiveness of this design arrangement.[11] The single point of contact can reduce the cultural, time zone and communication risks, as the client has better control over the on-site vendor engagement manager.

Another structure employed is the mirrored design, which is employed in close collaborative arrangements where there is the need for intensive and frequent communication.[12] The client and vendor have multiple levels

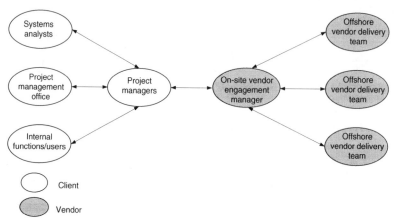

Figure 5.2   The funnel interface structure

of formalised communication, and structures in the client and vendor mirror each other. On the client side, the team leads report to each other and the development staff, including systems analysts and technical designers, who report back to the team leads. On the vendor side, the 'anchor' role corresponds to the client project manager, with the relevant team leads and development staff underneath. The vendor's development staff includes a mix of employees located on the client's site and in its nearshore or offshore operation. Although there are significant costs with this arrangement, it is suitable for managing complex, large-scale development projects.

An important influence on how clients manage software development projects with global vendors has been the Capability Maturity Model (CMM). The CMM was developed by Carnegie Mellon's Software Engineering Institute, and has become a global standard for software development processes. It has been employed to measure progress in software development and compare one software vendor's processes with another's. As well as being used as a tool for software process improvement, clients have been selecting vendors that are committed to the CMM as a way of co-ordinating processes in software development projects.[13] CMM is designed to facilitate communication, and enable smooth handoffs between the client and vendor at various phases of development. The CMM provides guidelines for embedding disciplined practices into various phases of the software development process. Companies can develop their software development and project management capabilities through integrating the practices associated with each certification level of the CMM.

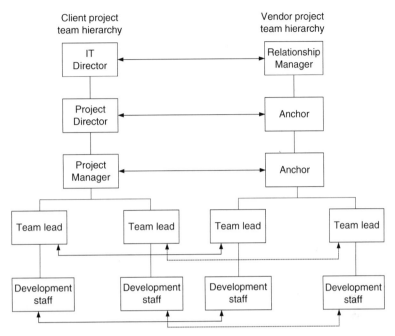

Figure 5.3   The mirrored design interface structure

Source: Kaiser, K. and Hawk, S. (2004). Evolution of Offshore Software Development: From Outsourcing to Co-sourcing, *MIS Quarterly Executive*, 3(2), 69–81.

There are a number of ways in which clients can co-ordinate work more effectively with the vendor's CMM activities:[14]

- Clients should attain the same level of certification in CMM as their vendors. Client personnel will find it difficult to work with vendor staff who are at a higher level of certification than themselves, as their specifications and documentation will not be sufficiently detailed.
- A major risk for the client is that the vendor will not understand fully its requirements, leading to expensive iteration to resolve any misunderstandings. One practice for mitigating this risk involves the vendor locating on the client's site a CMM Level V expert with no knowledge of the client's business. This expert can then identify any ambiguities in the requirements specification documentation that personnel in the vendor's offshore operations are likely to encounter.
- Clients should consider a flexible approach to CMM because of unnecessary documentation and associated costs. Minor changes to requirements can lead to extensive documentation to satisfy the relevant CMM

Illustration 5.1 The Capability Maturity Model

The CMM has its origins in the areas of quality and continuous process improvement, and was initially used as a tool for comparing vendor capabilities. Many software development projects are characterised by quality problems and cost overruns, primarily as a result of the way in which the software project is organised and co-ordinated. Software development has normally been a craft process, with no standard method or approach. Variations in both practice and performance have been enormous, often as a result of the lack of process activities or process performance standards. The CMM emerged as an approach to address these difficulties. The CMM maps the software development process onto a five-level system (initial, repeatable, defined, managed and optimised), with each level defining a greater level of management control and sophistication. There are a number of key activities associated with each level in the CMM, as shown in Table 5.3.

Achieving certification in CMM involves making significant investments in infrastructure, systems and people. Organisations have to compare their development and project management processes with the CMM framework, and identify aspects that have to be improved. Rigorous metrics have to be established to collect data in order to evaluate aspects of the development process, and to have audit systems to track non-conformance of best practice, process deviations and exceptions. Investment in training programmes is also an important aspect of improving process capability under the CMM. This involves ongoing training in new software process and project management skills for software developers and managers.

Software vendors in many countries have been very proactive in their efforts to become certified in the CMM. Level IV certification in the model is viewed by vendors as an important factor in winning outsourcing contracts in the global market for software services. In particular, Indian vendors have been extremely proactive in achieving Level IV certification in the CMM. However, the CMM has posed challenges to Western clients. The high level of documentation associated with the CMM has led to difficulties for clients when working with vendors at higher levels of certification. For example, when the software development project is undertaken locally, the requirements definition phase can be carried out informally, as system users are located on the same site. This contrasts with global development projects where extensive formal and informal communication among client systems analysts, systems users and vendor personnel has to take place in order to generate the required documentation. Clients have to assess carefully the CMM capabilities of the vendor during the vendor selection phase, because CMM certification levels are only assessed once. Although the vendor may have achieved CMM certification in the past, a lack of ongoing commitment to the CMM processes and high staff turnover in the vendor can weaken its capabilities in this area.

Table 5.3 Key activities in the CMM

Maturity level	Description	Key process activities
I. Initial	*Ad hoc* approach to software development with few defined processes	None
II. Repeatable	Basic, repeatable project management approaches to track costs, schedules and functionality	Software configuration management Software quality assurance Software subcontract management Software project tracking and oversight Software project planning Requirements management
III. Defined	Elements of effective management and software engineering embedded into a standard software development process	Peer reviews Inter-group co-ordination Software product engineering Integrated software management Training programme Organisation process definition Organisation process focus
IV. Managed	Collection and analysis of detailed measures of software process and quality	Software quality management Quantitative process management
V. Optimised	Organisation has all previous capabilities, and an environment that encourages continuous improvement and learning from experience	Process change management Technology change management Defect prevention

Sources: Davenport, T. (2005). The Coming Commoditization of Processes, *Harvard Business Review*, 83(6), 101–8; Ethiraj, S., Kale, P., Krishnan, M. and Singh, J. (2005). Where Do Capabilities Come From and How Do They Matter? A Study in the Software Services Industry, *Strategic Management Journal*, 26, 25–45; Jiang, J., Kelin, G., Hwang, H., Huang, J. and Hung, S. (2004). An Exploration of the Relationship between Software Development Process Maturity and Project Performance, *Information and Management*, 41, 279–88.

level requirements. Clients should only focus on the CMM processes that add most value. Vendors have begun to offer a flexible CMM model that delivers high quality and value, whilst minimising documentation costs.

Employ appropriate communication media

Effective communication between the client and vendor is an important element of any outsourcing arrangement. However, communication is even more important in global outsourcing arrangements where client and vendor personnel are separated by physical distance and time zone differences. Time zone differences between team members mean that queries and problems cannot be resolved as quickly as with local vendors, which ultimately slows down development times. Effectively employing communication media can reduce these difficulties and ensure that frequent and clear dialogue occurs between the client and the vendor's on-site and offshore or nearshore development teams. Table 5.4 provides an overview of the communication media used to co-ordinate global software teams.

Face-to-face interaction provides the richest form of synchronous communication, and facilitates the development of interpersonal relationships and team-building between client and vendor employees. Advances in information and communication technologies (ICTs) have increased the importance of technologies in facilitating communication in global teamwork – sometimes referred to as virtual teams.[15] Increasingly, rich synchronous communication such as video conferencing and less rich synchronous communication media such as desktop video conferencing have become substitutes for face-to-face interactions.[16] ICTs can be used to transfer knowledge in important phases of the development process including communicating client system requirements to the vendor, and transferring knowledge of policies, processes and systems from the on-site team to the offshore team. In addition, collaborative technologies such as group support systems, shared application development repositories, file-sharing and application-sharing technologies support communication in a global team environment. Lean synchronous communication media such as the telephone, conference calls on the Internet and instant messaging systems are also important tools for communication.

Although ICTs and other technologies are important communication media for managing global teams, they cannot be used exclusively to co-ordinate teamwork. Language and cultural differences can create communication difficulties, misunderstanding, and conflict between team

Table 5.4 Communication media and global software teams

Time	Location	Communication type	Communication media
Real time	Same location	Richest synchronous	Face-to-face interaction
Real time	Different location	Rich synchronous	Video conferencing, supported via group support systems and shared application development data repository.
Real time	Different location	Less-rich synchronous	Desktop video and audio conferencing, supported via group support systems, chat facilities, file-sharing etc.
Real time	Different location	Lean synchronous	Telephone, conference calls, instant messaging systems, chat facilities, group support systems, application development data repository etc.
Different time	Same or different location	Asynchronous	Email, file transfers, voicemail, group support systems and shared application development data repository.

Source: Adapted from Sakthivel, S. (2005). Virtual Workgroups in Offshore Systems Development, *Information and Software Technology*, 47, 305–18.

members. It is extremely challenging to build up trust in a team setting, which is particularly important in large-scale software development projects where communication takes place through technologies. Studies have found that people are less productive and less satisfied than those who work in a face-to-face team environment.[17] In addition, technologies such as desktop video conferencing are not suitable for all types of project task and people, and can adversely impact group performance.[18] There are a number of important factors that have to be considered when using technologies for managing communication in global software development teams.

Combination of communication media. Face-to-face interaction and physical proximity are still very necessary communication media, particularly in the case of complex software development projects that require high levels of collaboration. Collaborative tasks that require creativity, innovation and consensus require face-to-face interactions, as numerous and complex interactions have to occur between team members.[19] Therefore, the client and vendor have to combine rich communication media with ICTs to facilitate team co-operation throughout the development project. Some clients have established web portals with data repositories to serve as a central storage point for project-related information and communication. These technologies have been combined with face-to-face meetings, telephone conversations and instant messaging.[20] To build up stronger interpersonal relationships between client and vendor personnel, clients have created online communities, and client analysts have travelled to vendor operations, or vendor developers have visited client operations.

Alignment of communication media with the appropriate development phase. Certain communication media are more suitable to particular phases of the software development process. ICTs such as email, file transfers and shared data repositories are appropriate for clearly specified and structured tasks such as the coding phase, which is carried out in accordance with the system specification. In contrast, the requirements analysis phase demands intensive face-to-face interaction so that client personnel can convey user needs, and vendor personnel can understand the client's business domain. In addition, face-to-face interaction can be an effective medium for resolving misunderstandings and queries quickly, and generating ideas for system improvements.

Illustration 5.2 Creating socialisation in global software development projects

Socialisation can be used to improve collaboration between client and vendor personnel in global software development teams. Socialisation involves individuals acquiring the behaviours, attitudes and knowledge required to participate in a team environment. Socialisation facilitates the development of norms, identity and cohesion among team members, which improves communication and team performance. Socialisation in global software development projects is facilitated via two mechanisms, the deployment of ICTs and face-to-face (F2F) interactions. ICTs such as email, video conferencing, intranets and electronic meeting systems have been used to support socialisation between remote team members. F2F interactions are important for establishing interpersonal relationships between team members. F2F interactions positively influence team collaboration and performance through the development of one-to-one interactions between team members. However, there are challenges with using F2F interactions to create socialisation in global software development projects:

- F2F meetings are short and offer only limited social space to deal with cultural differences.
- Most of the time spent in F2F meetings involves dealing with project procedures and technical issues.
- F2F meetings are often selective as not all team members are invited to meetings.
- Short and infrequent F2F meetings facilitate sporadic interpersonal interactions between remote team members, which hinder the development of interpersonal relationships.

Oshri *et al.* carried out a study of SAP, LeCroy and Baan to understand how companies promoted socialisation in teams in global software development projects. They found that teams have to resocialise over time as circumstances change. For example, the introduction of new technology into development projects creates the need for the global team members to reacquire norms and work attitudes relating to new practices, tools and procedures. Companies also employed a number of mechanisms and processes to ensure socialisation is created and maintained throughout the project. Video conferencing as a means of introducing team members to the global team was useful for building up collaboration prior to F2F meetings. Making time during F2F meetings for social activities and one-to-one discussions was valuable in allowing remote team members to acquire norms, attitudes and behaviours. Reacquiring norms and attitudes throughout the project required additional mechanisms such as short visits and rich electronic communication media. Regularly reacquiring norms and attitudes is an important aspect of socialisation in large-scale software development projects. New team members often join at different phases of the project, which affects norms and attitudes. This can create disagreement and miscommunication between team members, which can lead to project delays, cost overruns and quality problems.

F2F meetings are important for creating interpersonal ties and socialisation. However, socialisation is not developed through F2F meetings alone. Activities employed before and after F2F meetings such as language courses, short visits, company newsletters and temporary co-location allowed teams to socialise and, where appropriate, reacquire norms and attitudes. Based upon their analysis, Oshri *et al.* proposed a three-phase framework for creating, maintaining and renewing socialisation in global software teams:

- *Introduction.* This phase relates to the initial stage of the project, or when a new member joins the project. Remote team members are introduced to the norms, attitudes and behaviours that govern collaboration in the global team.
- *Build-up.* This involves advancing the socialisation process through F2F meetings. This allows remote team members to negotiate communication procedures and resolve any collaboration issues. A large F2F meeting should take place at the beginning of the project, followed by additional meetings throughout the project with fewer remote team members involved.
- *Renewal.* This involves re-socialisation. As the interpretation of work and communication procedures by remote team members change, a 're-norming' process may have to take place. Much of this can be done through ICTs, as well as short visits and relocations.

Investing in the development of socialisation allows the client and vendor to achieve collaboration, leading to higher productivity and performance in the development project. Table 5.5 shows the activities involved in developing

Table 5.5 Activities for supporting socialisation

	Before F2F	During F2F	After F2F

Individual	Offer language courses
	Increase awareness of
	  communication styles
	Arrange short visits to
	  remote locations
		Facilitate one-to-one
		  interactions
		Provide sense of importance
		  of each member
		Adjust communication styles
			Offer visits to remote
			  locations
			Offer temporary co-location
			Establish real-time
			  communication channels

Team	Introduce new team members
	Increase awareness of
	  team composition
	Offer virtual F2F meetings
	Increase awareness of
	  communication protocols
	Establish mini-teams
	Establish contact person
	  for remote team
		Run start-up meeting
		Facilitate multiple
		  interactions between
		  team members
		Offer team-building
		  exercises
		Organise social events
		Discuss cultural differences
			Facilitate reflection sessions
			Facilitate progress meetings

Organisational	Distribute newsletters
	Create and offer shared
	  Internet space
		Discuss organisational
		  structure
		Discuss organisational
		  culture differences
			Establish direct
			  communication channels

Source: Adapted from Oshri, I., Kotlarsky, J. and Willcocks, L. (2007). Global Software Development: Exploring Socialisation and Face-to-Face Meetings in Distributed Strategic Projects, *Journal of Strategic Information Systems*, 16, 25–49.

> socialisation at the individual, team and organisational levels. These activities illustrate the multiple channels available for facilitating socialisation among remote team members.
>
> *Source:* Oshri, I., Kotlarsky, J. and Willcocks, L. (2007). Global Software Development: Exploring Socialisation and Face-to-Face Meetings in Distributed Strategic Projects, *Journal of Strategic Information Systems*, 16, 25–49.

Knowledge management

Sharing knowledge between the client and vendor is an important aspect of software development projects. This involves having mechanisms in place to ensure that the relevant knowledge is transferred, leveraged and shared between the client and vendor. Knowledge in software development projects includes technical knowledge on systems, technologies and tools and business knowledge on business processes, company functions and the industry. However, there are a number of properties of knowledge that make its management complex.[21] Firstly, knowledge is distributed on both sides of the relationship between the client and vendor. In a development project, the client possesses knowledge about its business needs from the application, and the vendor possesses technical knowledge on how to develop the software. Secondly, some of the knowledge is complex and context-dependent, which makes it difficult to articulate and transfer between the client and vendor. Exploiting this type of knowledge involves transferring it from the organisation in which it resides to the organisation that will use it. Finally, the client has to be careful not to share knowledge that is commercially sensitive and valuable to its competitors.

In routine software projects, where formal requirements and system design can be easily developed, knowledge-sharing is likely to be straightforward. The client can transfer knowledge of its requirements to the vendor, and the vendor does not need extensive knowledge of the client's business to develop the application. In complex development projects knowledge-sharing is extremely challenging. For example, where the project is novel and it is difficult to formalise requirements, knowledge transfer will be difficult, as the vendor may misunderstand client requirements. However, there are a number of ways of dealing with these challenges.

A potential solution for dealing with knowledge-sharing difficulties is not to outsource such a development project. However, where the client has to outsource project development, it should select a vendor with extensive knowledge of the client's industry, and ensure that the vendor can exploit knowledge gained from projects with its other clients. In addition, the client and vendor can establish arrangements to ensure that the right type of knowledge is exchanged in different phases of the development project. This will also involve understanding the different mixes of technical and business knowledge required in each phase.[22] Detailed requirements analysis will require more knowledge of the client's business processes and industry than the software testing phase. Frequent communication between the client and vendor is important for sharing knowledge in the initial phases of the project. Client and vendor business analysts working together on the client's site can facilitate this knowledge transfer.

Global vendors have been developing knowledge management practices to improve quality and productivity in project development. One important practice has involved putting in place mechanisms to facilitate bi-directional and frequent communication between staff located on the client's site and those offshore. Another valuable practice employed by vendors is applying knowledge gained from projects with other clients to current development projects. This allows vendors to reuse and develop standard applications, thus saving time and reducing development costs.[23] Vendors have also been formalising and storing important knowledge to mitigate the problems of high staff attrition rates. Illustration 5.3 outlines how Tata Consultancy Services has developed a strategy for managing knowledge, allowing it to share knowledge between its remote and dispersed software development teams and in turn strengthening its competitive position.

Illustration 5.3 How Tata Consultancy Services manages knowledge

In the software development area, clients and vendors have been employing practices to manage globally dispersed knowledge. Vendors, in particular, have been developing knowledge in new areas where teams are remote and dispersed in different locations. This involves retaining knowledge when employees move, which is important in the information technology (IT) area given the high rate of labour turnover. One such company in India that has developed a number of practices to manage and exploit knowledge is Tata Consultancy Services (TCS). It provides a range of services including business process outsourcing and IT maintenance and development to hundreds of clients globally. Its global delivery model involves projects handled by teams located remotely from the client and teams located on the client's site. Work is continuously transferred between the on-site and remote teams, and each team depends on the knowledge and expertise of the other until the project is complete.

TCS identified a number of areas where it could better manage knowledge. Firstly, in the relationship with the client, it believed it could better capture the client's knowledge at both on-site and remote locations to allow for uninterrupted service delivery and the provision of additional services. Secondly, it recognised that knowledge could be better managed in its own organisation, which involved capturing knowledge from an on-site team and refining and reusing it globally on other client projects. Previously, knowledge accumulated was seen as specific to a single project and was not shared with teams in other projects globally. TCS adopted a number of practices to deal with these issues.

How TCS managed knowledge in the relationship with the client

Mirror client organisational structure. A difficulty for client and vendor personnel was identifying the appropriate expert on the other team. Knowledge has to move between the client and the vendor, and at a certain project level, for example, from a vendor project manager. Therefore, TCS implemented an organisational structure that mirrored that of the client, which allowed both the client's personnel and remote TCS personnel to identify their counterparts.

Knowledge transfer. This involved transferring knowledge from client staff to on-site vendor staff, and then to remote vendor staff. Rather than using this knowledge purely for the current project in development and maintenance, TCS ensured that teams defined, captured, transferred and absorbed critical knowledge so that teams in other projects globally could deploy it.

Knowledge retention. TCS developed a strategy to ensure that knowledge transferred to and captured by remote teams was retained, even if staff left. This strategy involved a succession plan where managers selected successors by identifying individuals who would replace them in the event of them leaving a particular project or the company. In addition, this allowed these successors to be trained and prepared for the future role.

Monitor expertise development and retention. This involved linking expertise at the project and organisational levels. Although a project manager was aware of the expertise available at the project level, this expertise was not recorded at the organisational level. Therefore, centres of excellence monitored expertise globally and indicated how expertise could be upgraded when there was a gap between the existing and required knowledge on a particular project. This facilitated the transfer of specialist expertise between global development projects.

How knowledge is shared and leveraged within TCS

Expertise development as a key organisational value. Expertise development is a high priority for TCS and this is supported through learning within and across teams. Know-how and skills are developed through access to technical and business solutions, quality assurance best practices and important codified knowledge learned from client projects. Employees also expand their skills through learning about continuous improvements in process methodologies and processes.

Provide mechanisms to search for expertise. Allowing easy access to expertise is an important aspect of knowledge management. TCS integrates the search process for expertise with its mechanisms for developing and sharing expertise both at project and organisation level. At the project level, on-site and remote teams develop an expertise directory, with pointers to where knowledge resides. These pointers are updated during projects, as on-site and remote teams interact with each other to transfer and further develop their expertise. In addition, at the organisational level it has developed mechanisms to ensure that expertise outside a project can be quickly accessed on other projects globally.

Global reuse methodology. Many software development projects involve integrating a number of components that have already been developed and used in other projects. These components can be reused across a number of projects and replaced by advanced versions where there are compatible interfaces. TCS has developed an intranet to provide access to a database of reusable components from other projects. This intranet contains brief overviews and lessons learned from past projects. This has also allowed individuals to find information on projects, and contacts for advice on those projects.

Measure the contribution of reusable assets. – TCS uses metrics to assess the contribution of reuse and reusable assets to project success. This involves tracking usage rate, the nature of the application and the destination project. This allows TCS to identify those assets that are most successful and those that require improvement.

Source: Oshri, I., Kotlarsky, J. and Willcocks, L. (2007). Managing Dispersed Expertise in IT Offshore Outsourcing: Lessons from Tata Consultancy Services, *MIS Quarterly Executive*, 6(2), 53–65.

Managing culture

Dealing with cultural differences in a team setting is a particularly challenging aspect of global software development outsourcing. Different societies have distinct ways of working and communicating that lead to problems when attempting to build collaboration across different countries. There are a number of significant cultural barriers in a team setting.[24]

Direct versus indirect communication. Having a team of individuals with direct and indirect communication styles can create difficulties. For example, in cross-cultural meetings, the non-Westerner can understand the direct communications of the Westerner, whilst the Westerner has difficulties with understanding the indirect communications of the non-Westerner. Failing to understand these difficulties can create barriers to teamwork by reducing information-sharing and creating interpersonal conflict.

Differing attitudes to hierarchy and authority. The flat structure of cross-cultural teams can create difficulties for individuals from cultures where people are treated differently according to their status in the organisation. Their behaviour may be appropriate when they defer to individuals with higher status in a team predominantly composed of members from a hierarchical culture. However, their credibility and status may be damaged if most of the team comes from an egalitarian culture.[25]

Conflicting norms for decision-making. Different cultures influence decision-making styles, particularly with regard to how quickly decisions are made and to the level of analysis required in advance. For example, US managers often make decisions quickly with little analysis, compared with those from other countries. This can create difficulties in team-based projects where an individual from one culture is impatient for a decision, whilst an individual from another culture needs more analysis beforehand. Rather than one culture imposing its will upon the other, it is often more prudent to make minor concessions in the decision-making process, thus learning to adjust and respect the approach of others to decision-making.

Difficulties with accents and fluency. Communication difficulties can arise as a result of a foreign speaker's accent, lack of fluency, and from problems with translation. This can also influence perceptions of status and ability. In a team setting, although the non-fluent members may be the most knowledgeable and experienced, difficulties with communicating their knowledge make it hard for other team members to recognise and utilise their expertise. Conflict can arise when team members become frustrated with the lack of fluency.

Studies of clients in the USA, Western Europe and Japan and their experiences with vendors in India have highlighted the challenges of managing cultural issues in global software development projects.[26] Indian vendors have had to communicate with their clients in the USA and Japan in different ways. US clients normally work with detailed written agreements and documentation, supported by frequent and informal telephone and email contact. In contrast, Japanese clients prefer verbal communication, continuously negotiated agreements and more formal use of electronic media. Cultural challenges also arise in areas of social norms, attitudes towards authority and language. Clients in Norway prefer to use Russian vendors rather than Indian vendors, because of physical proximity, similar European values and the ease with which Russians can learn the Norwegian language.

As companies have become more experienced with global software development outsourcing, they have been adopting strategies to deal with cultural differences. For example, a cultural difficulty experienced by US clients with Indian vendors is that Indian employees are reluctant to communicate any difficulties during project development, for fear of offending the client. Some US clients have requested that vendors complete daily status reports to ensure they flag and identify any performance problems.[27] Staff rotation between the client and vendor sites is another means of familiarising staff with each other's culture. Some clients have used workshops and diversity experts to help their staff recognise, understand and accommodate the new diversities associated with working with vendors from different cultural backgrounds. There are a number of strategies companies have been adopting to manage culture in software development outsourcing projects.[28]

Project selection. Cultural barriers can be reduced through selection of appropriate projects. Software that can be specified in a culturally neutral way is suitable for outsourcing. The client should select projects where it can learn from the experience the vendor has gained on other project areas. Japanese clients have used vendors for telecommunications and e-business projects from India, because of the learning these vendors have gained in these areas from European and US clients. Outsourcing the development of software applications is only appropriate where in-depth working relationships can be developed between the client and the vendor. The cultural closeness between China and Japan means that relationships can be developed through linguistic closeness and similar ways of working and understanding user attitudes. Alternatively, German clients have not outsourced software development to India, primarily because of language and cultural barriers.

Relationship management. An important aspect of this strategy is the use of common systems and agreed co-ordination and control mechanisms to monitor project progress. The use of common processes such as software development methodologies and common technologies such as software systems and telecommunications links facilitates more effective relationship management. Differences in norms and values can be difficult to bridge, as they are based on significant differences in cultural background, education and working life. However, it is possible to form cross-cultural teams where a compromise working culture is achieved through employees in both the client and vendor modifying their behaviour to reflect the cultural norms of each other. This can involve staff in the client and vendor changing their working hours due to time zone differences, and the relocation of vendor staff on a long-term basis to the client's site.

Staffing issues. Although employees can be made aware of, and adapt to each other's culture, it is not possible for employees in one culture to act and behave like employees from another culture. This problem can be reduced through involving people that bridge cultures in outsourcing projects. Natives of India, with higher education and long-term residence in the USA, are often transferred to India as expatriate managers to manage complex outsourcing projects. In addition, the vendor can establish a mixed culture team in the client country, with local members performing roles such as sales management and interfacing with senior staff in the client company. Clearly, such an approach will increase costs. Recruitment and retention packages for staff must be adapted to both the cultural context and local labour markets. In Western economies, salary is the most important incentive, whereas in Japan, employees are more concerned about status within the company rather than salary alone. German companies have found it difficult to relocate managers to Asian development centres, because of the difficulties involved in adapting to the different living and working environments.

Training. This involves offering vendor employees cultural training in areas such as language and cultural practices. This should occur prior to the employee working on a specific project and throughout the outsourcing project. A formal approach to cross-cultural training will involve employees reflecting on their experiences throughout the project and sharing knowledge with colleagues. Training on the client side of the outsourcing project is also important to enable client staff to learn about the culture of the vendor. Of course, as both the client and vendor become more experienced with dealing with each other's culture, the need for training will be reduced.

Managing time zone differences

Time zone differences are often viewed as an advantage of using offshore vendors, as clients can have round-the-clock development processes to speed up development time and reduce costs. However, clients have to put in place additional resource to manage and monitor these arrangements. Where the client and vendor teams are involved in concurrent tasks, client personnel may have to work additional shifts to co-ordinate work with the vendor. Project delays can occur when the client has to complete project tasks before the vendor can begin certain other tasks. Clients have been pursuing a number of strategies to limit the impact of time zone differences. The client may decide only to outsource development work which is highly modularised with limited interdependencies between tasks performed by the client and vendor. The client can encourage the vendor to collocate some of its personnel onto the client's site, and ensure that these staff are responsible for resolving problems with the offshore development team. Moreover, the client can stipulate in the contract that the vendor synchronises some of its working hours with the client's to deal with time zone differences.

Time zone differences provide significant challenges to vendors as well. Vendors incur additional costs through their personnel working different shift patterns to mirror the client's working hours. Although collocating personnel onto the client's site is a means of dealing with time zone differences, this has also increased costs for the vendor. However, proactive vendors have been addressing these challenges to differentiate themselves from competing vendors and increase their attractiveness to global clients.

InfoSys, an Indian software service provider, pursued a number of strategies to overcome the challenges associated with time zone differences, and reduce the costs of software development.[29]

Organisational culture. The company has secured a greater commitment from employees, which involves working longer hours and working off-hours. Business analysts located on the client site are expected to work late into the evening to communicate with developers on the offshore site. Managers on the offshore site work longer hours, which involves overlapping with the time zone of the client. Moreover, flexible working arrangements are implemented through developers working from home.

Process approach. InfoSys has structured the development process to remove as many dependencies between phases as possible. Supported by the CMM, it has adopted a phase-based development approach, allowing certain phases to be carried out on the client's site and offshore. Requirements analysis is carried out at the client site with considerable involvement from InfoSys staff. Design, coding and initial testing are carried out offshore. Acceptance testing and full implementation are largely carried out on the client site. Formal weekly meetings and status reports are used as co-ordination mechanisms throughout the development process to overcome time zone differences.

Technology approach. Overcoming the challenges of time zone differences depends upon technologies such as mobile telephony, international telephony and Internet access. These technologies are combined with the company's approach to flexible working arrangements, allowing employees to check emails and make international calls from home. Table 5.6 summarises the practices employed by InfoSys to overcome the challenges of time zone differences.

Illustration 5.4 How Indian software vendors compete on capabilities

Indian software vendors have had considerable success in the global market for software services since the 1990s. Some of the largest Indian software vendors, including Tata Consulting Services, InfoSys, Wipro and HCL Technologies, are now competing directly with IBM and Accenture in the global market for software services. An important influence on the growth of the Indian software industry has been the increase in global demand for software services since the early 1990s. Several hundred software companies were established both to export software services and exploit the locational advantages India offered as a home base. These opportunities included 150,000 English-speaking software engineers graduating each year, minimal regulatory intervention and an advanced telecommunications infrastructure.

Initially, many Indian software vendors performed low-end, technically less demanding and labour-intensive tasks for global clients. Clients performed the more complex elements of software development internally, and employed Indian vendors, with lower labour costs, for the less complex tasks including coding, testing and maintenance. However, rather than relying solely on the advantage of lower labour costs to win business, Indian vendors recognised the importance of moving into more complex software development projects. Moreover, their competitive advantage in this area was being eroded as competitors such as IBM established subsidiaries in India to exploit the same labour cost advantage. Therefore, many Indian vendors shifted from merely implementing designs provided by clients to becoming actively involved in the design of client software applications. Two sets of capabilities have been important in enabling the most successful Indian vendors to move into more complex software development projects in the global market-place.

Client-specific capabilities

These capabilities have been developed through repeated interactions with the same client across a number of projects over time. As a vendor works with a client over time, it can develop client-specific patterns of interaction that allow it to reduce costs for the client. Through repeated interactions with the client the vendor not only develops a better knowledge of the client's business operations, but also gains important knowledge on how the software can improve the client's operations. Such knowledge has been developed through repeated interactions and a longer-term relationship with the client in various stages of the development cycle including requirements analysis, systems design, testing and installation. This knowledge is an important driver for winning repeat business from the client, and new business from others with similar needs. A further benefit of developing client-specific capabilities is that it has allowed vendors to build switching costs into the relationship with their clients. As the vendor develops a long-term relationship with the client, the client is less likely to switch to another vendor and incur the costs of finding a new vendor and developing a new relationship. In addition, as clients in many industries share similar software requirements, the vendors have been able to reuse and transfer important knowledge and technologies developed in one client setting to another.

Project management capabilities

These capabilities have been developed through investments in systems and processes, and in training to improve the vendor's software development processes. An important influence on the development of project management capabilities by Indian vendors has been the type of contract adopted by their clients. Although some clients have used time-and-materials contracts, the fixed-price contract, where the fee for services is negotiated at the beginning of the project, has been the most prominent contract employed. The vendor bears most of the risk in this contract. However, many Indian vendors have recognised the importance of developing strong project management skills both to mitigate the potential risks from project delays and cost overruns and to achieve higher returns on projects. Where the vendor has carried out the development project within the scheduled time and budget, it has been guaranteed higher profit margins. This approach has also created incentives for vendor staff to improve performance and productivity levels. Indian vendors have developed a number of important project management capabilities.

Software design and building capabilities. This involves having the capability to understand client requirements and design an appropriate software application to meet these requirements. It requires developing the system to conform to the design, and effectively co-ordinating the development process across different teams and locations.

Effort estimation and management capabilities. This involves estimating the resource required to develop and install the software application at the client's site. Identifying the personnel with the necessary skills and experience levels and using prior experience to derive accurate estimates of resource requirements are important elements of this capability.

Schedule estimation and management capabilities. This involves estimating the duration and schedule for completing the project. Important aspects of this capability include possessing the management skills to ensure project resources are deployed and managed to complete the project within the agreed time schedule.

Indian vendors have recognised the importance of the Capability Maturity Model (CMM) in developing project management capabilities. Many of the leading Indian software vendors have achieved Level IV or V certification in CMM. These vendors have further developed their project management capabilities through integrating many of the CMM-level activities into their operations. Indian vendors have also exploited their project management capabilities to modularise parts of the software development project, which has allowed them to disaggregate certain tasks to different geographic locations. Rather than developing and installing the application entirely at the client's site, vendors have been locating a few of their systems analysts at the client's site during the requirements analysis phase, and thereafter carrying out much of the development process in India in order to exploit lower labour costs.

Despite its success, the Indian software industry still faces challenges. Many vendors are still competing on price, rather than offering differentiated capabilities from their competitors. As some of their largest clients and competitors establish subsidiaries in India, Indian vendors have been competing both for people and business with these companies. Although India has a vast supply of software engineers, it does not have an unlimited supply of people with significant experience in software engineering and project management, and this has contributed to rising labour costs. The emergence of vendors from developing economies such as Russia and Eastern Europe has posed further challenges to India's dominance in the global software services market. As well as having developed infrastructures, advanced education systems and comparable labour rates, vendors in these countries have the advantage of being both geographically and culturally close to European and US clients.

Sources: Cusumano, M. (2006). Envisioning the Future of India's Software Services Business, *Communications of the ACM*, 49(10), 15–17; Ethiraj, S., Kale, P., Krishnan, M. and Singh, J. (2005). Where Do Capabilities Come From and How Do They Matter? A Study in the Software Services Industry, *Strategic Management Journal*, 26, 25–45; Athreye, S. (2005). The Indian Software Industry and its Evolving Service Capability, *Industrial and Corporate Change*, 14(3), 393–418.

Table 5.6 Strategies for overcoming the challenges of time zone differences

Time zone solution	Description
24-hour awareness	The organisation has a 24-hour culture where employees recognise they are part of a global organisation and must adjust accordingly. New recruits are trained on how to handle time zone differences.
Time flexibility	Time zones are not viewed as fixed by employees. Employees are expected to be available at all hours, and work longer hours. Employees 'time shift' by synchronising their work hours with clients.
Liaison	A middle manager acts as a human bridge between the distant geographic locations. Often the most effective liaison is an expatriate linking the organisation back to his or her home country.
Status reporting	Routine project reports are created to help with reducing co-ordination errors, and are stored in an open central repository.
Meetings	Routine, periodic and real-time meetings are called with participants from all locations, and are an important mechanism for co-ordinating tasks and dealing with errors.
Escalation protocols	These are guidelines for addressing problems and queries, and are designed to ensure that issues are dealt with promptly. Other aspects include which technology to use when dealing with an issue, and when to use voice messaging to resolve issues.
Awareness technologies	These technologies provide details on someone's availability, current work and location. They can include information on individual calendars, current time zone calendars and holiday schedules.

Source: Adapted from Carmel, E. (2006). Building Your Information Systems from the Other Side of the World: How InfoSys Manages Time Zone Differences, *MIS Quarterly Executive*, 5(1), 43–53.

5.6 Summary implications

- Organisations should have a formal strategy for maximising the benefits and mitigating the risks of global services outsourcing arrangements. Important aspects of this strategy include selecting the right project, developing a vendor strategy, managing people issues and developing vendor management capabilities.

• Organisations should have a vendor selection approach that allows them to achieve the objectives of the outsourcing strategy. Differences in legal systems, as well as geographical, time zone and culture differences between different countries, increase the challenges of contracting in global services outsourcing. Organisations have to form contract design teams with legal, functional and technical experts to develop and negotiate global services outsourcing arrangements.

• Structures have to be established to ensure communication between client and vendor staff. Effective structures will include clear lines of communication and co-ordination, and clear interfaces between client and vendor staff. Employing communication media can reduce communication difficulties, and ensure that frequent and clear dialogue occurs between client and vendor staff. Advances in ICTs have increased the importance of technologies in facilitating communication in global team environments.

• Mechanisms have to be put in place to ensure that knowledge is transferred, leveraged and shared between the client and vendor. Vendors can exploit knowledge management practices to improve productivity and service quality, which in turn strengthens their competitive position. In a software development context, this involves reusing and developing standard applications, applying knowledge learned from one client setting to another.

• Dealing with cultural differences is a major challenge in managing global services outsourcing arrangements. Cultural barriers in a team environment include communication styles, differing attitudes to hierarchy and authority, conflicting approaches to decision-making, and difficulties with accents and fluency. Client strategies for dealing with cultural differences include selecting an appropriate project for outsourcing, effectively managing the relationship, deploying the appropriate staff and training.

• Time zone differences pose challenges to clients and vendors in global services outsourcing. The client can incur transaction costs through having to put in place additional resource to manage and co-ordinate global vendors. Vendors incur costs through employing staff on different shift patterns to mirror the working hours of the client.

Notes and references

1 Vlaar, P., van Fenema, P. and Tiwari, V. (2008). Cocreating Understanding and Value in Distributed Work: How Members of Onsite and Offshore Vendor Teams Give, Make, Demand, and Break Sense, *MIS Quarterly*, 32(2), 531–51.

2 Sakthivel, S. (2007). Managing Risk in Offshore Systems Development. *Communications of the ACM*, 50(4), 69–75.

3 Sahay, S., Nicholson, B. and Krishna, S. (2003). *Global IT Outsourcing: Software Development Across Borders*, Cambridge: Cambridge University Press.

4 Benaroch, M., Lichtenstein, Y. and Robinson, K. (2006). Real Options in Information Technology Risk Management: An Empirical Validation of Risk–Option Relationships, *MIS Quarterly*, 30(4), 827–64.

5 See Sakthivel (2007) in note 2 above.

6 For a study on the role of business familiarity in determining how software development outsourcing projects are managed and priced to address risks, see Gefen, D., Wyss, S. and Lichtenstein, Y. (2008). Business Familiarity as Risk Mitigation in Software Development Outsourcing, *MIS Quarterly*, 32(3), 531–51.

7 For a study on the role of contracts in offshore software development, see: Gopal, A., Sivaramakrishnan, K., Krishnan, M. and Mukhopadhay, T. (2003). Contracts in Offshore Software Development: An Empirical Analysis, *Management Science*, 49(12), 1671–83.

8 Rottman, J. and Lacity, M. (2006). Proven Practices for Effectively Offshoring IT Work, *Sloan Management Review*, 47(3), 56–63.

9 See Rottman and Lacity (2006) in note 8 above.

10 Ranganathan, C. and Balaji, S. (2007). Critical Capabilities for Offshore Outsourcing of Information Systems, *MIS Quarterly Executive*, 6(3), 147–61.

11 Rottman, J. and Lacity, M. (2004). Proven Practices for IT Offshore Outsourcing, *Cutter Consortium Executive Report*, 5(12), 1–27.

12 Kaiser, K. and Hawk, S. (2004). Evolution of Offshore Software Development: From Outsourcing to Co-sourcing, *MIS Quarterly Executive*, 3(2), 69–81.

13 Davenport, T. (2005). The Coming Commoditization of Processes, *Harvard Business Review*, 83(6), 101–8; Adler, P., McGarry, F., Irion Talbot, W. and Binney, D. (2005). Enabling Process Discipline: Lessons from the Journey to CMM Level 5, *MIS Quarterly Executive*, 4(1), 215–27.

14 See Rottman and Lacity (2006) in note 8 above.

15 For additional reading on virtual teams, see Furst, S., Reeves, M., Rosen, B. and Blackburn, R. (2004). Managing the Life Cycle of Virtual Teams, *Academy of Management Executive*, 18(2), 6–20; and Maznevski, M. and Chudoba, K. (2000). Bridging Space over Time: Global Virtual Team Dynamics and Effectiveness, *Organisation Science*, 11(5), 473–92.

16 Sakthivel, S. (2005). Virtual Workgroups in Offshore Systems Development, *Information and Software Technology*, 47, 305–18.

17 Carmel, E. and Abbott, P. (2007). Why 'Nearshore' Means that Distance Matters, *Communications of the ACM*, 50(10), 40–6.

18 Townsend, A., Demarie, S. and Hendrickson, A. (2001). Desktop Video Conferencing in Virtual Workgroups: Anticipation, System Evaluation, and Performance, *Information Systems Journal*, 11(3), 213–27.

19 See Sakthivel (2005) in note 16 above.

20 See Ranganathan and Balaji (2007) in note 10 above.

21 Tiwana, A. (2004). Beyond the Black Box: Knowledge Overlaps in Software Outsourcing, *IEEE Software*, September–October, 51–8.

22 See Ranganathan and Balaji (2007) in note 10 above.

23 Herbsleb, J. and Moitra, D. (2001). Global Software Development, *IEEE Transactions on Software Engineering*, 18(2), 16–20.

24 Brett, J., Behfar, K. and Kern, M. (2006). Managing Multicultural Teams, *Harvard Business Review*, November, 84–91.

25 An egalitarian society affirms and promotes the belief in equal civil, economic, political and social rights for all its citizens.

26 Krishna, S., Sahay, S. and Walsham, G. (2004). Managing Cross-Cultural Issues in Global Software Outsourcing, *Communications of the ACM*, 47(4), 62–6; Nicholson, B. and Sahay, S. (2001). Some Political and Cultural Issues in the Globalisation of Software Development: Case Experience from Britain and India, *Information and Organisation*, 11, 25–43.

27 See Rottman, and Lacity (2006) in note 8 above.

28 See Krishna *et al.* (2004) in note 26 above.

29 Carmel, E. (2006). Building Your Information Systems from the Other Side of the World: How InfoSys Manages Time Zone Differences, *MIS Quarterly Executive*, 5(1), 43–53.

Recommended key reading

Brett, J., Behfar, K. and Kern, M. (2006). Managing Multicultural Teams, *Harvard Business Review*, November, 84–91. This paper highlights the cultural challenges of managing global teams and proposes a number of strategies for overcoming these challenges.

Carmel, E. (2006). Building Your Information Systems from the Other Side of the World: How InfoSys Manages Time Zone Differences, *MIS Quarterly Executive*, 5(1), 43–53. This paper examines how companies manage the challenges of time zones in global outsourcing. Using the experiences of InfoSys, the paper identifies ten practices for dealing with time zone challenges.

Ranganathan, C. and Balaji, S. (2007). Critical Capabilities for Offshore Outsourcing of Information Systems, *MIS Quarterly Executive*, 6(3), 147–61. This paper identifies ten capabilities required for success in IT offshore outsourcing.

Rottman, J. and Lacity, M. (2006). Proven Practices for Effectively Offshoring IT Work, *Sloan Management Review*, 47(3), 56–63. Based upon a study of US clients and Indian vendors, this paper identifies a number of emerging practices being employed to address the challenges of offshoring IT work.

Sakthivel, S. (2007). Managing Risk in Offshore Systems Development, *Communications of the ACM*, 50(4), 69–75. This paper provides a summary of the key risks associated with managing global software development projects.

6

Creating shared services arrangements

6.1 Introduction

Shared services arrangements involve consolidating and standardising common tasks associated with a business function in different parts of an organisation into a single services centre. These services are then provided by the service centre to other parts of the organisation. Shared services centres can be owned and operated by the organisation, or outsourced to independent vendors. Shared services have been increasing in prominence in both the private and public sectors, and encompass a range of back-office functions such as finance and accounting (F&A), human resources (HR), procurement, information technology (IT) and facilities management. Although many of the services provided by these functions are not visible to customers, they have a major impact on service quality, particularly when they are not performing properly. Indeed, senior executives often express dissatisfaction with service levels, despite the considerable expenditure involved in running these functions. Shared services have been viewed as a strategy for achieving both efficiencies and improved service performance levels, as organisations have strived to reduce costs and enhance performance in these back-office functions.[1]

Benefits of shared services

When effectively implemented, shared services arrangements offer a number of benefits.

Cost savings. Shared services arrangements allow organisations to reduce costs through process standardisation and economies of scale. Standardisation of processes in non-core functions such as HR, F&A and procurement reduces duplication across the organisation. Economies of scale are achieved through combining processes previously carried out independently.

Improved service. A shared services centre can specialise in a functional area, which then allows it to provide better service levels to users in the organisation. Through standardising services in a single location, it is possible to deliver services at an agreed performance level, with an emphasis on customer service. A culture of customer service is created in the shared service centre through committing resource to monitoring key performance indicators (KPIs) and meeting service level agreements (SLAs).

Enhancement of the strategic role of retained functions. Through transferring many administrative and transaction-oriented tasks into shared services centres, retained functions can take on a more strategic role and focus on more value-adding tasks. For example, in the case of F&A the retained function can focus on strategy issues, whilst the transaction-oriented tasks such as general accounting, accounts receivable and tax processing can be carried out in the shared services centre.[2]

Continuous improvement. Specialisation allows the operator of the shared services centre to drive improvements in both efficiency and service levels. In addition, more accurate and richer management information from the services centre allows the retained function to improve its performance.

Spin-off potential. Where an organisation sets up and operates a shared services centre, there is the potential to spin off the centre into a separate business offering the services to other clients. This allows the organisation to exploit its expertise in the service, and also fill any excess capacity in the centre.

Drivers of shared services arrangements

Organisations have been under pressure to reduce costs in back-office functions viewed as non-core, transaction-intensive, and adding little value to the corporate centre. Many tasks performed in back-office functions are often duplicated across different geographical locations. This situation has been further compounded as organisations have embarked upon acquisitions and inherited large swathes of support staff. Therefore, shared services arrangements have been a common strand among organisational restructuring efforts. Developments in information technology such as enterprise systems have allowed organisations to consolidate and re-engineer business processes from geographically dispersed business units into single services centres.[3] Enterprise system implementation is often accompanied by the redesign and consolidation of business processes.

Organisations have been locating shared services centres in lower cost global locations to further save costs. Some multinational organisations have established shared services units in regional centres globally, providing services in areas such as procurement, payroll and benefits administration and accounts management. Once organisations have rede-signed and consolidated processes associated with their back-office func-tions, they are in a better position to relocate the shared services unit to a geographically distant location. Global outsourcing of shared services has become more prominent as independent vendors in offshore locations offer shared services capabilities in back-office functions such as F&A and HR services.[4]

Illustration 6.1 Enterprise systems

An enterprise system – sometimes referred to as an enterprise resource plan-ning (ERP) system – is an integrated software application composed of a set of standard functional modules (including finance, human resource, sales, production etc.) developed by the vendor, and adapted to the specific needs of each customer. Enterprise systems attempt to integrate all the functions across an organisation onto a single software application that can serve the needs of those functions. Enterprise systems can replace complex and sometimes manual interfaces between different systems with standardised, cross-functional transaction automation. Traditionally, systems integration was achieved through effectively planning and implementing systems built internally or sourced from independent vendors. More recently, many com-panies have chosen to implement large enterprise systems that have built-in integration, and are often viewed as sourcing a complete ICT infrastructure. Implementing enterprise systems requires a process view of the organisation, and many systems have process templates that claim to incorporate best prac-tice in business processes.

Motivations and benefits of implementation

Many organisations have been struggling to deal with challenges such as globalisation, integrating and consolidating acquisitions, process standard-isation and changes in customer expectations. Implementing enterprise sys-tems has been viewed as a way of addressing these challenges, and is often an essential component of a wider business process re-engineering and organ-isational transformational project. Implementing an enterprise system allows an organisation to eliminate disparate and fragmented systems and replace them with a single, integrated set of applications for the entire organisation. A further motivation has been the increasing maturity of the market for ERP vendors including SAP, Oracle, JD Edwards, People Soft and BAAN. Table 6.1 shows the technical and organisational motivations for implementing enter-prise systems.

Effective implementation of enterprise systems can bring a number of sig-nificant benefits including: reduced operating costs; access to information to improve decision-making for better negotiating with customers and suppli-ers; no need for rewriting reports; and reliable figures available to analyse business performance. Enterprise systems can reduce costs by improving

Table 6.1 Technical and organisational motivations

Technical	Organisational
Disparate systems	Poor business performance
Poor quality and lack of available information	High cost structure
Business processes and systems not fully integrated	Lack of responsiveness to customers and/ or suppliers
Difficult to integrate acquisitions	Complex, inefficient business processes
Obsolete systems	Inability to support growth both locally and globally
	Inability to support new business strategies

efficiencies through computerisation, and enhance decision-making by providing accurate and timely enterprise-wide information. Enterprise systems can provide senior management with a clear view of the relative performance of various parts of the organisation, which can be used to identify areas for improvement and take advantage of potential market opportunities.

Problems with implementation

Many organisations have failed to achieve the benefits of enterprise systems, and implementation has proved difficult and led to expensive failures. The needs of organisations continually evolve and lead to new demands, thus making standardisation difficult. When organisations decide to extensively customise the system to meet their requirements, development costs increase and they fail to achieve the benefits of standardisation. Implementation can cause conflict within the organisation, a result of opposition from those functions or individuals affected by it. Some have argued that failure is a result of the technical complexity of a system that requires a considerable level of expertise, and of the mismatch between the technical specifications and the business requirements of the organisation. Some of the problems with implementation are related to the initial motivations. There are major technical challenges with replacing legacy systems, understanding business processes and infrastructural requirements. In addition, there are major people-related challenges including obtaining top management support, changing work practices, change management and inadequate training. Indeed, the misconception that implementation is a technical issue rather than a people-related business issue is the principal reason for enterprise system failure.

Source: Botta-Genoulaz, V. and Millet, P. (2006). An Investigation into the Use of ERP Systems in the Service Sector, *International Journal of Production Economics*, 99, 202–21.

This chapter uses the experiences of a public sector organisation to out-line the key tasks involved in creating outsourced shared services arrangements.[5] The shared services arrangement was part of a reform initiative to modernise and transform the HR function across a number of government departments. The arrangement involved replacing outdated IT systems, modernising payroll and HR processes and providing centralised administrative HR services from an outsourced shared services centre. Creating a shared services centre to handle routine queries and transactions allowed the HR function in the eleven departments to focus on more strategic and value-adding human resource activities. The HR services involved in the arrangement included external recruitment, employee relations, HR data management, internal recruitment, payroll and absence management, and performance management and learning development.

There were a number of major challenges with this arrangement. It was a highly complex, large-scale shared services arrangement involving almost 30,000 users of HR services. Determining the requirements for the new arrangement was extremely challenging. There were significant shortcomings with the organisations existing processes and systems, and there was a lack of knowledge internally on contemporary IT-enabled HR systems and service level determination. Implementing the arrangement required significant organisational change. Line managers, who traditionally passed all HR-related issues to departmental HR, were expected to take more control and ownership of HR issues. There were many disparate systems and widely varying interpretations of corporate policies across eleven departments, which made the task of enforcing a consistent and standardised approach challenging. Finally, as with any major IT implementation, there was risk of the project failing to meet the agreed budget and time-frame.

Figure 6.1 shows the stages involved in creating the outsourced shared services arrangement including planning and analysis, procurement and contracting, and implementation. The following sections provide a detailed overview of the key tasks involved in creating this outsourced shared services arrangement. These tasks included a structured approach to project management, business case development, vendor engagement, contracting, change management, stakeholder management, business process redesign and strategic partnership development. A number of these tasks, including a structured approach to project management and stakeholder management, were relevant to all the stages involved in creating the arrangement. Important insights are provided on the implications of creating outsourced shared services arrangements. Finally, summary implications are presented.

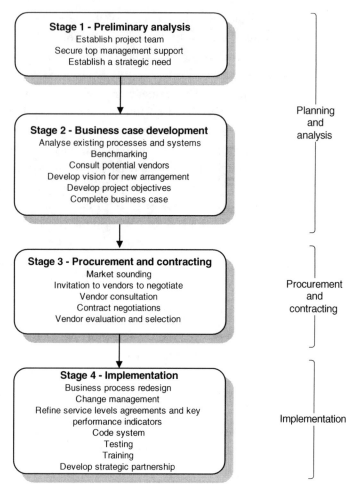

Stage 1 - Preliminary analysis Establish project team Secure top management support Establish a strategic need	Planning and analysis
Stage 2 - Business case development Analyse existing processes and systems Benchmarking Consult potential vendors Develop vision for new arrangement Develop project objectives Complete business case	
Stage 3 - Procurement and contracting Market sounding Invitation to vendors to negotiate Vendor consultation Contract negotiations Vendor evaluation and selection	Procurement and contracting
Stage 4 - Implementation Business process redesign Change management Refine service levels agreements and key performance indicators Code system Testing Training Develop strategic partnership	Implementation

Figure 6.1   Stages in creating outsourced shared services arrangements

6.2 Structured project management approach

Adopting a structured project management approach was regarded as important throughout all the stages in creating the shared services arrangement.[6] A project team was established in the preliminary phase of the project, which was led by the HR director at corporate level. The team leader was responsible for championing the project and selling it to important internal and external stakeholders. The team comprised procurement and business change specialists, along with twenty staff, drawn mainly from corporate and departmental HR. Involving staff from the departmental level was viewed as important to winning support for the project. In addition, senior management were careful to select team members with the necessary skills and knowledge of internal HR. Development of the IT system required in-depth and specific knowledge of HR systems and processes, including payroll in particular.

Governance structures were established to enable the project team to co-ordinate and manage the project. In the preliminary analysis stage, the governance structures created appropriate interfaces and communication channels between the various stakeholders involved at corporate level and HR department level. Meetings were held regularly, and stakeholders were allowed to raise concerns on the status and direction of the project. In addition, communication channels were created to provide updates on objectives, project scope changes and project status. The project team was responsible for carrying out a number of key tasks during the project.

Securing top management support. The project team was responsible for gaining support from a range of people in the organisation at a number of levels including ministers, department directors, department HR managers and HR staff and line managers. Securing top management support at corporate and department level was crucial to winning overall support for the project.

Stakeholder management Stakeholders are individuals, or groups of individuals, who are either directly or indirectly involved in the project, and have a vested interest in its successful (or unsuccessful) conclusion. The project team pursued a number of strategies to gain the support of potential opponents to the project, which included involving departmental HR in decision-making, training and providing ongoing communication on the status of the project.

Risk management. Throughout the project, the project team managed a risk register that identified potential risks and put in place procedures for mitigating them if they occurred. For example, the absence of data on the historical cost and performance of internal services made it difficult to determine objectively the benefits of moving to an outsourced solution. The project team carried out benchmarking and employed specialist consultants to assist with determining performance objectives in order to reduce this risk.

Managing project change. The project team had to assess and manage any changes during the project. In some cases, these were quite significant; for example, when the scope of the project changed from partial outsourcing to full outsourcing.

6.3 Business case development

A fundamental building block of shared services arrangements is the development of a business case. The business case should describe the business problem, and outline a proposal on how it could be overcome. The cost and complexity of shared services implementation means the business case should contain a logical and convincing justification for proceeding with such a project. The business case describes the work to be done, as well as a blueprint for the solution that the shared services arrangement will deliver if it is approved. The project team carried out a number of tasks to develop a business case.

Analysis of existing processes and systems

The project team analysed and documented the existing internal HR processes and systems. This analysis revealed the following problems:

- *Disparate systems.* Fifty-one systems were being used by the departments to maintain personnel data, along with the central HR systems. In addition, some of these systems were automated, and some were manual.
- *Lack of consistency.* Departments were interpreting policies and procedures in different ways. Although policies were developed at corporate level, they were being applied differently by departments in areas such as special leave or sickness absence.
- *Lack of a co-ordinated HR structure.* There was no co-ordinated structure for the delivery of HR services. Some departments were receiving HR services from another department, whilst pensions and external recruitment services were delivered from corporate level.
- *Ageing technical infrastructure.* Much of the technical infrastructure supporting the delivery of HR services had become obsolete.

Table 6.2 summarises the problems with the previous arrangement and the impact upon performance.

Development a 'vision' for the new arrangement

The project team explored a number of options for addressing the problems with the existing processes and systems. This assisted with developing a vision for the new arrangement, and involved carrying out a number of tasks:

- *Benchmarking.* Benchmarking was led by the project team along with input from the HR departments. The project team used published HR

Table 6.2 Business issues and performance impacts

Issue	Performance impact
HR services provided through an obsolescent technological infrastructure, and a number of delivery contracts due to expire.	• Higher maintenance costs. • Not exploiting advances in technology. • Disruption to service delivery.
Multiple data sources and lack of system integration.	No single definitive source of personnel-related data which was impacting service delivery in areas such as: • Duplication of work as satellite systems and manual work-arounds support current personnel system. • Lack of accessible historical data due to a number of fragmented systems.
Lack of ownership of personnel data. Analysis with departments revealed that basic staff information was not fully accurate as staff did not always provide full details of changes in circumstances due to a perceived lack of ownership of individual staff records.	Inaccurate personnel data led to errors in personnel processing as data was out of date.
Lack of common standards. There were inconsistencies using cumbersome coding structures and discrepancies in definitions.	Inconsistency of definitions led to distortion of similar information across departments. Staff time expended in resolving the resulting queries that arose.
Need to improve recruitment. Labour-intensive and time-consuming recruitment processes, and not exploiting more effective IT-enabled recruitment capabilities.	Adversely affecting the ability to recruit the best people with appropriate competencies for the defined job.
Need to match skills and competencies to jobs, and improve career management and HR planning.	Adversely affecting the ability to align career development with business objectives and match competencies to jobs.

industry benchmarking data, which included data from specialist HR service vendors. The project team compared performance in its HR services against numerical performance indicators reported in public sources. A difficulty with this exercise was the lack of valid performance measures used internally to measure HR service levels. However, benchmarking revealed some major weaknesses in areas such as under-investment in technology, poor management of information systems and duplication of processes.

Table 6.3 Project objectives

Objectives
Continuation of HR services – ensure the continued delivery of current payroll services through the implementation of a replacement solution prior to expiry of existing contracts.
Continuation of HR services – ensure, as a minimum, the continued delivery of current HR services through the implementation of an electronic HR solution prior to expiry of existing HR management system contract.
Increase efficiency of HR service delivery – increase the efficiency of HR services by 5 per cent through the implementation of modern HR support facilities, business process improvement and the phased introduction of employee and manager self-service.
Improve HR decision-making – improve HR decision-making through the provision of detailed, specific, timely, accurate and accessible personnel information.
Deliver consistent HR services – enable the delivery of consistent HR services through the implementation of common processes, systems and standards, where sensible and economically viable to do so.
Improve electronic HR capability – improve the delivery of HR services by ensuring that all transactions are capable of being provided electronically.
Reduce reliance on HR paper files – exploit information technology to reduce future reliance on HR paper files by 70 per cent by project completion.

- *External advice.* External HR consultants and expertise in other parts of the organisation were sought to identify ideas on how the project should proceed. The project team visited a number of other public sector agencies that had implemented innovative approaches to managing HR services.
- *Market sounding.* This involved inviting some vendors to contribute solutions and ideas on how internal HR could be improved. This was achieved by organising workshops and visiting vendor operations.

This exercise proved valuable for a number of reasons. It highlighted problems with existing systems, and emphasised the significance of the change required. Useful ideas and potential sourcing options were noted on how internal processes could be improved, which assisted in convincing senior HR staff at departmental level on the need to move to a new HR structure. Rough cost estimates were also developed for the new arrangement. Project objectives were established at this stage, as shown in Table 6.3. The findings from this exercise were the foundation for developing the business case for proceeding with the project. The business case involved a partial outsourcing of HR services, focusing mainly on the information technology development and maintenance elements. Full outsourcing of all HR services was not an option at this stage for a number of reasons. The project team believed there were no vendors with the scale and experience to take on the entire service portfolio because of its complexities. It was also felt that full outsourcing would have led to too much business and cultural change.

6.4 Vendor engagement

When the business case was approved, the project team proceeded immediately to procurement. Although the business case focused primarily on partial outsourcing, there was a degree of flexibility over the final sourcing option selected. The initial dialogue and consultation with vendors was viewed as a valuable opportunity to explore further ideas and suggestions on alternative sourcing options that would facilitate the transformation of the HR function. The project team recognised that they did not have the knowledge to specify clearly what they required from the new arrangement, and believed they could learn from vendors in this area. Vendor engagement proceeded through a number of phases.

Market sounding. An industry day was organised to which potential vendors were invited and informed of the details of the project. The industry day allowed vendors to identify and approach potential consortium partners to determine whether they were interested in being involved in the bidding process. As a result of this event, three consortia comprising vendors with specialist expertise in HR shared services arrangements were invited to compete for the contract.

Invitation to negotiate. These three consortia were invited to negotiate. This was regarded as a sufficient number to ensure competition in the procurement process. It was thought that inviting more than three bidders would have increased the cost, complexity and duration of the procurement process.

Consultation. This phase gave each bidder the opportunity to understand the existing processes and organisation of the HR function at corporate and departmental level. The project team organised a number of meetings and over 200 workshops with the bidders and various HR service specialists across the departments. The project team carried out site visits to the bidders' operations to view potential service arrangements they were operating with other clients. The consultation phase ended with the submission by each bidder of a 'blueprint' and outline costs for the delivery of the services. This exercise allowed the project team to explore with the bidders different levels of outsourcing beyond those outlined in the business case.

Vendor engagement had a significant impact on the overall direction and scope of the project. Following a review of the blueprints and site visits, the project team decided to expand the scope of the project. Rather than having an in-house shared services centre and partial outsourcing of some services, it decided to invite bidders to submit bids for a fully outsourced service including:

- A shared services centre including an HR contact centre providing transactional and administrative support in the areas of resourcing and employee relations
- An HR contact centre logging calls and providing advice and guidance on current HR policy and procedures
- A fully managed payroll service
- A fully managed ICT service providing a personnel database and online information and self-service facilities for policy advice and decision support to line managers and employees
- Provision of professional HR support on detailed casework on a consultancy basis.

There were a number of reasons for expanding the scope of the project. Firstly, the project team recognised the need to transform the HR function, which they believed would not have been possible with the partial outsourcing option. Through visiting and observing vendor operations with other clients, they observed how a fully outsourced option could deliver the required benefits and transform the HR function. Examples were found of how outsourced shared services centres were delivering efficiencies and a demand-driven customer service culture. This would not have been possible through an internally managed shared services centre with existing employees who had been accustomed to working in a supply-driven culture, rather than in a demand-driven culture where the service is purchased at an agreed fee and service level.

Secondly, transforming the retained HR function in the departments would entail a major change programme, and the project team lacked the required skills and experience to drive this change. In addition, it lacked the depth and experience required to redesign its existing business processes to create an efficient and effective internally managed shared services centre.

Finally, there was a high degree of complexity associated with managing the different internal and outsourced services of the partial outsourcing option. Rather than attempt to co-ordinate and manage complex interfaces and interdependencies between services provided by internal departments and external vendors, it was more appropriate to establish a single sourced option where there was a prime contractor responsible for managing the relevant services involved.

6.5 Contracting

Negotiation

The negotiation phase required extensive knowledge of internal HR processes and systems, procurement skills, supply market knowledge and legal advice. The project team faced a number of challenges including poor internal performance measurement systems and a lack of internal skills in contracting and service level development. Although the project team had developed baseline performance measures for the business case, there were difficulties in applying these in a contractual context. Therefore, the project team sought advice in this area, and consultants were employed to develop KPIs and SLAs. This facilitated the development of a baseline position against which to measure any future improvements, and provided a framework for ongoing performance monitoring and comparison during the management of the outsourcing arrangement. The project team also lacked the legal skills required to translate the requirement into appropriate contractual language. As well as seeking advice from other government agencies, extensive legal input was necessary for drafting and refining the development of requirements schedules.

Illustration 6.2 Service level agreements and outsourcing

A service level agreement (SLA) is a contract that defines the services that the vendor will deliver, and comprises information on the agreement including its term, the parties and the ways in which disagreements or changes are to be negotiated. An SLA is fundamental to managing the outsourcing relationship. An SLA can help the client to precisely define its requirements, facilitate negotiations between the client and vendor, communicate agreements reached, and provide mechanisms for changing the agreement and monitoring vendor performance. There are a number of important aspects of SLAs in outsourcing arrangements. Prior to outsourcing an organisation should analyse and specify the outsourced services involved. There are a number of units of analysis in this exercise:

- *Service.* Refers to the service being provided; for example, the provision of meals to patients in a hospital.

- *User group*. Refers to a group of service users with homogeneous needs. For example, patients can be categorised as vegetarian, those needing help with food or those with special dietary requirements.
- *Service element*. Refers to an element of the service. For example, the service can be broken down into breakfast, lunch and dinner.

Direct services are the outputs of the process such as transferring funds into an employee's bank account. Indirect services are used to measure vendor performance and calculate payments and vendor penalties.

Service level clauses

Outsourcing contracts normally include service level clauses (SLCs), which relate to a service used by a single group of users. The following are examples of some SLCs in contracts:

- *Service provided*. For example, a delivery service will include elements such as the location where goods are to be delivered, the method of packaging and allowable delivery times.
- *Client obligations*. For example, the client will have to provide details of employee changes to a vendor which is delivering a payroll service.
- *Performance targets*. A means of measuring improvements. For example, data on network performance for an IT system will involve measures of response times, downtime and security breaches.
- *Bonus or penalty calculations*. The SLA should specify how performance bonuses or penalties are to be calculated. Calculations will be based on targets and formulae relating to performance measures.

Taxonomy of service attributes

There are a number of attributes relevant to accessing service quality in outsourcing arrangements. The relevance of these attributes will differ depending upon the type of service and customer. Some of the more important attributes are:

- *Accessibility*. A service is accessible if it is working correctly and is usable by customers. Access to automatic teller machines (ATM) is not available if there is none within a reasonable distance, or if existing ones are not usable by those with disabilities.
- *Availability*. This refers to the scheduled time that a service is functioning. For example, an ATM that is scheduled to be working from 6 a.m. to midnight but is down for thirty minutes has availability of 97.2 per cent.
- *Performance*. Performance criteria can vary depending upon the type of service. The criteria used to measure the performance of HR services are likely to differ from those used for facilities maintenance.
- *Time*. This includes a number of criteria such as response time, queuing time, performance time and turnround time. Response time is important for call centre services where it is important that customers should not

have a long waiting time. Queuing time is the gap between the scheduled and actual start of a service. Performance time refers to the time taken to perform a service once started. Turnround time is the time between a customer requesting a service and the service being delivered.

- *Capacity and flexibility.* Capacity involves the vendor's ability to meet the client's additional demand beyond normal demand patterns. Vendors can often cope with peaks in demand through flexible working arrangements. Flexibility refers to the vendor's ability to customise services or deal with exceptional service requirements. Capacity and flexibility can be difficult to measure, and often rely on the judgement and experience of management in the client.
- *Empathy and ambience.* These criteria are important in the case of personal services such as service in a restaurant. However, these are difficult to measure objectively as they are based on intangible factors, and customer opinions can differ depending on personal preferences.

Source: Beaumont, N. (2006). Service Level Agreements: An Essential Aspect of Outsourcing, *Services Industries Journal*, 26(4), 381–95.

Evaluation

Once negotiations were complete, each bidder submitted a best and final offer. As part of this process, a risk register was prepared and shared with each bidder to reflect information gathered through site visits and references from clients to whom the bidders provided similar services. These visits identified further risks for the client, which were openly discussed with bidders and this allowed bidders to propose and/or take action to mitigate the risks. The site visits were viewed as an important element in identifying and mitigating the risks arising from the complexities and novelties of the project. The open discussion of the results of evaluation and risk registers enabled bidders to improve their final proposals.

Consortium selection

The final evaluation and selection decision was based on a qualitative and quantitative assessment of each bidder. The successful bidder had a clear cost advantage over the others, and the project team regarded their offer as having the lowest quantifiable risk. The successful consortium consisted of four companies:

- *Prime contractor.* Responsible for the implementation and overall management of the ICT services, which involved implementing the Oracle software application to deliver the HR services. This contractor was responsible for managing the other companies in the consortium.

- *Shared services operator.* Responsible for managing and operating the shared services centre through a front-office employee HR contact centre, and a back-office operation providing transaction services, casework and professional support to managers and employees.
- *Specialist HR consultancy.* Responsible for providing support on deploying best practice, business process redesign and HR transformation.
- *Oracle.* Responsible for providing specialist Oracle consulting services, and working with the prime contractor's development staff.

The client signed a public–private partnership (PPP) agreement.[7] The contract was for up to fifteen years with an option for the client to terminate at any time after the 10th year. The arrangement was projected to be cash-neutral as the cash savings achieved from implementing the new services and systems would be allocated as a contribution to future contractor service charges. Previously, there had been 900 staff involved in the provision of HR services, giving a full-time-equivalent (FTE) ratio of 1:32.[8] Under the new arrangement, 350 staff were retained internally in the HR function, giving a FTE ratio of 1:80. Around 500 staff were redeployed internally to other suitable posts, and there were no compulsory redundancies or internal staff transferred into the shared services centre.

Although contracting was an extremely challenging process, the project team believed that the KPIs and service levels would be of benefit to other public sector organisations outsourcing HR services. There were a number of important elements of the contract.

> *Payment and performance.* Operational services were paid for on the basis of *availability* and at the agreed *performance level*, i.e. no service, no fee. The abatement regime was used to calculate the deductions required when operational services failed to meet the minimum required service levels for availability and performance. For example, abatements of up to 100 per cent of the charge for services were put at risk in the case of under-performance.

> *Charging model.* A number of charging mechanisms were employed. One mechanism involved charging for the service on the basis of the number of internal employees using the service. The shared services centre and ICT services were both charged on a cost per qualifying employee. A further mechanism was based on allocating a unit cost per transaction. Pay and reward was charged on a cost per payslip, whilst

recruitment was charged on a cost based on the type of competition. There were two payment points for each type of competition: at pre-interview list, post-sift list or post-assessment list; and at final outcome stage (e.g. issue of letters, publication of final list). Specifically scoped packages of work required by the client were charged on daily rates.

Benchmarking. Provisions were included for benchmarking at various stages in the contract, which included the appointment of independent benchmarking consultants to undertake a full comparative study of all the services involved. The outcome of this exercise involved the client and contractor agreeing an action plan, which involved a review of service levels, reasons for under-performance, possibly reduced service charges, and plans for service improvements.

Continuous improvement. There was a commitment to continuous improvement in the contract, which was resourced through the specialist HR consultancy providing four full-time equivalents to work with the client and contractor to drive improvement. Through an annual review of service levels and benchmarking, the client expected to achieve service levels in HR that would place them in the top quartile for public sector employees.

The structure of the new HR arrangement which developed from contract negotiations with the successful consortium had a number of elements, as shown in Figure 6.2.

Online service

This was a self-service facility for staff with online access, and had two elements:

- *Source of information.* Online access for staff to the HR Handbook, containing information on all HR policies and procedures. This service provided a single, up-to-date, online source of information on HR policies and procedures.
- *Transaction capability.* Staff could carry out some HR administration transactions online including reviewing and updating personal information, checking holiday balances, applying for leave, trawling for job opportunities and searching for and booking training. Some of the capabilities provided to line managers included approving annual leave requests for staff online, recording absences, managing staff over time, pay allowances, performance management and learning and development.

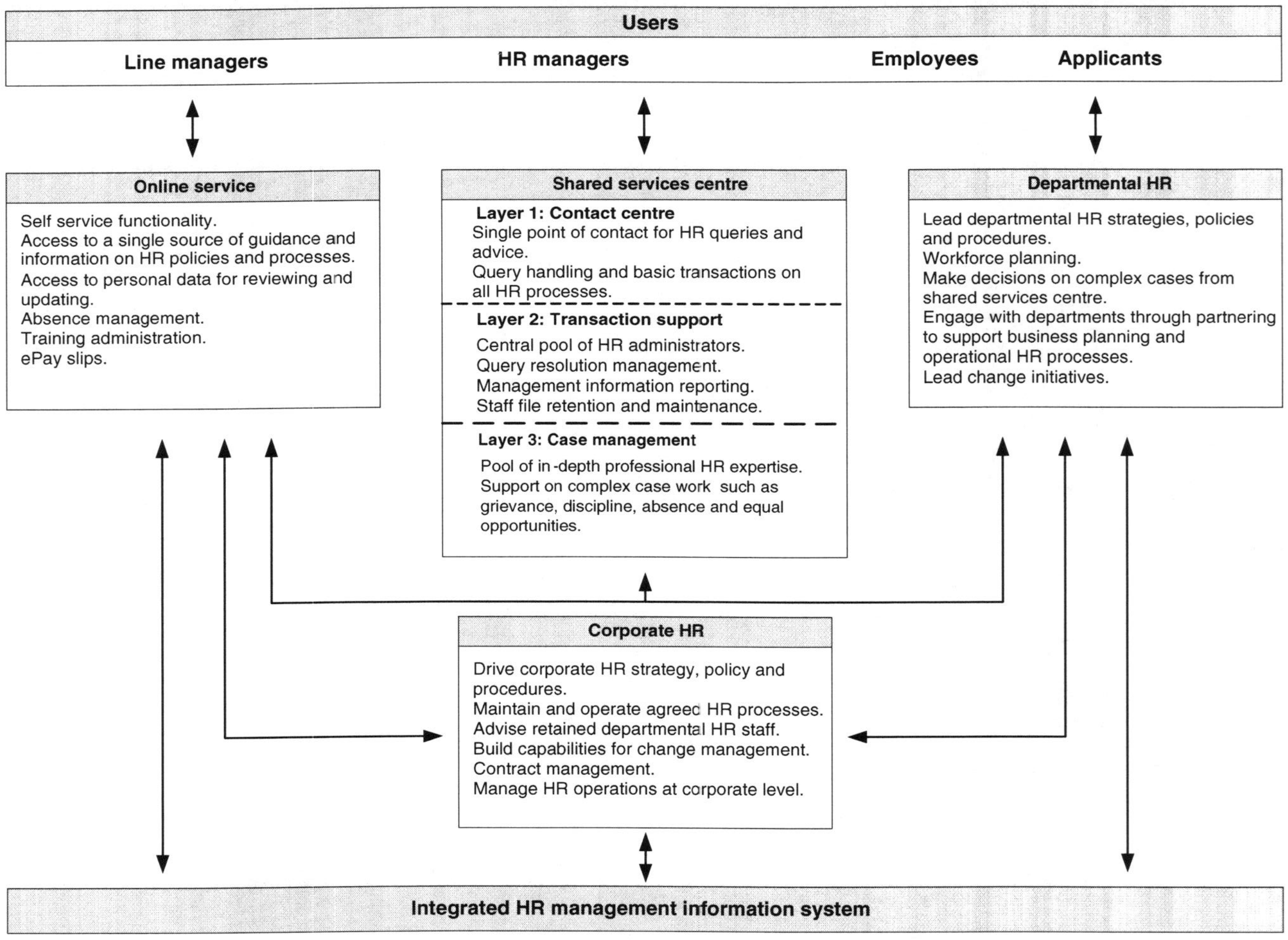

Users
Line managers
HR managers
Employees
Applicants
Online service
Self service functionality.
Access to a single source of guidance and information on HR policies and processes.
Access to personal data for reviewing and updating.
Absence management.
Training administration.
ePay slips.
Shared services centre
Layer 1: Contact centre
Single point of contact for HR queries and advice.
Query handling and basic transactions on all HR processes.
Layer 2: Transaction support
Central pool of HR administrators.
Query resolution management.
Management information reporting.
Staff file retention and maintenance.
Layer 3: Case management
Pool of in-depth professional HR expertise.
Support on complex case work such as grievance, discipline, absence and equal opportunities.
Departmental HR
Lead departmental HR strategies, policies and procedures.
Workforce planning.
Make decisions on complex cases from shared services centre.
Engage with departments through partnering to support business planning and operational HR processes.
Lead change initiatives.
Corporate HR
Drive corporate HR strategy, policy and procedures.
Maintain and operate agreed HR processes.
Advise retained departmental HR staff.
Build capabilities for change management.
Contract management.
Manage HR operations at corporate level.
Integrated HR management information system

Figure 6.2 Structure of the new HR arrangement

Shared services centre

Staff who did not have access to a PC or who had more complex queries could talk to an advisor in the shared services centre who was trained and had access to corporate policies and procedures. The shared services centre had a number of layers:

- *Layer 1: Contact centre.* Accessible by email, telephone and text to all employees, managers, departmental staff and job applicants. It was anticipated that up to 70 per cent of queries would be resolved at this first point of contact. Under the previous arrangement, these queries were dealt with by HR staff in the departments.
- *Layer 2: Transaction support.* The bulk of transactional tasks such as the administration of recruitment competitions and payroll processing were carried out at this level. Queries escalated from Layer 1 that required a further degree of HR input were dealt with at this layer. Another aspect of this transactional role involved the vendor retaining and maintaining all personnel data in line with the client's policies for data retention.
- *Layer 3: Case management.* Involved teams of HR caseworkers providing personal high touch service in terms of investigating and reporting on complex cases in areas such as grievance, discipline and absence. These teams provided case analysis and recommendations. However, all HR decision-making remained within the client.

Departmental HR

Departmental HR took on a business partnering role, which involved focusing on advising the business areas and line managers on areas such as business planning, providing support in complex cases such as grievance and disciplinary matters, and communicating how new policies and procedures would impact on their departments. Departmental HR was no longer the first point of contact for simple queries on HR policies or procedures.

Corporate HR

Corporate HR worked with departmental HR teams to develop HR policy.

6.6 Change management

Although change management is recognised as an important aspect of implementing shared services outsourcing arrangements, organisations struggle to deal with change management issues such as winning support from those affected. Organisations often ignore the fact that the success of such arrangements is heavily dependent upon the attitudes and commitment of employees.[9] The shared services arrangement in this case had significant change implications for a number of individuals or groups across the organisation.[10]

HR professionals

The concerns of HR professionals had to be managed carefully, as they were being directly affected by the shared services outsourcing arrangement. Outsourcing can lead to resistance, and also have an adverse impact upon morale due to legitimate fears of job losses. In this case, it was made clear from the beginning of the project that there would be no redundancies, and that individuals affected would be redeployed to other parts of the organisation. Previously the HR functions at departmental level spent 80 per cent of their time on administrative-type activities, and 20 per cent of their time solving problems for departmental and line managers. Under the new arrangement HR professionals were expected to spend 80 per cent of their time solving problems in areas such as absence management, morale and motivation problems. By implementing the new arrangement senior management were attempting to effect an attitudinal change, and transform HR into a customer-service-oriented function. A number of strategies were pursued to achieve this transformation.

> *Training and development.* Implementing these changes required developing new skills and competences in HR professionals both at director and lower levels. HR directors undertook ongoing executive development courses in areas such as business partnering, change management and project management throughout implementation. The HR professionals at departmental level were encouraged to take part in training and development courses on business partnering, developing negotiation skills, data analysis and communication skills.
>
> *Redeployment opportunities.* The HR directors recognised that some HR staff in the departments would not be comfortable with moving away from a primarily administrative role towards a business partnering role. HR staff unwilling to embrace this new role were offered the opportunity to transfer to other parts of the organisation.
>
> *Consultancy* – Implementing the shared services arrangement meant HR departments had to change their bureaucratic structures to become more customer-focused, and act as strategic partners delivering value-added services. Therefore, expertise from the specialist HR consultancy agreed in the contract was employed to advise and implement these required changes.

Line managers

A key objective of the new arrangement involved increasing line manager involvement, and ownership of HR tasks and decisions. Line managers were in a better position to deal with HR issues as they had better knowledge of departmental needs. Previously, line managers had passed HR-related tasks to their HR department, regarding such issues as not their responsibility. Some line managers resisted the new arrangement because they viewed it as additional to their existing workload. However, senior management made it clear to line managers that these HR tasks were part of their existing responsibilities and workload. Two practices were adopted to win the support of line managers for the necessary changes:

- *Benefits communication.* The benefits of the new arrangement were communicated to line managers. A key benefit of the system for line managers was the rapid processing of HR tasks electronically, in contrast to previous paper-based systems.
- *Training and support.* Extensive training opportunities were provided for line managers via workshops and e-learning packages. In addition, a small number of staff in each department were given extensive training to provide support in the event of any difficulties with the system.

Employees

Previously, employees carried out many HR tasks manually, and sought assistance by speaking directly with an HR person in their department. Under the new arrangement, employees had to seek information and assistance online or via the contact centre. Again, the project team placed particular emphasis on selling the benefits of the new arrangement to employees. These included the ability to perform HR tasks such as processing leave requests more quickly, and the availability of a single point of contact in the shared services centre for HR queries. Employees were provided with training via e-learning packages, and employees with extensive training were on hand in each department to deal with queries.

6.7 Stakeholder management

Managing the expectations of stakeholders in large-scale projects such as shared services arrangements can have a critical influence on achieving a successful outcome.[11] The project team regarded stakeholder management as an important approach to gaining the support of potential opponents, and also creating greater ownership and support among important stakeholders. Through engaging with stakeholders from the outset, the views and opinions of important stakeholders could shape the development of the project, which would ensure greater support. Analysing the expectations and needs of stakeholders made it possible to anticipate their likely reactions, and put in plans to win their support for the project. Communication was a key element of the project team's strategy for engaging with stakeholders. A range of media were used in communications including the staff intranet and portal, regular news updates, training communications and post-release support.

Illustration 6.3 Stakeholder management

Stakeholder management has become an important aspect of a range of disciplines including project management and strategic management. Stakeholders are individuals or groups of individuals who have an interest in the outcome of a project. Stakeholders in a software development project include system users, managers of users, systems analysts, senior managers and any other individual impacted by the development of the system. Stakeholder management involves identifying stakeholders, determining how stakeholders are likely to react to project decisions, understanding their level of influence, and accessing how they will interact with each other and the project management team to affect the chances of a successful outcome. The ability to understand the power and influence of stakeholders has become a critical skill for successful project managers. Stakeholders can be a valuable asset, contributing important knowledge, insights and support for the project, which can lead to a more successful outcome.

There are a number of benefits of stakeholder management. Project managers can involve stakeholders at an early stage to inform the development of the project. This will help secure their support and lead to a more successful outcome. Through winning support from key stakeholders such as senior management, project managers are more likely to secure the required resource. Communication is an important tool in stakeholder management. Through communicating early and frequently, stakeholders will more fully understand the potential benefits, and therefore provide support whenever necessary. Understanding the needs and concerns of stakeholders allows the project team to anticipate their reactions and put in place mechanisms to win their support.

One of the most common techniques used to manage stakeholders is the power/interest matrix, as shown in Figure 6.3. Stakeholders are classified by their degree of power to influence the project and degree of interest they have in the outcome of the project. The position of stakeholders within this matrix provides guidelines on how they should be managed:

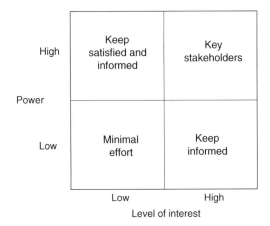

Figure 6.3 Stakeholder power/interest matrix

- *High power/high interest.* These are key stakeholders and most attention should be given to satisfying their expectations and needs.
- *High power/low interest.* Efforts should be made to keep these stakeholders satisfied and adequately informed.
- *Low power/high interest.* These stakeholders should be kept adequately informed, and efforts should be made to ensure that no problems arise. Involving these stakeholders in project decisions can create greater ownership and support for a successful outcome.
- *Low power/low interest.* Minimal effort should be given to these stakeholders. However, the expectations of these stakeholders should be monitored, and regular communication used to inform them of developments in the project.

Stakeholder mapping can be used to understand some of the following issues:

- Identifying the key supporters and opponents of the project, their likely reactions, and potential strategies for responding including education and involving them in some aspects of project decision-making.
- Assessing whether it is feasible or desirable to reposition certain stakeholders. For example, the influence of key stakeholders could be reduced, or key stakeholders could be encouraged to champion the project in order to win the support of other stakeholders.
- Maintaining the level of interest and power in the project is important. Endorsement of the project by senior management can increase the level of interest and in turn maintain the involvement of some stakeholders in the project.

> Conflicts that can arise in large projects between stakeholders are an important aspect of stakeholder management. Conflict between stakeholders can be reduced through clarifying rights and responsibilities. The rights of a stakeholder group can include project managers clearly articulating the details of the project; identifying and understanding their requirements; being receptive to suggestions or ideas; and treating them with respect. The responsibilities of a stakeholder group can include issues such as providing resources to support the project team; committing time to explain their requirements to the project team; respecting the judgement of a project manager; reviewing and providing timely feedback; and promptly communicating changes to requirements.
>
> *Sources:* Johnson, G., Scholes, K. and Whittington, R. (2008). *Exploring Corporate Strategy: Text and Cases*, 8th edn, Harlow: FT Prentice Hall; Maylor, H. (2005). Project Stakeholders, *Blackwell Encyclopaedia of Management: Operations Management*, 2nd edn, Oxford: Backwell, 243–4.

The project team adopted a number of approaches for engaging with the following stakeholder groupings.

Senior staff at corporate and departmental level

Key stakeholders at corporate level included ministers, permanent secretaries[12] and corporate HR, whilst key stakeholders at departmental level included HR directors, departmental HR, departmental senior managers and trade union representatives. A key objective of engaging with these stakeholders was to obtain their commitment and support in actively and visibly promoting the project in the departments. Managing the expectations and needs of these stakeholders was important throughout all phases of the project. At the preliminary analysis stage the project team paid close attention to gaining support from senior staff such as departmental HR directors for the project. This was particularly critical when the project team increased the scope of the project to include the transformation of HR services, as well as an outsourced shared services centre. HR directors were invited to the site visits of the vendors to see the benefits of moving towards a total outsourced shared services centre.

Departmental HR staff

Securing the support of all HR staff at departmental level was another important feature of stakeholder engagement as they had both a high level of interest and influence over the success of the project. The traditional role and processes of HR were being changed, and there was the potential for resistance from HR staff. In addition, departmental HR staff were expected to commit a lot of time and resource to the project, particularly in the implementation phase. Therefore, it was important that the benefits of the project were communicated to them, and that they did not feel threatened. Particular attention was given to emphasising that there would be no job losses in HR as a result of the project. Gaining their support ensured that they worked closely with vendors in the procurement phase to describe existing processes and future requirements. In the implementation phase, HR staff worked closely with the vendor to develop and implement the new arrangement. Crucially, they had in-depth and specific knowledge of departmental requirements, which was of particular importance in the case of payroll processing.

Line managers

Line managers were also key stakeholders who had to be managed carefully. Much of the stakeholder engagement activity with line managers involved selling the benefits of the system to them, which involved meetings and conducting training workshops. Table 6.4 shows the benefits messages communicated to line managers prior to implementation.

The project team introduced a mechanism for monitoring where stakeholders were positioned in relation to their support for the project, which was used to inform the type of engagement required. A stakeholder engagement curve was developed to assess where each stakeholder was currently positioned, and where they needed to be in relation to their support for the project. The stakeholders were positioned on the engagement curve which plotted both their current and desired level of support for the project. The curve began at the awareness stage and moved along to understanding, engagement, support, commitment and ownership. For example, departmental HR needed to be committed to the programme whereas staff needed to be supportive of the programme. This mapping process enabled the project team to decide which form of engagement would move each stakeholder to the desired position on the engagement curve. The maps were used by the project team and each department to monitor how each stakeholder was progressing towards the desired future state of engagement.

The project team learned a number of lessons in stakeholder management as the project developed and adapted their approach in some areas. They implemented mechanisms to measure the effectiveness of communications in stakeholder management. One mechanism involved consulting staff in each department to gather opinions on communications, and how

Table 6.4 Key benefits messages to line managers

Key benefits messages	
Better visibility of and access to information	• Access to a single set of policies and procedures via the HR handbook (easier to understand, better navigation, user guide, search functionality, FAQs). • Single integrated solution from which line managers could extract information more efficiently to support better decision-making. • Better visibility of staff absence, enabling more effective management.
Efficient processes	• Streamlined, integrated and quicker HR administration. • Less paper. • Single point of contact for queries. • Consistent processes and systems across all departments.
More focused HR support	• More business-oriented and better information for HR staff. • Continued support for difficult decisions and cases. • Business partners will not support day-to-day HR transactions and queries.
More proactive role in management of personnel matters. Decision-making moved from HR to line managers	• Have the right information to take decisions. • Decisions taken at the appropriate level.

they might be improved. In addition, the project team decided to differentiate between key stakeholder groups, as some stakeholders were more critical than others for communications activities. For communications purposes, it divided key stakeholders into the following tiers:

- *Tier 1 key stakeholders* were defined as key stakeholders who played a pivotal role in briefing other groups of key stakeholders and included the HR director and the deputy HR director at corporate level, the departmental HR directors and departmental project managers.
- *Tier 2 key stakeholders* were those who were to be briefed by a Tier 1 stakeholder.

Rather than adopt a standard communications approach to all key stakeholders, the project team used Tier 1 key stakeholders to brief other key stakeholders, as shown in Figure 6.4. For example, departmental HR directors were briefed very closely by the project team at various stages of the project and then were responsible for briefing departmental senior management teams and HR staff.

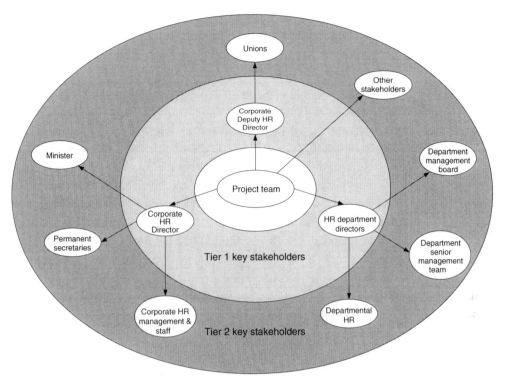

Figure 6.4   Key stakeholder category communication approach

6.8 Business process redesign

An important element of the implementation phase was business process redesign, which involved analysing and redesigning the HR processes that were being transferred into the shared services centre. The outputs from this exercise were used to develop technical specifications for coding the information technology element of the system. Business process redesign presented a number of challenges. Analysis for business case development revealed significant process duplications and inconsistencies in interpretation of corporate policies in areas such as absence management. There was a lot of customisation required because of the specific nature of the organisation's requirements. Differentiating between activities that should remain in the HR department and those that should move to the shared services centre was challenging. There was a risk that HR staff would try to retain processes in their departments, and hold onto their own specific way of performing certain processes rather than agree to the adoption of standard processes applied across all departments. However, the project team believed that effective management of this process would yield a number of significant benefits. Outdated and idiosyncratic work practices would be eliminated, and significant costs would be reduced through standardisation of duplicated activities into the shared services centre. The shared services centre would provide higher service levels for internal users through continuous improvement. Leveraging the specialist expertise of the HR consultancy in contemporary HR practices had the potential to transform the HR function.

Process mapping was an integral part of business redesign process. Staff participated in workshops to develop and refine process maps. This exercise was led by the specialist HR consultancy and involved staff from the prime contractor and staff across the client organisation, including those from the project team, corporate HR and HR staff at departmental level. Process mapping included fully documenting the processes, which involved developing diagrams to show inputs, automated processes, manual processes, decision points and outputs. Lines of responsibility were identified for each process, along with the interfaces with other processes. Process maps went through a number of iterations and the following criteria were applied to process maps during the exercise:

- *Standardise* – ensuring that processes were standardised to capture the benefits of economies of scale, whilst maintaining appropriate service to users.
- *Simplify* – reducing process complexity, where possible, to reduce costs.
- *Eliminate* – eliminating processes that created little or no value-added to service users and increased costs.
- *Automate* – designing the process so that the most effective technical solution would be deployed.

Throughout this exercise, idiosyncratic work practices associated with certain departments were removed. The project team adopted a number of practices to gain the support of departments in this exercise. The commitment of employees at both corporate and departmental level was obtained through involving relevant staff in the design of the new arrangement in design workshops. In addition, buy-in to the necessary changes was achieved through demonstrating the benefits of standardising the process. The specialist HR consultancy used its expertise to show how process performance could be improved, and introduced standard processes developed from working with other clients – often industry-standard HR practices. Departments were encouraged to contribute ideas for improvement in order to create greater buy-in and participation in the exercise.

However, some issues did arise that slowed down business process redesign. During the process analysis phase, it was found that a number of corporate policies had to change prior to implementation as a result of outdated procedures or a lack of consistency. Updating policies involved renegotiations with a number of stakeholders including unions, which caused delays in implementation. Leadership and authority were required to deal with disagreements from departments when having to relinquish previous practices and accept new and standard processes. Although it was recognised there would have to be exceptions for departments in certain areas, senior staff at corporate level became involved in certain instances to ensure that departments were not holding onto inefficient processes.

6.9 Strategic partnership development

The scale and complexity of the project made a strategic partnership agreement essential. The contract included a number of provisions to facilitate a partnership ethos including the equal sharing of efficiency savings annually, and opportunities for 'gain sharing' during the contract period, when profits by the contractor exceeded a threshold profit margin of 7.5 per cent. The high level of dependency between each party meant attempting to build partnership relations could help to deal with potential difficulties and drive improvements. Open-book arrangements that involve sharing and understanding each other's costs to estimate margins and drive continuous improvement required the development of interpersonal relationships and frequent communication, essential characteristics of partnerships.

Both the client and the vendor envisaged that a partnership would be helpful in creating flexibility in the relationship. This was important as the SLAs and charging models had to change during the implementation and management phases of the contract. As both the client and vendor became more experienced with the shared services arrangement, more sophisticated SLAs and charging techniques would be required. Indeed, during implementation the client agreed to reduce the number of KPIs specified in the contract, as it was felt they were over-elaborate and diluted the significance of what was being measured. A key objective of the shared services arrangement was improving performance. However, the client and vendor recognised that performance management would have to be conducted in a spirit of openness. Effective management of the contract required the client putting in place internal mechanisms for monitoring the service quality that internal users were getting from the shared services centre. This involved developing a scorecard that included metrics highlighting performance levels in the areas of customer satisfaction and operational and financial performance.

6.10 Summary implications

- Adopting a structured project management approach is an essential element of creating shared services. Clearly defined project objectives and strong leadership are required at corporate level. Departmental staff are likely to resist shared services arrangements because such projects consume scarce resource and management time. Therefore, leadership at corporate level is important for gaining the necessary commitment and support from departments and other stakeholders. The project team should be properly convened with the appropriate mix of skills, and representation from parts of the organisation impacted by the shared services arrangement.
- A strong business case should be developed to describe clearly the problems with existing systems and processes, and outline how these problems can be overcome, along with the benefits of moving towards a shared services arrangement. A convincing rationale for proceeding with a shared services arrangement will assist in winning the support of key stakeholders.
- The scale and complexity of outsourced shared services means that clients often lack the skills to determine requirements and a detailed outline of the shared services delivery model. Therefore, engaging with potential vendors in the procurement phase is a valuable means of exploring potential sourcing options, gaining ideas and refining requirements. Specialist vendors have superior levels of knowledge and experience. Engaging with vendors offers the potential to exploit these capabilities to improve the performance of functions affected by shared services.
- Significant attention has to be given to contract negotiations. Determining KPIs and SLAs is a complex process, and requires specialist skills often lacking in the client. Contracting becomes even more challenging where existing client processes and performance measurement systems are weak. External legal advice and expertise in performance measurement and procurement should be employed to address the challenges of contracting. Such expertise is essential when the client has relied on the vendors to suggest potential sourcing options during the vendor engagement phase.

- Change management is an important aspect of shared services. The perspectives and responses of employees affected by shared services outsourcing arrangements have a significant impact on successful implementation. Much of the change management effort has to be given to the function directly affected. For example, a key objective of HR shared services arrangements involves transforming the retained HR function into a customer-service-oriented function, which requires a significant attitudinal change on the part of the HR professional. Training and professional development are important elements of facilitating this change.

- Engaging with stakeholders is valuable for winning support from key individuals or groups of individuals. Powerful stakeholders can be used to brief and increase support from less enthusiastic stakeholders. Important mechanisms for engaging with stakeholders include timely and properly directed communication, and involving potential opponents in project decisions and tasks. The effectiveness of stakeholder management activities should be monitored throughout the project. This involves consulting stakeholders on the effectiveness of communications, and monitoring how the support of certain stakeholders is changing.

- Standardising and improving process performance presents a number of challenges including the reluctance of departments to relinquish long-held practices, highly specific client requirements and weaknesses in corporate policies. It is essential to standardise as many processes as possible in order to achieve the potential benefits of shared services. Although exceptions to a standardised approach have to be included in certain circumstances, these should not adversely affect performance. Incorporating too many exceptions to standards, and making changes to corporate policies, is likely to create complexity for the vendor, and lead to delays in implementation. Analysing and eliminating deficiencies in corporate policies is an important exercise for the client prior to implementation.

- The complexity and scale of outsourced shared services necessitates the development of a partnership relationship between the client and vendor. Strong interpersonal relationships between the client and vendor are important in both the implementation and relationship management phases. Adjusting KPIs and SLAs from those agreed in the contract in the implementation phase requires good client–vendor relations. Benchmarking and continuous improvement, key elements of relationship management in outsourced shared services, are more likely to succeed in a climate of openness and trust between the client and vendor.

- Outsourced shared services arrangements pose enormous challenges to the affected function. The retained function has to move from a transaction-intensive mode to one of value-adding. In the case of HR, this involves developing a business partnering role, becoming more strategic, formulating effective policies and managing external relationships with outsourcing vendors. Where an outsourced shared services centre is established, and the retained function fails to take on a more strategic role, it is likely to become a target for further outsourcing initiatives at the corporate level.

Notes and references

1 Cooke, F. (2006). Modelling an HR Shared Services Centre: Experience of an MNC in the United Kingdom, *Human Resource Management*, 45(2), 211–27; Davis, T. (2005). Integrating Shared Services with the Strategy and Operations of MNEs, *Journal of General Management*, 31(2), 1–17; Quinn, B., Cooke, R. and Kris, A. (2000). *Shared Services: Mining for Corporate Gold*, London: FT Prentice Hall.

2 Cecil, B. (2000). Shared Services Moving Beyond Success, *Strategic Finance*, 81(10), 64–8.

3 Lacity, M. and Fox, J. (2008). Creating Global Shared Services: Lessons from Reuters, *MIS Quarterly Executive*, 7(1), 17–32; Wang, S. and Wang, H. (2007). Shared Services beyond Sourcing the Back Offices: Organisational Design, *Human Systems Management*, 26, 281–90.

4 For further reading on HR outsourcing, see Hesketh, A. (2006). *Outsourcing the HR Function: Possibilities and Pitfalls*, London: Accenture/CRF; Klaas, B., McClendon, J. and Gainey, T. (2001). Outsourcing HR: The Impact of Organisational Characteristics, *Human Resource Management*, 40, 125–38; and Greer, C., Youngblood, S. and Gray, D. (1999). Human Resource Management Outsourcing: The Make or Buy Decision, *Academy of Management Executive*, 13, 85–96.

5 The analysis presented in this chapter concerns a shared services arrangement in the public sector. Important contract details are not included to protect the confidentiality of the organisation involved. The primary source of data collection involved semi-structured interviews with personnel at both corporate HR and departmental level in the client organisation, and with personnel in the vendor. Data were collected on key aspects of the project including business case development, vendor selection and contracting, stakeholder management, implementation and business process redesign. It should be stressed that the analysis is not intended to illustrate the effective or ineffective management of creating shared services, as data collection took place during the early stages of the services going live. However, the analysis provides many important insights into the issues involved in creating shared services arrangements.

6 For additional reading in project management, see Meredith, J. and Mantel, S. (2006). *Project Management: A Managerial Approach*, 6th edn, New York: Wiley; Levene, R. (2005). Project Management, *Blackwell Encyclopaedia of Management: Operations Management*, 2nd edn, Oxford: Blackwell; and Maylor, H. (2003). *Project Management*, 3rd edn, London: FT Prentice Hall.

7 A public–private partnership (PPP) is an agreement between government and the private sector for the provision of public services or infrastructure. The goal of PPPs for government is to access the management skills of the private sector, and reduce the capital expenditure involved in large projects.
8 Ratio of the number of HR staff to employees in the organisation.
9 McIvor, R. and McHugh, M. (2002). The Organisational Change Implications of Outsourcing, *Journal of General Management*, 27(4), 27–48.
10 For general reading on change management, see Hayes, J. (2007). *The Theory and Practice of Change Management*, 2nd edn, New York: Palgrave Macmillan; and Burnes, B. (2004). *Managing Change: A Strategic Approach to Organisational Dynamics*, 4th edn, Harlow: FT Prentice Hall.
11 For further reading on stakeholder management, see Lund, A. and Eskerod, P. (2009). Stakeholder Analysis in Projects: Challenges in Using Current Guidelines in the Real World, *International Journal of Project Management*, 27(4), 335–43; Johnson, G., Scholes, K. and Whittington, R. (2008). *Exploring Corporate Strategy: Text and Cases*, 8th edn, Harlow: FT Prentice Hall; and Boonstra, A. (2006). Interpreting an ERP Implementation Project from a Stakeholder Perspective, *International Journal of Project Management*, 24(1), 38–52.
12 'Permanent secretary' is the term used to describe a senior civil servant who runs a major government department in the UK.

Recommended key reading

Adler, P. (2003). Making the HR Outsourcing Decision, *Sloan Management Review*, 45(1), 53–9. This paper identifies six key factors that organisations should consider when making the HR outsourcing decision. Particular attention is given to the landmark HR outsourcing deal between BP and Exult Inc.

Cooke, F., Shen, J. and McBride, A. (2005). Outsourcing HR as a Competitive Strategy, *Human Resource Management*, 44(4), 413–32. This paper provides a critical review of the reasons for, and effectiveness of, HR outsourcing. It explores the implications of HR outsourcing for the role of the HR function.

Davis, T. (2005). Integrating Shared Services with the Strategy and Operations of MNEs, *Journal of General Management*, 31(2), 1–17. This paper provides a history of shared services arrangements in the USA, Europe and Asia.

Lacity, M. and Fox, J. (2008). Creating Global Shared Services: Lessons from Reuters, *MIS Quarterly Executive*, 7(1), 17–32. This paper presents lessons from the experiences of Reuters in creating a global shared services model for its finance operations.

Zeynep, A. and Masini, A. (2008). Effective Strategies for Internal Outsourcing and Offshoring of Business Services: An Empirical Investigation, *Journal of Operations Management*, 26, 239–56. This paper examines various configurations of shared services, and explains why and under what circumstances some of these configurations deliver superior performance.

Services outsourcing and performance management

7.1 Introduction

Outsourcing is increasingly being employed to achieve performance improvements across the entire business. However, many organisations have had mixed results with outsourcing, and have failed to achieve the desired performance improvements. Some have argued that organisations have not understood fully the implications of outsourcing and performance management.[1] Organisations have outsourced poorly performing processes without understanding the causes of poor performance. Services providers often cannot deliver the required performance improvements because of poorly designed processes or the idiosyncratic requirements of clients. Organisations also have difficulties assessing vendor performance during the outsourcing relationship, as they have not established effective performance measures for the process prior to outsourcing.

This chapter focuses on performance management and the outsourcing process. A framework is presented which provides an outline of the stages involved in integrating performance management into the outsourcing process. The framework employs a number of performance management techniques including cost analysis, benchmarking, workflow mapping and continuous improvement. The chapter is structured as follows. Initially, an overview of the relationship between outsourcing and performance management is presented. This is followed by a detailed description of a framework for integrating performance management into the outsourcing process. Illustrations from a financial services organisation (FSO) are introduced throughout the chapter to demonstrate the practical implications of performance management for the outsourcing process.[2] The challenges and benefits of performance management and outsourcing are outlined. Finally, summary implications are presented.

7.2 Services outsourcing and performance management

As organisations outsource larger and more complex processes, perform-ance management has become increasingly challenging. Performance management is more complex in business services than in manufactur-ing. Whereas many manufacturing processes can be standardised and modularised, it is more difficult to standardise service processes, thus increasing the difficulties of developing effective performance measures for use in outsourcing arrangements. Services lack the tangible attributes of physical products, and include many attributes that are difficult to spe-cify in measurable terms, which often leads to incomplete specifications of both requirements and service levels.[3] This makes it difficult to make meaningful comparisons across organisations, and understand the causes of variances in process performance. Organisations struggle to identify what should be measured and how to normalise data across different organisational contexts.[4] Even when organisations know what to meas-ure, they fail to achieve accuracy, as performance data are not defined or collected consistently. Moreover, the approach to data collection for performance management in many organisations is driven by the require-ments of financial cost reporting, rather than understanding the factors affecting performance.[5]

Effective performance management is acknowledged in the literature as a critical influence on successful services outsourcing. There is a consen-sus on the need to link outsourcing and performance management with the business strategy of the organisation.[6] In fact, performance manage-ment and business strategy are closely linked, as performance measures and management are critical elements in translating an organisation's strategy into reality.[7] Performance management is a way of making the mission of an organisation tangible and establishing objectives and performance meas-ures that can be understood. The motives of organisations in outsourcing decision-making are often dominated by performance concerns. The use of the core/non-core logic by practitioners in outsourcing decisions is driven by performance considerations. Organisations should perform internally 'core' processes where they have a superior performance position that is difficult to replicate, whereas they should outsource 'non-core' processes where vendors have superior performance positions.

As well as impacting business strategy, performance management has implications for both the decision to outsource and implementing and managing the outsourcing arrangement.

Performance management and outsourcing evaluation

In making the decision to outsource a process, organisations often focus on processes with which they are experiencing performance problems. This creates significant difficulties when organisations outsource such processes. Organisations assume that external vendors can provide processes at a higher performance level than internal functions. Often, vendors cannot meet client performance expectations because of problems that were present in the process when it was performed in-house. Failure to understand the causes of poor performance may also lead an organisation to outsource processes, often labelled as 'problem processes', that are critical to competitive advantage. Prior to outsourcing, organisations should have an understanding of the key measures that indicate performance in a process relative to vendors or competitors. Analysing the causes of poor process performance in areas of cost and service quality expands the range of sourcing options available – ranging from outsourcing to internal process improvement.

As well as costs, the relative performance along a number of other dimensions such as quality, flexibility and service should be considered in outsourcing evaluation. Indeed, as organisations have become more experienced with outsourcing, they have begun to introduce continuous improvement techniques to assist with evaluation.[8] For example, process mapping and cost analysis approaches can be used to understand cost drivers and potential ways of achieving efficiencies by redesigning processes. Benchmarking is particularly valuable in an outsourcing context and can be used to compare operations, work practices and business processes. The purpose of benchmarking comparisons is to enable organisations to determine where and how performance can be improved. It is concerned with searching for and implementing best practice and performance improvement so that organisations can understand and incorporate process or product innovations that have been successful in other contexts.[9]

Performance management and managing outsourcing arrangements

In the case of managing outsourcing arrangements, effective performance management has a number of important implications.

Performance management capability. A major source of difficulty for organisations when measuring outsourcing performance is that they have never effectively measured the performance of the process when it was performed internally. This means that the organisation is developing performance measures for the first time when the process is outsourced. These performance measures are often ineffective and create difficulties in the outsourcing arrangement. For example, a major difficulty with poor performance management in the outsourcing process is that organisations have no way of knowing whether the external vendor has performed the process better or worse than the internal department previously. Indeed, some have argued that organisations should create metrics to measure the quality of processes for a while, and improve performance internally before outsourcing.[10] Ineffective performance measures also mean that performance milestones established in the initial phases of the outsourcing arrangement are unrealistic, and lead to relationship difficulties as the client becomes disappointed with the performance of the vendor.

Over-emphasis on measurement. An over-emphasis on specifying requirements and measurement, rather than understanding the influences on performance, creates difficulties in outsourcing. This is particularly prevalent in outsourcing arrangements that are dominated by efficiency considerations, rather than effectiveness. In this case, the contract is dominated by obligations that are over-specified and the flexibility of the vendor is constrained. For example, in a call centre context, efficiency-dominated outsourcing contracts reward the vendor for strictly adhering to efficiency measures of the time to answer a call and the average talk-time per call.[11] However, the focus on efficiency reduces the incentive and ability of the vendor to focus on areas that contribute to effectiveness, such as enhancing service quality and customer satisfaction. The client has to strike a balance in the outsourcing arrangement between sourcing the most efficient service, and creating the context where efforts at contributing towards effectiveness are encouraged.

Opportunism potential. Ineffective performance management in outsourcing arrangements can also lead to vendor opportunism. Difficulties with measuring performance create problems in the relationship, as the client must expend additional resource on monitoring vendor performance. The client–vendor relationship can be damaged as a result of disputes in relation to the performance measures chosen and the measurement process. Disagreements can arise on which performance criteria should be chosen for measurement and the frequency of measurement. There are a number of performance-related factors in an outsourcing arrangement that can create opportunism. High levels of interdependency between processes and functions in both the client and vendor make it extremely difficult to determine the causes of poor performance, and therefore assign responsibility for any performance shortcomings. Changes in requirements from the client throughout the outsourcing arrangement can lead to changes in both performance measures and the level of performance required. Such a situation can lead to disputes, particularly in instances where there is a lack of trust in the relationship.[12]

Any failings on the part of the client to understand the outsourced process and how to measure performance can be exploited by opportunistic vendors. Mistakenly, the client may adopt the set of performance measures proposed by the vendor, which are often imbalanced. Indeed, as with many aspects of outsourcing, the prior experience and skills of the client will be an important influence on how effectively they manage performance throughout the arrangement. This is particularly relevant when incorporating performance considerations into the outsourcing contract. Performance management is an essential element of effective contracting.[13] Performance requirements must be clearly established at the outset and incorporated into the contract. This will assist in ensuring that incentives can be built into the contract to encourage performance improvements and also improve the nature of the client–vendor relationship.

7.3 Integrating performance management into the outsourcing process

This section provides a detailed overview of the stages involved in integrating performance management into the outsourcing process. The decision tree in Figure 7.1 shows the stages. Stages 1 to 3 focus on the evaluation phase, and the decision on whether it is appropriate to outsource the process. Stages 4 to 6 focus on the implementation and management phase where an organisation has decided to outsource a process. These stages are now discussed in detail.

Stage 1: Cost analysis

Cost analysis involves assessing the cost position of the client in relation to both vendors and competitors in a process. The major cost drivers associated with a process should be identified. For example, cost drivers associated with customer service processes include labour rates, location of facilities, number of customers served, sales per customer and service levels offered. Cost drivers differ across organisational processes. For capital-intensive processes the major cost drivers are likely to be the cost of equipment, whilst for highly labour-intensive processes, the major driver of costs is labour rates. At a general level, there are a number of drivers

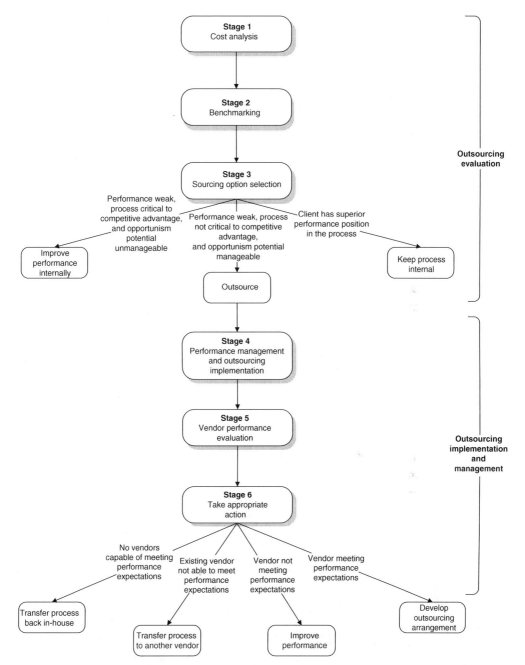

Figure 7.1   Integrating performance management into the outsourcing process

of costs that impact upon the cost position of an organisation relative to those of vendors and competitors:[14]

- *Factor costs.* One of the most prominent influences in cost analysis of the outsourcing decision is that of factor costs. Factor costs refer to the inputs that are used to perform organisational processes and include labour, capital, land and raw materials. Vendors may have a significant cost advantage in a number of areas as a result of having lower factor costs. Perhaps the most common influence on factor costs is that of labour rates. Many organisations can realise significant cost reductions by outsourcing to vendors that have much lower labour costs, often due to their location.

- *Economies of scale.* These can be achieved through internal development or outsourcing to vendors. Economies of scale in certain processes can be realised internally through the achievement of high relative market share in the client's respective product markets. Alternatively, vendors are often in a position to realise scale economies, as they are supplying the same services to a number of clients and achieving the benefits of specialisation.

- *Experience.* Often as a result of specialisation, costs can be reduced through experience built up over time that competitors can find extremely difficult to replicate.

- *Complexity.* The range of products and services offered by an organisation influences costs. Also, enhancing value for customers through adding unique product or service features is likely to increase costs. Complexity can dilute the impact of reduced costs associated with other cost drivers such as scale economies. Introducing a constant stream of new and innovative services can make it extremely difficult to realise scale economies.

Illustration 7.1 Cost analysis in outsourcing

This illustration outlines how the FSO analysed the costs associated with mortgage processing, which involved undertaking in-depth cost analysis of mortgages both internally and with one of its European sister operations. The ability to process mortgage applications quickly and accurately was a major priority for the FSO – due to a phenomenon referred to as 'churning'. Churning involves the loss of mortgage business to other providers during the life of a loan. Customers are often offered better terms by other lending institutions, and are encouraged by the financial press to seek better mortgage deals. Churning had become a major problem for the FSO. Prior to this analysis, 13.2 per cent of its mortgage business was lost and new business was required to compensate for this loss. The FSO had calculated that if the level of churn reached 20 per cent, it would have to sanction 5,888 new mortgages per annum to achieve sales targets. Therefore, it had to limit the loss of customers as a result of taking too long to process their applications and not being price competitive. One strategy the FSO was considering was outsourcing mortgage processing. Understanding the costs associated with processing mortgages was a key aspect of outsourcing evaluation. An example of how the FSO assessed costs in the mortgage process is shown in Table 7.1.

Table 7.1 shows that on average it was costing the FSO £550 to process a mortgage application. The mortgages sold outside the branch network cost £20 more than those sold at a branch, which was due to higher staff and marketing costs. In addition, insurance was not being sold outside the branch network, which meant there was greater opportunity to increase revenue in a branch. However, the value per product was far greater in the branches, averaging £1,330 compared to £766 sold outside, which was reflected in the much higher margin per product sold. Therefore, the branch network was far more effective at selling mortgages of a higher value.

The method used by the FSO to calculate cost per product sold involved adding together all the costs associated with processing a mortgage, splitting them into in-house and other, and dividing them by the number of products sold. The costs of any mortgage applications that were not converted into sales were being absorbed into the costs of those that were. Thus, the bank was not looking at a process cost per product, but the total cost of an actual sale. Using the data above, the FSO calculated the net income per product sold and also the margin (surplus of income over expenditure) per product sold and used them as a baseline for benchmarking purposes. When the FSO compared the average cost (£550) of processing a mortgage application with one of its European sister organisations, it found that the average cost per product sold was much less at £188. The sister operation benefited from economies of scale through processing a greater number of mortgages and was more heavily automated.

The lower half of Table 7.1 provides details of the productivity and efficiency of the staff in the FSO and its sister organisation. Within the FSO, there was no difference in number of mortgages processed by each staff member per annum nor in the turnround time. In contrast, there was a significant difference in the speed of processing mortgages, with the sister organisation being considerably faster (seven days as opposed to fourteen days). However, the small difference in productivity should be noted. Despite the automation employed by the sister organisation, each member of staff only processed twenty more mortgages per annum (175 versus 155) – a difference of 13 per cent. Therefore, despite the lower levels of automation, members of staff in the FSO were more efficient in their working practices.

However, there were a number of limitations with the cost analysis. The information provided for both the FSO and the sister organisation, and for

Table 7.1 Mortgage processing cost analysis

	Sold at branch	Sold outside branch network	Totals per annum	Sister organisation
Direct costs (£'000)				
Staff (total)	3,464	1,782	5,246	5,469
Marketing	231	118	349	
Procurement & legal fees	558	288	846	
Other	n/a	n/a	n/a	459
Total costs	4,253	2,188	6,441	5,928
Income (net) (£'000)				n/a
Mortgage	10,303	2,975	13,278	
Insurance	249	0	249	
Total income	10,552	2,975	13,527	
Surplus of income over expenditure	6,299	787	7,086	
Number of products sold	7,896	3,882	11,778	31,500
Average revenue per product sold (£)	1,330	766	1,150	n/a
Average cost per product sold (£)	540	566	550	0.188
Average margin per product sold (£)	790	200	600	n/a
Number of staff	51	25	76	180
Mortgages processed per staff member per annum			155	175
Turnround time			14 days	7 days

Notes:
[a] The figures have been altered in the interests of confidentiality, and the sister organisation's figures have been converted from euro to sterling.
[b] Staff costs include the salaries of staff at branches and at Head Office, plus any overtime payments. Overtime is counted as a direct cost as it is a necessity.

> ^c Procurement and legal fees are deemed to be a central cost. For convenience, they have been allocated on a proportional basis, i.e. products sold.
>
> ^d The breakdown of costs such as marketing and procurement and legal fees was not available for the sister organisation. However, it had another category, 'other', which might include these costs.

the FSO's internal and external operations (i.e. outside the branch network) was not always directly comparable. The FSO did not use well-known methods to analyse costs when providing the financial figures, and it was difficult to get a full picture of costs. For example, marketing was classed as a direct cost, yet most organisations would class it as an indirect cost or overhead. Furthermore, there were a number of gaps in the information. The legal and procurement costs for the FSO were not broken down, and were allocated between sold at branch and sold outside branch on a pro rata basis, which may not have been totally accurate. No revenue costs were provided for the sister organisation, and so it was not possible to calculate average revenue per product sold or average margin per product sold.

Stage 2: Benchmarking

As well as considering costs, an important element of capability analysis in outsourcing evaluation involves assessing the relative performance along a number of dimensions including quality, flexibility and service. Analysis along these additional dimensions is important given the experiences of organisations that have embarked upon outsourcing primarily on the basis of costs. Initial analysis may reveal that a vendor possesses a lower cost position, while at the same time being weaker in areas such as quality and service. Organisations must have an understanding of non-financial performance measures that indicate performance in a process relative to vendors or competitors. Benchmarking is a valuable approach for assessing an organisation's performance relative to potential vendors and competitors.

It is important to understand and prioritise the processes under scrutiny in order to integrate benchmarking into the outsourcing process. It is not feasible to undertake an extensive benchmarking exercise for every potential outsourcing candidate. In fact, the evaluation of outsourcing for an organisation is likely to focus on one or a limited number of processes as a starting point rather than on every organisational process. The prior experience of the organisation in the area of benchmarking is a key consideration. Where it is the organisation's first experience with benchmarking it may be beneficial to undertake a brief and highly focused exercise that is likely to deliver a high impact. This section outlines a number of the critical aspects involved in undertaking a comprehensive benchmarking exercise for outsourcing purposes.

Select benchmarking approach

This involves deciding who should undertake the benchmarking exercise. An organisation can use internal staff alone or involve external consultants to assist with the benchmarking exercise. A team should be formed to carry out the benchmarking of the processes under scrutiny. This team should be composed of personnel involved in outsourcing evaluation, such as senior management, as well as representatives from the process under scrutiny.

Analyse the process

From an outsourcing perspective, it is important to analyse the process under scrutiny to understand the process, complexities, problems and process interdependencies. Process analysis assists with providing a benchmark against which improvement can be measured. The level of analysis will depend significantly on the impact of the process on competitive advantage. In the case of a process deemed to be of critical importance, it is necessary to conduct extensive analysis to determine the strategic options in terms of either internal improvement or using an external vendor. This more extensive analysis will involve carrying out a number of tasks including: identifying the people and their roles in the process; determining the role of vendors in the process; and mapping and documenting the process by interviewing relevant people involved in the process and analysing organisational documents and reports.

Process maps are detailed diagrams comprising a flowchart of tasks that make up some process. Obtaining co-operation from the staff involved in the process can significantly enhance the validity of process maps. Process maps can also be used to compare performance across organisations to identify areas for improvement. As a result of mapping the process a key outcome is the identification of performance metrics. This is necessary since, before comparing performance with external vendors, a clear understanding of internal performance is required. The choice of key metrics to be used for benchmarking purposes must be based on how well they measure process performance.

Illustration 7.2 Process analysis in outsourcing

This illustration shows how the FSO carried out a detailed analysis of the mortgages process as part of the outsourcing evaluation benchmarking exercise. A five-step process was followed.

Step 1: Personal interviews

Semi-structured interviews were conducted with each staff member of the mortgages processing unit. The objective was to obtain information on the job role of each person and their experience, as this would provide an overview of both the processes involved and the role of personnel. Information gathered in the analysis of each process included: details of procedures and work systems; details of information technology used to support the process; explanation of reporting lines; communication procedures; and description of any prior initiatives to improve the process. Information gathered on each member of staff included: a description of the individual's job role and responsibilities; duration of service in the role; extent of training provided; level of management support available; assessment of time management skills; level of personal motivation; and perceived career opportunities. Each individual was asked to submit a sample of all documentation which they used or to which they had access.

Step 2: Work-study observations

Work-study observations were carried out to analyse the mortgages process and associated sub-processes in practice. These observations proved to be a very valuable mechanism for understanding the processes, and highlighted that there was inadequate flexibility in the system to cope with absences – due to either planned annual leave or illness. Such issues had not been raised during the personal interviews in the previous stage. Observations also revealed that staff training sessions did not actually take place with the frequency that personnel would have wished. Observing staff perform their jobs also revealed additional problems in terms of working conditions and a lack of basic equipment. It was also evident that some key staff spent a lot of their time answering telephone branch queries, which diverted them from their operational duties. The FSO realised that the requirements of the mortgages process had evolved over time and that new requirements and changes appeared to have been introduced on an incremental basis. There was a lack of emphasis on formally documenting the changing requirements of the branches.

Step 3: The development of workflow charts

Workflow mapping involved documenting the steps in each process, which meant employing various modelling techniques to identify the essential

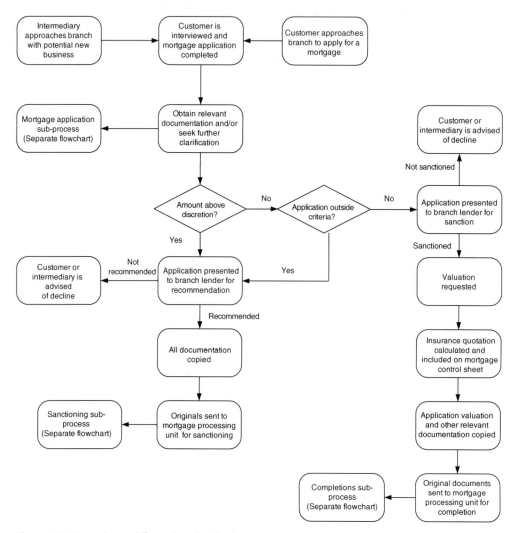

Figure 7.2 Sample workflow chart for the mortgages process

aspects of each process and sub-process. Workflow diagramming methods such as cross-functional workflows and cause-and-effect diagrams were created to visually represent the business processes. Flowcharts indicating the flow of materials, people and information through each sub-process were produced. In relation to mortgages processing, ten A4 sub-process flowcharts were produced. These included charts for the sub-processes of mortgages application processing, sanctioning, completions, deeds-in, deeds-out, redemption quotations, capital reduction, full settlement and maintenance.

A sample workflow chart for mortgages processing is shown in Figure 7.2. Workflow mapping involved determining the distinctive tasks required to accomplish the process objectives, choosing the ideal sequence that tasks should follow and determining who should be responsible for performing each task. As well as highlighting areas for process improvements, the flowcharts greatly assisted the development of performance measures for the process.

Step 4: Focus groups to confirm workflows

Once the process flowcharts had been developed, focus groups, consisting of continuous improvement specialists and key employees in the mortgages processing unit, were formed. These focus groups had a number of objectives. The opinions of staff members were important in verifying the workflows. Once this had been achieved, the processes were critically evaluated to identify problems or deficiencies and highlight any duplication of effort. Ideas for process improvements to enhance quality and speed of throughput were identified and evaluated:

Step 5: Identification of performance metrics

An important outcome of process analysis was the development of performance measures. The project team spent a considerable amount of time with senior management and staff from each area to ensure that appropriate measures were identified. The following performance metrics for mortgages processes were developed:

- Number of draw-downs
- percentage straight-to-offer
- percentage of redemptions
- Application sanctioning speed
- Speed of redemptions
- Speed of overall turnround
- Customer satisfaction
- Cost of processing

Process analysis for mortgages processing was a valuable exercise for the FSO. Although senior managers were aware of some of the problems through monthly reports, process analysis revealed major problems including disjointed processes, a lack of an effective performance management system and high levels of manual intervention in the process. Costs had increased significantly as the increasing demands for mortgage products were being met through the introduction of excessive overtime. Through this analysis, senior management obtained a better understanding of the internal and external dependencies, cost drivers, suitable performance measures and activities, as shown in Figure 7.3.

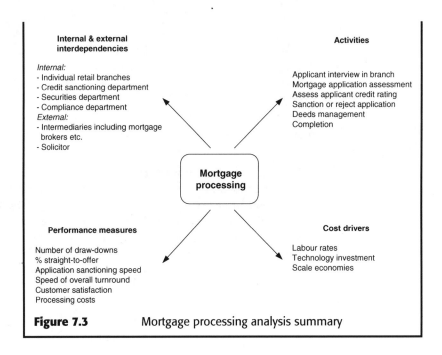

Figure 7.3   Mortgage processing analysis summary

Identify potential partners

Once processes have been analysed and understood, suitable benchmark partners should be found. Based on the mapped processes and the metrics developed, the development of a partner profile can assist in identifying companies carrying out similar processes. In the context of outsourcing, the most competent vendor of the process is a valuable benchmarking partner. Information from vendors can be much more readily obtained than from competitors, which are likely to have a natural reluctance to share commercially sensitive information. In relation to competitors, benchmarking can act as an imperative for strategic action. For example, where an organisation establishes the performance benchmark for its competitors, this can serve as a reliable indicator of competitive advantage. In relation to the use of partners in other industries, access may be more readily achievable than to direct competitors. With full access obtained it may then be possible to determine whether there is the potential to improve performance rather than considering the outsourcing option. Alternatively, the exercise may reveal too significant a disparity in performance, which may lead an organisation to outsource the process to a more competent vendor.

Collect and analyse data

Effective benchmarking involves ensuring that the right information is collected and then analysed. The first phase involves designing a questionnaire based on the partner profile. The benchmarking questionnaire should be a clear, formal agreement and understanding about what data and information are to be collected and shared. Rules need to be agreed with the partners in relation to the level of access to, and use of, confidential information. As well as a questionnaire, internal reports, site visits and interviews can be carried out with key staff within the partner organisation. The success of the benchmarking exercise will depend upon the organisation understanding the results and consequences.

Illustration 7.3 Benchmarking and outsourcing

The first step for the FSO in benchmarking involved an analysis of the internal mortgage processing unit. A process mapping exercise was undertaken, which involved interviewing staff, observing work practices, developing workflow charts and identifying potential performance measures for benchmarking purposes (refer to Illustration 7.2). The FSO identified a number of companies to benchmark including one of its sister operations and a specialist mortgage vendor. This vendor had three processing centres managing assets of £24 billion and had a number of major UK banks as its clients. It had 15,000 different mortgage products available and assisted clients in bringing new products to market within six weeks, which was considerably quicker than the FSO could achieve internally. The FSO adopted a three-tiered benchmarking process, which identified benchmarks at the strategic, operational process and sub-process levels, as illustrated in Figure 7.4. It can be seen from strategic level indicators in Figure 7.4 that the most critical strategic indicator was the speed of mortgage application processing. This strategic indicator was further analysed at the operational process and sub-process levels to illustrate how the benchmarking exercise was carried out.

Step 1: Strategic level indicators

The strategic level indicators were broadly based on critical success factors[a] (CSFs) identified by the FSO in corporate strategy development. These CSFs included factors such as lower processing transaction costs, improving customer value-added and understanding customer needs better. For purposes of evaluation at this stage, the senior management team in the FSO subjectively quantified the performance of both the sister organisation and the external vendor using a 1–10 scale, with each unit on the scale equalling ten percentage points. For example, where one of the entities processed mortgage applications twice as quickly as the FSO, the score next to the indicator comparing its own performance with that of the entity would be −10, as it

Step 1: Strategic level indicators

Financial services organisation	Sister organisation	External service provider
Strategic level Indicators		
The elimination of all non-value-adding processes to keep costs low.	→–30%	→–40%
Process mortgage applications quickly.	→–100%	→–100%
Process mortgage applications accurately.	→–10%	→–10%
Keep processes up-to-date through innovative practices.	→–30%	→–40%
Ensure level of resources is appropriate for volume of transactions.	→–20%	→–30%
Ensure compliance with Financial Services Authority regulations.	←→	←→

Step 2: Operational process level

Financial services organisation	Sister organisation	External service provider
Performance measures for 'Process mortgage applications quickly'		
Number of draw-downs	→–23%	→–28%
Applications sanctioning speed	→–25%	→–27%
Speed of redemptions	→–21%	→–20%
Time spent dealing with telephone enquiry		→–27%
Time spent dealing with written enquiry		→–20%

Step 3: Sub-process level and key performance indicators

Financial services organisation	Sister organisation
Key performance indicators for 'Applications sanctioning speed analysis'	
Quantity of applications input per day/hour	→–30%
Quantity of applications sanctioned per day/hour	→–35%
Quantity of letters of offer checking per day/hour	→–38%
Quantity of queries dealt with per day/hour	→–25%
Quantity of management interventions per day/hour	←3%

Key

→ Better than benchmarked organisation

← Worse than benchmarked organisation

←→ Comparable with benchmarked organisation

Figure 7.4 Benchmarking at the strategic, operational and sub-process levels

was 100% slower than the benchmarked organisation. However, it must be stressed that the senior management team acknowledged that the measurement process was fairly subjective.

Step 2: Operational process level

At the operational process level the strategic factor of *processing mortgage applications quickly* was broken down into five process measures. Initially, the only performance measure used by the FSO was *number of draw-downs*. However, through analysis of the two benchmarking partner organisations, four additional measures were identified. The second and third measures came from the sister organisation, as a result of the emphasis it placed on mortgage turnround time. The external vendor measured this process at the highest level of detail. Consequently, a further two measures (measures four and five) were identified by the benchmarking team. These reflected the remote nature of processing delivered by the external vendor. Both the sister organisation and external vendor were quicker in all areas that were measured, as shown in Step 2 in Figure 7.4. For example, they were 25 per cent and 27 per cent quicker, respectively, when it came to sanctioning applications.

Step 3: Sub-process level and key performance indicators

The next stage compared the FSO with key performance indicators at the sub-process level. The measures identified in Step 3 in Figure 7.4 relate only to the performance measure *applications sanctioning speed* since this was highlighted in Step 2 as the poorest overall performer. It should also be noted that the external vendor would not divulge information on metrics at this level of detail and only those for the sister organisation are indicated. Apart from one area, *quantity of management interventions per day/hour*, the sister organisation outperformed the FSO, being over a third quicker in two areas.

The FSO used this analysis to further understand performance weaknesses and how they should be addressed. In the case of its sister operations, it found that their operational performance levels were better, and they also invested more resource in information technology to automate a number of key processes. In the case of the specialist mortgages vendor, it found that it invested a considerable amount of resource in information technology and had considerable experience in offering mortgages processing services to other leading UK financial services organisations. Their systems were capable of dealing with customised mortgage profiles, with a range of different rest periods, interest profiles, repayment plans and early settlement and flexibility features. Senior management also found that the vendor had clearly defined processes and provided detailed performance measures that it was using with its major clients.

[a] Useful general references on critical success factors include van Veen-Dirks, P. and Wijn, M. (2002). Strategic Control: Meshing Critical Success Factors with the Balanced Scorecard, *Long Range Planning*, 35, 407–27; Ward, B. (1990). Planning for Profit, in T. Lincoln (ed.), *Managing Information Systems for Profit*, Chichester: Wiley; and Rockart, J. F. (1979). Chief Executives Define their Own Data Needs, *Harvard Business Review*, 57(2), 81–92.

Stage 3: Sourcing option selection

Employing cost analysis and benchmarking provides an organisation with a number of potential sourcing options, as shown in Figure 7.1:

- *Outsource.* In this case, the analysis will have revealed that vendors are more capable in performing the process than the client organisation. This option is most appropriate when the process is not critical to competitive advantage and/or the opportunism associated with outsourcing is manageable.
- *Continue to perform the process internally.* In this case, the analysis will have revealed that the client organisation has superior performance relative to potential vendors. This option is most appropriate when the process is critical to competitive advantage and/or the opportunism associated with outsourcing is unmanageable.
- *Invest to perform the process internally.* In this case, the analysis will have revealed that the client organisation is less competent at performing the process than vendors or competitors. This option is most appropriate when the process is critical to competitive advantage and the client can replicate and advance upon the performance of vendors.

Once an organisation has decided to outsource a process, it should have an evaluation and control process to ensure that the outsourcing arrangement is accomplishing its performance objectives. Essentially, this involves comparing actual performance with desired results and providing feedback, so that management in both the client and vendor can evaluate the results and take corrective action. Performance measures provide the following functions in an outsourcing arrangement:

- *Control.* Performance measures allow the client to evaluate and control the performance of processes for which vendors are responsible.
- *Communication.* Performance measures are essential for communicating performance to management in the client and vendor for purposes of control. Well-designed and communicated performance measures provide management in the client with a sound understanding of what the vendor has to deliver, without having to understand fully the intricacies of the processes. Poorly developed and communicated performance measures can lead to frustration and create difficulties in the relationship between the client and vendor.

- *Improvement.* Performance measures identify the disparity between actual and anticipated performance. Identifying and understanding any performance disparities can serve as a basis for developing an improvement strategy. In many instances, the onus will be on the vendor to make the improvements. However, in some instances the client may have to make adjustments to their internal operations to allow for performance improvements.

Stage 4: Performance management and outsourcing implementation

Establish outsourcing objectives

Many companies embark upon outsourcing without establishing clear objectives for what they intend to achieve. The absence of clear objectives can create difficulties in managing the outsourcing process in a number of areas including selecting the most appropriate outsourcing relationship, drawing up the contract and managing performance in the outsourcing relationship. Typical outsourcing objectives include reducing costs, enhancing service quality and obtaining higher levels of service in the provision of the process. The objectives established will reflect the underlying motives for the organisation considering outsourcing as an appropriate strategy. For example, in many cases, organisations outsource with the objective of obtaining higher quality service at a lower cost from external vendors. In this case, the key objectives will provide valuable direction for managing the outsourcing process. This will involve the organisation ensuring that it is selecting the most capable vendor in terms of cost and quality. Moreover, the client must ensure that the chosen vendor maintains and improves its performance throughout the life of the outsourcing relationship.

Determine requirements

This involves determining what is required from the vendor and dissecting the process to determine the skills and resources required to perform the process. At the most basic level, this will include a specification of the process the vendor should provide for the client. This step will involve determining the interdependencies between the outsourced process and other internal and outsourced processes. Where the interdependencies are clearly understood, it should be possible to derive effective performance measures for the outsourced processes. However, the greater the number of process interdependencies, the more difficult it will be to specify performance measures at the outset of the outsourcing arrangement. In addition, where the needs of the client are changing in relation to the process during the relationship, performance measures may have to be amended.

Establish performance measures and standards

There are a number of steps in establishing performance measures and standards. The client should firstly decide on which aspects of the outsourced process should be measured. Priority is often given to the most important aspects of the process, and those that account for the highest proportion of cost, or the greatest number of problems.

Performance measures should then be developed. They should be verifiable, which means they are based on an agreed set of data and a well-understood and documented process for converting this data into the measure.[15] Performance measures should be expressed in meaningful terms and, therefore, be fully understood by the vendor. The performance measures should capture the characteristics or outcome of the outsourced process in a numerical or nominal format.

Finally, performance standards should be established as a reference point for acceptable performance. Standards can be based on past performance measure values used when the process was performed internally, or externally published benchmarks. Each standard will normally include a tolerance range, which will define acceptable performance deviations from the vendor. These performance measures and standards will be incorporated into the service level agreement (SLA).

Illustration 7.4 Performance management and outsourcing implementation

This illustration outlines how the FSO integrated performance management into the implementation phase outsourcing of the cheque clearing process. The cheque clearing process required the transfer of cheques between bank branches and different banking organisations to exchange funds. Whilst the cheque clearing process involved significant investments in technology, the capability for efficient cheque clearing did not impact significantly on the FSO's competitive position. The FSO established an independent outsourcing services provider for cheque clearing processes with one of its competitors. As well as offering cheque clearing services to the parent companies, the vendor would offer these services to other financial services organisations to allow it to further grow its business. The implementation phase of this arrangement had the following steps.

Establish outsourcing objectives

The FSO established a number of objectives for outsourcing the cheque clearing process. Firstly, outsourcing cheque clearing would reduce operational costs in a number of ways. The vendor would achieve economies of scale, and staff could be employed at lower labour rates than experienced banking employees. Secondly, it was anticipated that a specialist vendor would deliver higher service levels than if the process was performed internally. Thirdly, outsourcing cheque clearing would reduce capital expenditure investments in information technology hardware and software. Finally, experienced banking staff previously involved in cheque clearing would be redeployed into higher-value-adding processes such as customer services management.

Determine requirements

The first month of implementation involved establishing the requirements for the newly appointed vendor delivering the cheque clearing process. A project team was established to work on this task, which comprised senior management, cheque clearing staff and other stakeholders. A series of in-depth interviews was conducted with bank stakeholders to agree on the key aspects of the outsourcing arrangement. This involved considering client requirements, IT architecture and the functional specifications associated with the process, which informed the development of the contract.

Establish performance measures and standards

The development of performance measures for the SLA required detailed process analysis and workflow mapping to establish the tasks involved in executing the process and associated levels of performance. This involved identifying and defining the tasks, choosing the ideal sequence that tasks should follow and determining who would be responsible for performing them. This process analysis exercise included the development of graphical workflow diagrams indicating the flow of materials, people and information through the process. The workflow mapping exercise influenced the selection of performance measures. As well as establishing what should be measured, it was necessary to consider the required frequency of measurement, the required frequency of reporting and how the measurement would take place. In the case of cheque clearing, the FSO sub-divided the process into a number of sub-processes: out-clearing, debit in-clearing, encoding and credit referencing/settlement. A detailed analysis of each sub-process was performed using workflow mapping techniques.

This analysis highlighted the key tasks involved and influenced the development of the performance measures that were used in the SLA. Employing this approach allowed the organisation to concentrate on the procedures and performance measures that would allow the vendor to better understand and meet its requirements. Furthermore, the key performance measures were developed under the criteria of quality and timeliness for each of the cheque

Table 7.2 Key performance indicators for debit in-clearing sub-process

Criterion	Key performance indicator	Required activity level
Quality	Receipt of all exchange items and high-level balancing.	99%
Quality	All code lines for each item to be captured on day of receipt.	95%
Quality	All capture files transmitted correctly to mainframe to enable updating with exception code	99%
Timeliness	Capture files to be transmitted regularly during the day up to an agreed cut-off time of 16:00 hours.	
Timeliness	Presentation of work – all items boxed and labelled for collection at 15:30 hours.	

clearing sub-processes. It was agreed that any changes in the scope of the agreement would be charged for by the provider. Table 7.2 illustrates the complexity of the SLA by providing a sample of the key performance measures associated with quality and timeliness for the debit in-clearing sub-process. The required service levels were stepped through time, i.e. performance improvement targets were built into the SLA. Penalty clauses were agreed for non-achievement of service.

Stage 5: Vendor performance evaluation

Many difficulties associated with outsourcing arise from the failure of vendors to deliver and meet the requirements and performance expectations of the client. In order to reduce these risks and pre-empt vendor failure, the client must have a formal mechanism to determine whether the vendor is meeting the performance levels set and whether the objectives in its approach to relationship management are being achieved. Evaluation of vendor performance involves determining whether the vendor is meeting the required performance standards set out in the SLA. Having an effective mechanism for evaluating vendor performance can also serve as a basis for comparing performance levels with those of other potential vendors in the supply market.

The approach to assessing performance will depend upon the nature of the relationship and the complexity of requirements. For example, in a cost-focused outsourcing arrangement for standard call centre services, the client is likely to focus on measuring the performance of the vendor quantitatively against a number of criteria including average speed of answering calls, first-time call resolution, total calls handled and call abandonment rate. The focus is on inspecting the outcomes of the process rather than attempting to diagnose the causes of poor performance. The responsibility for performance rests solely with the vendor with little or no assistance provided from the client to resolve problems.

Where the client's needs are highly complex and specific, the approach to performance evaluation will differ considerably. The increased dependency between the client and vendor necessitates a relational contracting outsourcing relationship, where the evaluation of performance is a joint endeavour, with both the client and vendor attempting to identify and deal with the causes of poor performance in any areas. As both the client and vendor are responsible for the success of the relationship, the focus should be on performance improvement. This focus on improvement not only centres on cost reduction but also can encompass any performance area such as service, flexibility and responsiveness. There is also an onus on the client to effect performance improvements. The client may attempt to achieve improvements in its own internal operations that can assist the vendor in meeting the required performance levels. Therefore, both the client and vendor must be aware of the other's performance expectations. The development of relational contracting outsourcing relationships will involve the client and vendor working jointly over the long term to improve performance levels and meet each other's expectations.

There are a number of important aspects to effective vendor performance evaluation during the outsourcing relationship.

Resource commitment

It is critical that both the client and vendor have the necessary resources and skills to analyse and understand performance, particularly in the initial phases of the relationship. There are a number of influences on the level of resource commitment. The complexity of the client's requirements will influence the resource required. Where the client's requirements are highly complex and specific, both the client and vendor have to commit substantial resource to deal with any difficulties and performance problems. For example, visits by personnel from both the client and vendor to their respective facilities are essential in creating a mutual understanding of each other's needs and capabilities. Face-to-face interaction is an important means of understanding the needs of both parties, and it can be a valuable investment by the outsourcing vendor to install a relationship manager in the client operations. In addition, the strategic importance of the outsourced process is an important influence on resource commitment. In the case of strategically important processes, the client will have to commit considerable resource to working with the vendor to improve performance. Achieving performance improvements in such processes has the potential to differentiate the client from its competitors. Where the focus of the outsourcing arrangement is on less complex and strategically important processes, less resource is required. The relationship interface is likely to be confined to a single manager in both the client and vendor, often with limited involvement from the strategic level of each business.

Flexibility

There should be flexibility in the selected performance measures and measurement systems to reflect the dynamic nature of many outsourcing arrangements. A flexible approach to performance management is important, particularly in outsourcing arrangements that are characterised by highly complex client requirements and uncertainty. Although the client should specify as much detail as possible at the outset, it often difficult to fully specify all the requirements and performance levels for the entire outsourcing contract. In complex information technology development projects, where a wide variety of processes and technologies is involved, it is not possible to fully specify all requirements and performance measures during the contracting phase and changes are often required during implementation and relationship management.

In order to deal with highly complex requirements and uncertainty, a relational contracting outsourcing relationship is essential to compensate for any gaps in requirements unanticipated at the beginning of the relationship. This allows any gaps in requirements and performance measures to be adjusted, as the client and the vendor develop their knowledge of the processes involved. It is often argued that contracts should be as complete as possible, and the client should invest considerable efforts in specifying requirements and service levels at the outset. However, such a strategy can be inappropriate in complex outsourcing arrangements. Such efforts consume a considerable amount of resource and lead to the development of performance measures that are ineffective. In addition, attempting to enforce such performance measures may damage the relationship from the outset and create a climate of mistrust that is difficult to eliminate.

Illustration 7.5 Performance management and managing the outsourcing relationship

This illustration outlines the FSO's approach to performance management in the outsourcing of cheque clearing. In the initial phases of the relationship, two senior managers from the FSO were seconded on site to the vendor. These managers were responsible for developing an understanding in the vendor of the performance levels required and providing training for the workforce. Evaluating the performance of cheque clearing involved a resource commitment on the part of both the FSO and the vendor. Senior managers in the FSO and vendor met monthly to assess the performance of the cheque clearing service. In the FSO, a relationship promoter was appointed. The senior management team was involved primarily in the measurement and examination of the performance of the vendor against the SLA. The relationship promoter, along with the internal users of the cheque clearing process in the FSO, was involved in creating an environment in which the agreed service levels were met. Furthermore, the relationship promoter was responsible for dealing with changes in the FSO's requirements and implementing contract variations. The service delivery manager in the vendor was responsible for resolving operational problems and managing routine changes in accordance with the SLA. This manager liaised directly with the relationship promoter in the FSO to address any performance problems.

Even though considerable resource was committed to establishing the outsourcing arrangement, some difficulties arose in the initial phases of the relationship. The FSO failed to understand fully the cheque clearing process, which had an adverse impact upon service levels. For example, initial problems with the cheque processing software had a detrimental impact on processing times and resulted in additional costs due to the need for additional overtime. This problem also highlighted that training for staff in processes linked to cheque clearing had not been adequate. There was a lack of adequate investment in IT, which meant that the processes feeding cheque clearing could not be delivered at the performance levels required. In addition, in the initial phases of the relationship the FSO viewed the performance difficulties as the sole responsibility of the vendor and there was a lack of emphasis on understanding the causes of performance problems.

The FSO recognised that it would have to adopt a more collaborative relationship with the vendor to address these performance difficulties. As the vendor and FSO began to collaborate in addressing the problems associated with quality and timeliness, the vendor was able to achieve the efficiencies necessary to reduce the levels of overtime working. The parties realised that although the outsourcing arrangement was primarily transactional in nature, there were some complexities and collaboration was necessary. Indeed, collaboration allowed the parties to come together to agree procedural modifications to comply with changes to cheque clearing recommended by the Office of Fair Trading (OFT). Maximum times were established for the cheque clearing cycle. These recommendations reduced the time available to complete the cheque clearing cycle and had a positive impact on performance levels in the SLA for the vendor.

Stage 6: Take appropriate action

Evaluation of vendor performance leads to a number of potential outcomes and the need for appropriate action, as shown in Figure 7.1. Where the vendor is meeting or surpassing performance expectations, the client is likely to continue with the outsourcing arrangement. Indeed, it may be necessary to amend upwards the initial performance standards, as the vendor surpasses performance expectations. In addition, in the case of a high-performing vendor, the client may decide to outsource more processes to strengthen the relationship.

However, when the vendor is not meeting performance expectations, corrective action is required. A lot of the onus will be on the vendor to address performance problems. In the case of complex processes with changing requirements, the client will have to work with the vendor to understand the causes of poor performance. Dealing with performance problems may also require that processes are redesigned, and that revised performance measures are developed.

In some instances, the vendor may not be able to meet performance expectations, and the client may have to transfer the process to another vendor. In the case of a complex process, this is an extremely difficult decision and will have come after considerable efforts at addressing performance problems in the vendor's operations.

When the vendor cannot meet performance expectations, the client may have to bring the process back in-house – often referred to as backsourcing. This option is most likely when there are no other capable vendors available, and the client has retained some internal capability in the process involved.

The approach to performance management will have to change as the outsourcing arrangement evolves. Performance measures established at the outset of the outsourcing arrangement may lose their relevance and ability to distinguish between strong and weak performance. This is particularly important when the requirements of the client have changed during the relationship. Such changes can make initial performance measures redundant and necessitate the development of new performance measures. In addition, as the vendor becomes more familiar with client requirements and delivers improved performance, the frequency of measuring performance may have to change. As the relationship between the client and vendor develops, the approach to performance management extends beyond straightforward reporting to creating mechanisms for identifying improvement opportunities and anticipating future problems.

7.4 Challenges and benefits of performance management in the outsourcing process[16]

Cost analysis in outsourcing evaluation is challenging for a number of reasons. Unless the client and the vendor have standardised processes, it is not possible to derive fully objective cost comparisons. Objective cost comparisons are difficult because of different costing systems used by vendors. A further challenge involves the amount of cost data that vendors are willing to divulge on account of the risks of competitors accessing such sensitive data. However, cost analysis prior to outsourcing can be beneficial from a number of perspectives. It provides an understanding of the reasons for cost differences between the client and vendors. This can provide a mechanism for identifying how costs can be reduced via process redesign internally or outsourcing to a vendor. Cost analysis allows the establishment of a benchmark for which the client can aim either through internal improvement or outsourcing.

There are a number of challenges associated with benchmarking in the outsourcing process. It is difficult to compare processes in the client organisation with those of vendors because of the presence of idiosyncratic practices and process interdependencies. Superior performance in a certain process may be the result of interdependencies among other processes that are difficult to isolate. Moreover, the lack of effective internal performance measures associated with a process makes objective comparisons with other organisations difficult. However, benchmarking can play a beneficial role in outsourcing evaluation. Benchmarking external vendors allows an organisation to identify and develop performance measures for processes that can be used to assess performance for an outsourced process or one retained in-house. In particular, where organisations outsource processes without developing performance measures they have no way of knowing whether vendors are executing processes better or worse than internal departments. Benchmarking vendors can create a greater awareness of vendor capabilities, which can alert the client to further opportunities for outsourcing additional processes.

Process analysis is an important aspect of benchmarking in outsourcing evaluation. Although process analysis is time-consuming and difficult, it is an important element of outsourcing in a number of areas:

- Analysing and determining causes of poor performance
- Understanding internal and external process interdependencies
- Understanding and determining process requirements

- Determining performance measures for the contract and SLA
- Determining required vendor capabilities
- Clearly communicating requirements to the vendor
- Selecting the most appropriate outsourcing relationship.

Effective performance management during the outsourcing relationship requires appropriate skills in both the client and vendor, not only to understand performance but also to drive performance improvements. Often, the client does not commit sufficient resource to addressing performance problems, primarily as a result of viewing problems as the responsibility of the vendor. An over-emphasis on measuring performance by the client in the outsourcing arrangement can damage the relationship, as the vendor views it as a mechanism for extracting more favourable terms in future contract negotiations. However, effective performance management in the outsourcing relationship has a number of benefits. Determining effective performance measures prior to and during the relationship can serve as a benchmark for improvement. A strong emphasis on performance management is necessary for creating a culture of continuous improvement in the outsourcing relationship. Of course, the client has to align the outsourcing relationship with its desired performance objectives from outsourcing. Where the client is seeking continuous improvement, the outsourcing relationship should be on a collaborative basis, dominated by a joint approach to addressing performance problems and driving improvements.

7.5 Summary implications

- Cost analysis and benchmarking of vendors is an extremely challenging aspect of outsourcing evaluation. Unless the client and the vendor have standardised processes it is not possible to derive fully objective cost comparisons. A key benefit of cost analysis and benchmarking is that they provide a mechanism for identifying how costs can be reduced via internal process redesign or outsourcing.
- Organisations must have robust performance management systems in place to effectively evaluate and manage the outsourcing process. Effective performance management can assist in identifying causes of poor performance prior to outsourcing. Outsourcing processes without developing effective performance measures means an organisation will not know whether vendors are executing processes better or worse than when they were performed internally.

• Organisations must have a clear understanding of the relationship and interdependencies between business processes prior to outsourcing. Failure to understand the interdependencies between internal and outsourced processes can make vendor performance assessment an extremely difficult task. Performance management techniques such as workflow mapping are important for improving performance in the outsourcing process. Workflow mapping can be employed to remove inefficiencies from processes both prior to outsourcing and during outsourcing arrangements.

• Understanding clearly the nature of processes prior to outsourcing is an important prerequisite for successful performance management with the vendor. Detailed requirements analysis will facilitate the development of an effective SLA, which can be used to measure vendor performance. When designing an SLA, an organisation should consider the impact of allowing the vendor to focus its service delivery and performance management exclusively on the metrics within the agreement. It is likely that there may be gaps in the SLA, which need to be amended over time. Therefore, the SLA should be flexible enough to enable the updating of performance metrics on an agreed basis between client and vendor.

Acknowledgements

I would like to acknowledge the support of the Chartered Institute of Management Accountants (CIMA) for providing funding to collect and analyse the data in the financial services organisation. In addition, I would like to thank Paul Humphreys, Alan McKittrick and Tony Wall for their contributions to the collection and analysis of data presented in this chapter.

Notes and references

1 Aron, R. and Singh, J. V. (2005). Getting Offshoring Right, *Harvard Business Review*, 83(12), 135–43.

2 The principles of the outsourcing framework presented in this chapter were applied in a UK financial services organisation over a three-year period. The financial services organisation offered a range of financial services including deposit-taking, current account facilities, residential and commercial mortgages and other tailored products and services. These services were offered across a number of segments including individuals, small and medium-sized commercial organisations and large corporate clients. A case-study methodology was applied to the research, which involved engaging directly with the

organisation throughout the outsourcing process. The research focused on a number of processes that the organisation had outsourced, and examined the performance management implications of the outsourcing process.

3 Ellram, L., Tate, W. and Billington, C. (2008). Offshore Outsourcing of Professional Services: A Transaction Cost Economics Perspective, *Journal of Operations Management*, 26(2), 148–63.

4 Harman, E., Hensel, S. and Lukes, T. (2006). Measuring Performance in Services, *McKinsey Quarterly*, 1, 30–9.

5 For additional reading on performance measurement, see Kennerley, M. and Neely, A. (2002). A Framework of the Factors Affecting the Evolution of Performance Measurement Systems, *International Journal of Operations and Production Management*, 22(11), 1222–45; Kaplan, R. and Norton, D. (2001). *The Strategy-focused Organisation: How Balanced Scorecard Companies Thrive in the New Business Environment*, Boston: Harvard Business School Press; and Neely, A. (1999). The Performance Measurement Revolution: Why Now and What Next? *International Journal of Operations and Production Management*, 19(2), 205–28.

6 A number of authors have argued that outsourcing and performance management should be linked with business strategy, including Langfield-Smith, K. and Smith, D. (2003). Management Control Systems and Trust in Outsourcing Relationships, *Management Accounting Research*, 14(3), 281–307; Roy, V. and Aubert, B. (2002). A Resource-based Analysis of IT Sourcing, *Database for Advances in Information Systems*, 33(2), 29–40; Insinga, R. C. and Werle, M. J. (2000). Linking Outsourcing to Business Strategy, *Academy of Management Executive*, 14(4), 58–70; and McIvor, R. (2000). A Practical Framework for Understanding the Outsourcing Process, *Supply Chain Management: An International Journal*, 5(1), 22–36.

7 Melnyk, S., Stewart, D. and Swink, M. (2004). Metrics and Performance Measurement in Operations Management: Dealing with the Metrics Maze, *Journal of Operations Management*, 22, 209–17.

8 McIvor, R., Humphreys, P., Wall, A. and McKittrick, A. (2009). Performance Management and the Outsourcing Process: Lessons from a Financial Services Organisation, *International Journal of Operations and Production Management*, 29(10), 1025–48.

9 Harris, S. (2007). Formal Benchmarking in Outsourcing Contracts: TPI's Position, TPI Research Report, London. www.tpi.net/pdf/papers/FormalBenchmarkingInOutsourcingContracts.pdf.

10 See Aron and Singh (2005) in note 1 above.

11 Tate, W. and van der Valk, W. (2008). Managing the Performance of Outsourced Customer Contact Centres, *Journal of Purchasing and Supply Management*, 14, 160–9.

12 Williamson, O. E. (1985). *The Economic Institutions of Capitalism: Firms, Markets and Relational Contracting*, New York: Free Press; and Williamson, O. E. (1975). *Markets and Hierarchies*, New York: Free Press.

13 Barthélemy, J. (2003). The Seven Deadly Sins of Outsourcing, *Academy of Management Executive*, 17(2), 87–98.

14 McIvor, R. (2005). *The Outsourcing Process: Strategies for Evaluation and Management*, Cambridge: Cambridge University Press.
15 See Melnyk *et al.* (2004) in note 7 above.
16 The benefits and challenges outlined in this section are drawn from the experiences of the financial services organisation and the analysis presented in the chapter.

Recommended key reading

Aron, R. and Singh, J. V. (2005). Getting Offshoring Right, *Harvard Business Review*, 83(12), 135–43. This paper provides valuable insights into performance management in the context of offshore outsourcing. Particular attention is given to the link between performance and risk.

Harman, E., Hensel, S. and Lukes, T. (2006). Measuring Performance in Services, *McKinsey Quarterly*, 1, 30–9. This paper focuses on performance management issues in services. It highlights some of the difficulties of measuring performance in services and makes a number of recommendations for implementing a performance management system.

Harris, S. (2007). Formal Benchmarking in Outsourcing Contracts: TPI's Position, TPI Research Report, London. www.tpi.net/pdf/papers/FormalBenchmarkingInOutsourcingContracts.pdf. This report discusses how benchmarking can be used as an effective tool in outsourcing relationships.

Tate, W. and van der Valk, W. (2008). Managing the Performance of Outsourced Customer Contact Centres, *Journal of Purchasing and Supply Management*, 14, 160–9. This paper examines customer contact services, and shows that focusing on effectiveness rather than efficiency can benefit the overall performance of the vendor. It is argued that quality improvements in both process and service delivery lead to lower costs.

Services outsourcing and the spin-off arrangement

8.1 Introduction

Spinning off non-core functions into separate businesses has become increasingly prevalent as organisations restructure and specialise in core areas. The spin-off arrangement is often used as an alternative to outsourcing functions to an independent vendor. Organisations have spun off parts of their operations into separate profitable businesses in an attempt to concentrate further on their core business, or as an alternative to outsourcing the function to an independent vendor. The spin-off arrangement can be an attractive alternative to straightforward outsourcing as the staff transferred will have an intimate knowledge of requirements, and the parent will still have significant influence over the spin-off business. Some have argued that spin-offs are important in unleashing entrepreneurial potential, both by creating dynamic new enterprises and by creating leaner, competitive and more focused parent companies.[1] An often-cited example of a spin-off is the case of Mercedes-Daimler AG spinning off its information technology (IT) function into a separate company, DaimlerChrysler Services. Mercedes-Daimler AG regarded the expertise in this department as world-class with significant potential to generate additional revenue. This spin-off competed in the IT market against established companies, while still delivering IT services to its parent.[2]

There are a number of reasons why companies spin off businesses. The efficient management of certain parts of the business often requires skills and capabilities that are not present in the parent company. Consider a manufacturing firm that is operating in an industry that requires specialist skills in research and development. The skills involved in managing the manufacturing parts of the business are very different from those involved in managing a research and development operation. Where the core skills of the firm are not aligned with a particular part of the business, that part of the business is often spun off into a separate entity. Companies may spin off parts of their operations to free up capital to invest in other parts of the business. Large firms often have constraints on capital, and may need to spin off part of their non-core operations to raise capital to invest in other core parts of the business. With the growth in supply in the market for business services, companies have spun off parts of their business to offer services to other clients. Companies have successfully spun off high performing internal functions such as human resource (HR), IT and finance and accounting (F&A) to take advantage of these opportunities. Moreover, as a result of a lack of investment in technology and inefficient processes, companies have spun off under-performing parts of their operations, and formed alliances with vendors.[3] The capabilities of the spin-off operation can be developed through partnering with the specialist vendor.

The success of spin-offs depends on the ability to attract a critical percentage of sales from new customers – rather than sales primarily from the parent company.[4] The success of a spin-off will also depend upon whether it has a viable product to attract external customers, and the ability to develop the commercial and marketing skills required to expand the spin-off. In fact, management and employees in the spin-off face a steep learning curve when they move into a competitive market, particularly where the required capabilities and resources are under-developed. A further important consideration for success is the stage of development of the intended target markets for the products and services of the spin-off company. Under-developed markets with the need for the capabilities of the spin-off may provide rich potential for sales growth. Indeed, the increasing market for business services driven by business process outsourcing (BPO) has fuelled the trend towards spinning off business functions, as organisations seek to generate additional revenue streams. However, in the initial stages of development the spin-off business may require additional resource from the parent company to establish a presence in target markets.

Although the spin-off arrangement has been increasing in prominence, there are few studies that provide detailed insights into the development and implementation process – from idea generation in the parent company through to the spin-off developing a full client base. Lacity *et al.* provide valuable insights into how Lloyds of London successfully commercialised its claims administration function by forming a partnership with Xchanging and creating a separate company.[5] Although this study provides a detailed account of how the function was radically improved, it does not fully examine how the new company developed its client base, and the impact upon service levels to the parent company. As in other studies of spin-offs in the literature the spin-off business was established through forming a relationship with a strategic partner. For example, Barclays also established a new company in partnership with Lloyds of London and Unisys to commercialise its cheque processing operation. However, none of these studies focuses on companies that have successfully spun off separate businesses without entering into partnerships with existing vendors. In addition, few of these studies place sufficient emphasis on how the growth of the spin-off business impacts upon the relationship and services being provided to functions in the parent company.

Illustration 8.1 Transforming back-office performance through spin-off arrangements

Some of the earliest examples of spinning off businesses were in the manufacturing area.[a] Advances in engineering and production technologies allowed manufacturers to decouple internal capabilities and create specialists in areas such as component manufacture and design. More recently, spinning-off capabilities in business services areas have become prominent, primarily as a result of standardisation, advances in information and communication technologies and the increasing demand for back-office services. Normally, companies spin off part of their operations in order to exploit an internal capability, and create shareholder value through generating additional revenue. This was the case when General Motors spun off its internal IT operation, to create Electronic Data Systems (EDS). However, companies have begun to spin off internal back-office functions both to generate revenue and improve performance.

Many large companies have back-office functions that are under-performing as a result of under-investment, inefficient processes and a piece-meal approach to technology utilisation. Improving performance internally is often infeasible because of a lack of internal skills and resource. Outsourcing is probably the most common option used to address under-performance in back-office functions. However, some companies have recognised the opportunities of partnering with a specialist vendor to create a spin-off company and transform performance. Barclays Bank used such an arrangement to transform its cheque processing operation. Under-investment in technology meant that performance in cheque processing had been suffering, and additional investment was not feasible because of declining volumes. Senior management recognised that other banks were facing the same problem and identified the potential for a market in cheque processing services. Barclays spun off their cheque processing operation, and partnered with Lloyds of London and Unisys to assist with investment and commercialisation. The newly formed company was called Intelligent Processing Solutions Limited (IPSL), and has been profitable from its initial start-up position.

Bank of America pursued a similar arrangement in the human resource (HR) area. The bank's HR function was over-staffed, inefficient and had duplicated processes, primarily as a result of acquisitions. Consequently, to transform its HR operations, the bank partnered with a start-up company, Exult. The bank had an equity stake in Exult and was guaranteed significant cost reductions and performance improvement in HR services. Exult was able to deliver these benefits through centralising and standardising processes, and also to achieve scale economies through growing its client base. Lloyds of London commercialised its claims administration through partnering with a specialist vendor. Previously, its claims bureaux had never been fully integrated, and customers had to deal with a range of people and processes when submitting different types of claim. The lack of investment in claims administration led to high staff attrition rates and poorly motivated staff. Lloyds recognised that improving performance in claims settlement could attract more customers, and also allow it to offer a valuable service to other insurance companies. Therefore, it formed an enterprise partnership with Xchanging, called Xchanging Claims Services (XCS), in order to acquire resource and expertise. XCS rapidly delivered cost savings, improved performance and generated revenue through winning contracts with other clients.

Note:
[a] 'Commercialising functions' is another term used to explain the spin-off phenomenon.

Sources: Lacity, M., Willcocks, L. and Feeny, D. (2004). Commercialising the Back Office at Lloyds of London: Outsourcing and Strategic Partnerships Revisited, *European Management Journal*, 22(2), 127–40; Mack, D. and Quick, J. (2002). EDS: An Inside View of a Corporate Life Cycle Transition. *Organizational Dynamics*, 30(3), 282–93.

This chapter focuses on a privatised electricity utility company that spun off a number of functions into a separate commercial organisation.[6] This organisation marketed services in the areas of information technology, call centre management, training, revenue management and supply chain services in the utility and general service sectors. As well as developing a strong client base, particularly in the area of IT services, the spin-off continued to provide services to subsidiaries in the utility company. This arrangement was regarded as an extremely successful one, principally because the company disposed of the spin-off business for a sum of £155 million seven years later, having only invested around £60 million in acquisitions during the development of the spin-off. However, the development and implementation of this spin-off arrangement was far from straightforward, and faced a number of difficulties along the way. This chapter considers this spin-off arrangement from the initial idea generation through to the development of its client base and eventual disposal. The development of the spin-off is considered along with the implications for the subsidiaries in the utility company that were sourcing services from the newly formed spin-off business. The chapter provides many important insights on the implications of outsourcing via the spin-off configuration. In particular, a number of important implications are identified for outsourcing and spin-off arrangements.

8.2 Background to the spin-off

In the early 1990s the UK electricity industry was privatised and a five-year review cycle by an industry regulator was imposed. Prior to privatisation, the UK government perceived electricity utilities as inefficient, over-staffed and poorly performing organisations. The utility company in this case was no exception, having an unwieldy hierarchical management structure with no incentives for performance improvements, mainly because of its monopoly position. The company suffered from a number of problems including bureaucratic and inefficient processes, lack of employee motivation and little focus on improving customer service. It was privatised in 1993 and an industry regulator was appointed to protect and advance the interests of consumers by promoting competition and imposing regulations where appropriate. As a result of an evaluation of the business by the regulator, the utility company had to reduce its cost base by 2 per cent below inflation over a five-year period and achieve a return of 7 per cent on capital employed. Between 1993 and 1994 the company conducted a major internal re-engineering exercise, which involved redesigning business processes and reducing staff levels through voluntary severance schemes. Part of this strategy involved outsourcing relatively straightforward activities such as printing, grounds and building maintenance, cleaning and security – what the company termed 'quick hits'. Undertaking these changes allowed the company to achieve these objectives and satisfied the requirements of the regulator for the five-year period from 1992 to 1997.

The regulator undertook a second price control review, which was more stringent than the first post-privatisation review. It placed the company in a very difficult situation as it was being faced with a further reduction in capital and operational expenditure, more stringent service delivery targets and pressures to reduce the unit price of electricity for its customers. In fact, senior management challenged this review, which led to protracted negotiations over a three-year period and consumed a considerable amount of management time. As a result of the process the requirements in the initial review were relaxed. However, during the process senior management in the utility company realised that they were now in a much more challenging operating environment. Although management had succeeded in having the requirements of the regulator relaxed, it still faced considerable challenges as a result of the demands of its key stakeholders. Post-privatisation the company not only had to satisfy the requirements of the regulator but also meet the demands from shareholders and large institutional investors for increased profitability.

8.3 Motives for establishing the spin-off arrangement

Senior management believed it would not meet the challenges in its operating environment without outsourcing a wider range of processes to external vendors. One area that senior management identified was billing and revenue. The supply division of the business was responsible for billing customers and collecting revenue for the transmission and distribution of the electricity division. Processes in this area included meter reading, bill production, query and complaint handling, revenue and debt recovery. The company also had an IT department that provided the systems and infrastructure to automate many of these processes. Therefore, the initial view among senior management was that billing and revenue should be outsourced.

The search for a vendor

The company searched for an external vendor for this area of the business. Initial analysis revealed that there were no vendors outside the utility sector with the scale to deliver the required services. In particular, the utility company had huge billing and engineering systems that were highly specific to the utility industry. However, they identified one potential vendor in the utility sector – Vertex. Vertex was created in 1996 as a result of a merger of the electricity utility Norweb and water utility Northwest Water to form United Utilities. Vertex was created as a separate business to offer support services in the UK utility industry. The utility company embarked upon detailed negotiations with this vendor over a six-month period. Negotiations focused on establishing a joint venture with this company to provide the required services. These negotiations and analysis of this vendor proved to be an important learning experience for the utility company. Senior management began to realise that they could perform many of the processes involved at the same if not better levels of performance than this vendor. Senior management were also impressed by the success of this spin-off, as it achieved quite rapid growth and a strong position in the market-place. Benchmarking studies of other utilities in these processes during this time had revealed that the utility company was achieving comparable levels of performance in many areas.

Recruitment of external expertise

Crucially, the company had recruited a number of executives with commercial experience outside the utility industry prior to the negotiations with Vertex. One of these recruits was quick to recognise the existing capabilities and potential that resided inside the business. He was instrumental in making senior management aware of capabilities that the organisation possessed in areas such as IT and call handling that had the potential to compete in external service markets. This senior manager did not become involved in the ongoing argument with the regulator over the price control, and focused on identifying areas of the business that had the potential to develop additional revenue streams. He was fully aware that other privatised water and electricity companies had been successfully spinning off parts of their businesses to create additional sources of revenue. Moreover, he recognised other areas, including finance, property and telecommunications, as having potential to compete as separate businesses. Creating separate businesses would allow the company to create additional revenue streams and generate greater value for shareholders.

8.4 The structure of the spin-off arrangement

In 1998 senior management in the utility company established a holding company which was comprised of both regulated and unregulated businesses. Activities in the regulated part of the company included the procurement of power from generating companies, transmission and distribution of electricity, maintenance and refurbishment of the network and the supply business which included the billing and collection of customer accounts. A number of separate businesses were created in the unregulated element of the company including a telecommunications services company, a property company, a financial services company and a business services outsourcing provider. The spin-off would market services in the areas of information technology, call centre management, training and revenue management and supply chain services in both the utility and other service sectors. This involved transferring a number of departments from the previous company structure, including information technology, warehousing and logistics, accounts payable, call handling and training and development. A departmental breakdown of the staff that were transferred is shown in Table 8.1.

The information technology element of the spin-off company was regarded as key to the success of the venture. At the time of the spin-off the IT services market had been growing rapidly as a result of many large firms outsourcing their IT requirements.

Table 8.1 Departments and staff breakdowns

Department	Staff numbers (approximate)
Information technology	250
Warehousing and logistics	50
Accounts payable	15
Call handling	60
Training and development	30

The IT department had a strong skills base as it had pay scales that were extremely competitive in the IT market and attracted highly qualified graduates at that time. The area of call handling was viewed as another potentially lucrative area as demand for call centre services was starting to grow in the UK at that time. The company also believed that other areas in the service portfolio could be offered to other utility companies. In particular, the analysis of the industry and negotiations with Vertex had led senior management to believe that the spin-off company could compete successfully as a BPO vendor in the UK utility industry.

As well as offering services to other companies, the spin-off would continue to provide its existing service portfolio to other subsidiaries in the company, which was another major attraction of the spin-off arrangement to senior management. This meant that they would not have to untangle all the processes involved and transfer them to an external vendor. They believed that the prior relationships and experience that departments had within the spin-off company would allow it to deliver better service levels than if it had to source these services from a vendor. The experience of the people in the departments also meant that they understood the specific requirements of each subsidiary in the company. The utility company would have had to expend considerable effort in untangling the processes involved and deriving detailed requirement specifications if it were to employ an independent vendor. The situation was further complicated because another vendor would have to provide services to all the subsidiaries in the company, and understand the idiosyncrasies and linkages between them.

A major element of the service portfolio to the subsidiaries in the company was the provision of IT services. Another substantial part of the service portfolio involved providing meter reading, customer billing, call handling, debt management, printing and mailing services to the electricity supply business. A seven-year commercial agreement was established with the spin-off company. It was envisaged that this arrangement would be a partnership built on trust, co-operation and information-sharing for mutual benefit. In addition, it was expected that the transfer of staff to the spin-off would foster this collaboration through prior working relationships and having a detailed insight into the requirements of each subsidiary. As part of the commercial agreement, subsidiaries within the company could not procure these services from other vendors. It was anticipated that the guarantee of business from the parent company would underpin the development of the spin-off and allow it to develop other markets for its service portfolio. Service level agreements (SLAs) for the processes were developed by staff who were transferred to the spin-off in co-operation with the relevant staff that remained in the company. The costings for each service were developed from an analysis of materials, labour rates and overhead allocations.

8.5 The development of the spin-off arrangement

A number of important strategies were employed by both senior management in the utility company and the spin-off company to successfully commercialise the spin-off in the initial development phase.

Recruitment of commercial expertise into the spin-off

The success of the venture was based very much on the ability of the spin-off to compete in the IT industry. However, the experience of the people transferred into the spin-off business resided primarily in the public sector. Consequently, a senior management team with experience in the commercial IT sector was recruited. In particular, a number of senior managers from a local IT company were recruited and charged with developing the spin-off business. Senior management in the utility company recognised the importance of bringing in this commercial expertise and integrating it with what was largely a number of public sector departments. This was particularly relevant in the IT area of the business where having a more dynamic culture was viewed as important to successfully competing in this market.

Selection of target markets

In the early phases of development, senior management in the spin-off undertook a significant amount of market research on which markets they should target with their IT services portfolio. Although at the outset they regarded the UK public sector as an area where they would win business, they quickly realised that they did not have the scale to compete with larger IT companies for large-scale government contracts up to the value of £100 million. However, they identified smaller public sector contracts up to the value of £20 million in education and local government as areas in which they could compete. At this time education bodies and local government were outsourcing much of their IT requirement. In particular, many local government authorities in the UK required IT systems to automate the billing and collection of council taxes. The UK government was promoting greater use of the Internet to link citizens and businesses with local government agencies through its *Modernising Government* initiative.[7]

Capability development through acquisitions

The newly recruited senior management team had extensive experience of winning contracts in local government. However, they recognised that they would have to develop their internal capabilities and service portfolio to take advantage of opportunities in local government and education. Consequently, they embarked upon an ambitious acquisitions strategy, which was funded largely by the utility company. Within a two-year period they acquired six companies with IT capabilities in the areas of education and local government. The first two companies they acquired possessed IT applications skills with clients in the education sector. Four companies with IT capabilities in the local government sector were then acquired. One of these companies had specialist skills in network management, whilst another had skills in IT maintenance and support. The other two companies specialised in developing local government applications. One of these companies specialised in the development of building control and town planning software, whilst the other developed applications for housing revenue collection and housing benefits and had 50 per cent of the market in local government at that time. Pursuing this strategy allowed the spin-off to win a number of important contracts in the education and local government sectors. In the education sector, they won a large contract to supply IT to the schools sector within an entire UK region, and they won a number of contracts with large local government authorities. The acquisitions strategy allowed the spin-off to sell its IT services into the existing customer bases of the acquired companies.

These strategies allowed the spin-off to achieve tremendous growth. From its initial start-up in 1998 the spin-off achieved stunning success, increasing its turnover from £31 million to £109 million in 2000. The growth achieved through increasing its customer base and acquisitions meant that staffing levels had increased from 380 to 1,300. Moreover, this growth played well with shareholders and senior management in the utility company, who were impressed with the results delivered by the spin-off company. The utility company was demonstrating its ability to grow other sources of revenue in the unregulated elements of the business, which had a positive impact upon its share price. The strong growth and buoyancy in the IT market meant that the spin-off was viewed as a key contributor to the development of unregulated business. Indeed, senior management in the utility company were very bullish about the performance and the future prospects at the time. Unregulated business had grown from zero profitability to £17.6 million from 1998 to 2000 and senior management in the utility company believed there were no limits on how far this area would grow.

8.6 Difficulties in the spin-off arrangement

Although the spin-off company experienced considerable growth initially, difficulties began to emerge in 2001 during a downturn in the IT sector. These difficulties emerged for a number of reasons.

Failure to integrate acquisitions effectively

The rapid growth in turnover and the rush towards acquisitions had created significant difficulties. The spin-off company had struggled to integrate the various systems of each acquisition into the overall business. As senior management in the spin-off acquired companies, they had failed to implement the required financial controls. They had been operating in an environment where insufficient attention was given to financial controls and business planning, which meant that decisions were taken without fully understanding the consequences. Senior management in the utility company had given the spin-off too much latitude in allowing it to grow the business. During the initial phase of development the emphasis was on growing revenue without sufficient consideration being given to profit levels.

Lack of expertise in acquisitions

There was a belief in the utility company that the spin-off company had overpaid for some of the acquisitions. Although the funding was available to make the acquisitions, senior management in both the utility company and the spin-off had no experience in this area. None of the senior managers had any experience of acquiring companies, which led to a limited understanding of how companies should be acquired and effectively integrated into the business. The lack of financial controls meant that management did not know which client contracts were profitable and which were unprofitable, which had become a major issue during the downturn in the IT market. These problems came to a head when one of the companies acquired for its specialist expertise in the area of local government experienced delays with delivering a key Internet-based product, and this began to impact the ability of the spin-off to win contracts in this sector.

Overdependence on the IT services market

At this time senior management in the utility company became concerned at the lack of success the spin-off business was having with selling its non-IT services to other clients. Although they were aware of some difficulties during the period when the IT services portfolio had been growing rapidly, it had become a concern when the IT industry experienced a downturn. There was a perception that senior management in the spin-off had focused primarily on the IT side of the business, and had not given sufficient attention to growing its client base in other areas of its service portfolio. This was understandable given that the majority of the senior management team recruited for the spin-off came from an IT background and had focused on developing the business in this direction. However, prior to the initial start-up it was anticipated that the spin-off business would win business from other utility companies across its entire service portfolio. Although the spin-off tendered for a number of large contracts, it was unable to compete against the larger utility service providers. A number of other utility companies in the UK, privatised prior to the utility company in this case, had established service providers and these companies had won a number of large contracts, which allowed them to build strong market shares.

Efforts were made to develop a number of areas outside the IT portfolio, albeit with limited success. Although a few contracts were won in the area of call handling services, they found the margins on these contracts were much tighter than on its IT services portfolio. Furthermore, they found that when they tendered for larger contracts they did not have the capabilities to compete with specialist call centres. They were competing against larger call centres with much greater scale and lower cost bases. At this time senior management in the utility company and the spin-off began to challenge the logic of some of the processes that were transferred into the spin-off business. The spin-off did not achieve any success in areas such as warehousing and logistics. It could not compete with other vendors in these areas and senior management in the spin-off did not seek out clients for these services. Indeed, there was a view that these processes were transferred into the spin-off to give the business a 'critical mass', rather than because of the potential to compete in external service markets.

8.7 Relationship difficulties

In the initial phases of development the focus of senior management in the utility company had been on allowing the spin-off to grow its client base. However, as the spin-off developed, difficulties began to emerge in both the service levels and the relationship between subsidiaries in the utility company. Prior to the establishment of the spin-off it was anticipated that the utility company would benefit from lower costs and higher service levels across the portfolio of services as the spin-off achieved the benefits of specialisation through growing its customer base. However, the anticipated benefits did not materialise for a number of reasons.

Lack of focus on the needs of its largest client

As the spin-off began to develop other sources of revenue and new clients, it lost focus on meeting the needs of its largest client – the subsidiaries in the utility company. Service levels began to deteriorate as it won contracts with new clients. The fact that the spin-off had a guaranteed income from its main client meant that there was no urgency in improving service levels. Although the spin-off invested in the area of IT, it failed to invest in the utility-related services delivered to the utility company. Difficulties were occurring in areas that were perceived as routine processes. For example, poor performance in the meter reading process was creating difficulties in the area of revenue collection and call handling. Failure to obtain actual meter readings meant that many customer bills were based on estimates, which led to customers disputing bills via the call centre and additional visits to customer homes. This situation was slowing down the revenue collection process and led to escalating levels of customer debt. The absence of a formal contract was a major limitation of the arrangement, as the subsidiaries in the utility company could not seek alternative vendors for the services.

Ineffective service level agreements (SLAs)

When problems arose with service levels in certain areas, it was difficult to drive improvement because of shortcomings in the SLAs. In the initial phase of the arrangement the emphasis was on growing the spin-off rather than on imposing stringent performance targets on the services provided to the utility company. The service levels in the SLAs in many areas were not clearly specified and were too general. To further exacerbate this problem, many of the SLAs had been hurriedly developed by staff who were transferred into the spin-off. There had been a feeling when the spin-off was established that any shortcomings in the SLAs could be improved as the relationship developed. However, important knowledge had been transferred into the spin-off, which left the utility company in a weaker position. Most of the skill set relating to the processes now resided in the spin-off, which meant that it was very difficult for staff in the utility company subsidiaries to drive performance improvements.[8]

Ineffective governance arrangements

Throughout these difficulties the relationship between staff in the spin-off and the utility company had deteriorated. Staff in the utility company believed that they were paying too much for some of the services. They supported their claims by pointing to the lack of success the spin-off was having with winning contracts for services outside the IT portfolio. In fact, they believed that many of the services could be delivered at a lower cost in-house. Another difficulty in the relationship was the lack of formal governance arrangements for managing the relationship with the spin-off, and dealing with service problems across each subsidiary in the utility company. There were no formal procedures for dealing with ongoing issues or changing requirements, which led to an *ad hoc* approach to dealing with change. The situation was further compounded as people on each side of the relationship who were previously colleagues were now dealing with each other in a commercial arrangement. Prior relationships with former colleagues created difficulties in addressing performance problems and encouraging improvements as the lack of formal governance arrangements meant that there was no agreement on whose responsibility many of the ongoing problems were. Staff in the spin-off regarded the problems as a result of poorly specified requirements from subsidiaries in the utility company. Conversely, the subsidiaries believed that staff in the spin-off should be using their experience and knowledge to re-engineer the processes and deliver an improved service.

8.8 The turnround strategy

Senior management in the utility company recognised that they had to take decisive action to address the difficulties in the spin-off and also in its relationship with the subsidiaries.

Restructuring the spin-off company

In 2001 the utility company embarked upon a major restructuring of the spin-off which involved replacing a number of the senior management team. Senior management in the utility company recognised that they had given the spin-off business too much autonomy in growing the business and therefore took firm action. No further acquisitions were made by the spin-off and the utility company became more proactive in the running of the spin-off and implemented tighter internal controls. Implementing a greater level of control had revealed weaknesses in some of the businesses the spin-off had acquired and allowed them to better integrate the more successful acquisitions. The company also sold off the training and development part of the business. Adopting this approach facilitated the restructuring of the business, which involved refocusing on its core and the more lucrative IT services portfolio.

During this restructuring programme, senior management in the utility company began to recognise the difficulties of managing a portfolio of companies in diverse business sectors. Although the restructuring of the spin-off was successful, it highlighted the different cultures of senior management in the utility company and the spin-off company. For example, senior management in the utility company operated in a stable environment where they had over 700,000 customers and it was possible to forecast revenue streams accurately three years ahead. This contrasts with the dynamic IT sector where senior management in the spin-off had to make rapid decisions to compete for important contracts. When senior management in the utility company became more involved in the management of the spin-off, there was a belief in the spin-off company that it had become too risk-averse and was missing out on contracts that they should have won. The utility company was also coming under pressure to focus on its core energy business interests. Therefore, in 2004 the utility company decided to prepare to dispose of the spin-off business. It had already made significant progress with restructuring the business. However, prior to disposal it recognised that it would have to address the difficulties in the relationship between its subsidiaries and the spin-off as the contract with the company would be a major selling point for any prospective buyer of the spin-off business.

Addressing the relationship difficulties

The utility company pursued a number of strategies to address the relationship difficulties between its subsidiaries and the spin-off.

> *Backsourcing.* This involved the utility company bringing a number of areas back in-house including warehousing and logistics and debt collection. It was believed that performance in these processes would be improved by carrying them out internally. The transfer of these areas back in-house was eased, as the spin-off had no other clients for these processes.

Redesigning the SLAs. This addressed the problems in the service levels and the relationship between subsidiaries in the utility company and the spin-off business. This involved establishing clear services agreements (SLAs) for the services sourced from the spin-off. A benchmarking exercise was carried out to compare performance with that of other utility service providers. This exercise revealed that the spin-off was providing a number of services at a lower level of performance and higher cost than competing providers. It also showed that many of the processes had not been improved since the establishment of the spin-off. The results of the benchmarking exercise allowed senior management in the utility company to negotiate and develop with the senior management team in the spin-off a programme for action.

Fostering a continuous improvement culture. The Six Sigma quality approach was adopted to improve performance in the services delivered to the utility company. This involved recruiting additional staff with expertise in this area. Adopting Six Sigma required taking the results of the benchmarking exercise and working jointly with staff in the spin-off to redesign and improve processes. Undertaking this analysis allowed the utility company to eliminate complex interdependencies among many of the processes involved. In the case of the spin-off being disposed, it was quite possible that in the future the utility company would have to consider sourcing some of the current service portfolio from other vendors. Using the improvement programme to remove complex interdependencies would allow processes to be transferred and sourced from other vendors. The presence of complex interdependencies among processes would have increased the switching costs of moving to another vendor. Each of the processes was redesigned and improved in stages and the entire initiative lasted almost twelve months. Once the processes were redesigned, baseline performance measures were established for each process and agreed performance targets with the spin-off.

Illustration 8.2 Six Sigma

Six Sigma is a continuous improvement programme for eliminating waste and improving performance in business processes. Statistical and scientific methods are at the heart of Six Sigma, both in developing an optimum process specification, and in reducing defects in the process to almost zero.[a] Six Sigma was pioneered by Motorola in the 1980s, and has since been applied successfully by companies such as GE, Sony, Caterpillar and Texas Instruments. Six Sigma has developed from a defect elimination programme to become an organisation-wide initiative to reduce costs through process efficiencies and increase sales revenue through process effectiveness. Although Six Sigma was pioneered in manufacturing, it has been widely applied in business services to improve service quality and customer satisfaction. There are three key practices associated with Six Sigma implementation.

Role structure

Implementing Six Sigma involves a group of improvement specialists – normally referred to as champions, master black belts, black belts and green belts. The logic of Six Sigma is that improvement initiatives are only successful if significant training and resources are devoted to implementation. Therefore, improvement specialists receive training to improve their knowledge and skills in areas such as statistical methods, project management, process design and problem-solving techniques. Improvement specialists are assigned roles and responsibilities to drive continuous improvement efforts across the organisation. There is a hierarchical co-ordination mechanism for implementation, where senior management champion long-term, strategic improvement plans, and black belts lead Six Sigma projects and monitor the performance of green belts. Top management support is necessary for overcoming employee resistance and fostering a culture that is receptive to the associated change.

Structured improvement procedure

A structured approach to managing improvement activities is applied in Six Sigma. This is often represented by the Define–Measure–Analyse–Improve–Control (DMAIC) cycle used in process improvement:

- *Define*. Identify an improvement area and define project scope and the process involved.
- *Measure*. Determine which aspects of the process require improvement. Identify critical input variables that can be controlled and affect the output. Define unacceptable levels of process performance, and collect data on process performance.
- *Analyse*. Use performance data to document current performance. Where possible, benchmark performance against internal or external processes.
- *Improve*. Eliminate causes of poor performance. Where no special causes of poor performance can be found, the improvement effort may have to focus on the process design.
- *Control*. Verify and embed the process change, and share experiences and knowledge with other process improvement teams.

Six Sigma specifies quality management tools and techniques to use within each step. Using Six Sigma structured procedures and tools and techniques in improvement projects assists in developing the team's experience and knowledge base.

Focus on metrics

Six Sigma incorporates quantitative metrics to set improvement objectives. Explicit and challenging improvement objectives can increase the scale of performance improvement, reduce the variability in project performance and drive employee commitment to improvement and quality. Six Sigma integrates strategy performance measures, process measures and project metrics into a co-ordinated review process that allows managers to measure and manage overall business performance. Moreover, similar to other continuous improvement programmes, Six Sigma is a continuous process of repeatedly challenging the detailed working of processes in order to drive improvements.

Note:
[a] Six Sigma gets its name from the Greek letter sigma that is used to denote the standard deviation, or the amount a process varies from the mean. Six Sigma requires that the natural variation of processes (+/− 3 standard deviations) should be half their specification range, i.e. the specification of a product or service should be +/− 6 the standard deviation of the process. The number of defects in the process is expressed in terms of defects per million, and the defects per million measure is used to emphasise the drive towards a zero-defect objective.

Sources: Zu, X., Fredendall, L. and Douglas, T. (2008). The Evolving Theory of Quality Management: The Role of Six Sigma, *Journal of Operations Management*, 26, 630–50; Betts, A. (2005). Six Sigma, *Blackwell Encyclopaedia of Management: Operations Management*, 2nd edn, Oxford: Blackwell; Hammer, M. (2002). Process Management and the Future of Six Sigma, *Sloan Management Review*, 43(2), 26–32.

Formalising the governance arrangement. This involved formalising the relationship between the utility company subsidiaries and the spin-off. A formal contract was introduced which included performance bonuses and penalties. A system for formally dealing with change controls was implemented. Previously, changes were being dealt with through informal mechanisms such as telephone calls or *ad hoc* meetings, which meant that in many cases, changes were not logged and often forgotten. Adopting a more formal approach to the relationship involved the utility company and spin-off appointing personnel to manage the relationship for each of the service lines. Throughout the improvement process a number of senior managers in the utility company were actively involved in driving through these changes. This ensured that senior management in the spin-off were fully involved and committed the necessary resource to address the difficulties. The extent of the changes and improvements was made possible because the spin-off business was part of the utility company rather than an independent vendor. Senior management in the utility company still had considerable influence over the spin-off, which meant that the necessary changes could be implemented.

In 2005 the utility company disposed of the spin-off for £155 million. This was an opportune time to sell as the IT market had recovered and was growing rapidly, which raised the attractiveness and price of the spin-off business. The acquiring company was a major supplier of software applications and outsourcing solutions to the public services, human resources and corporate markets in the UK. The strong presence of the spin-off in the local government and education sectors was a major attraction. Another was the £15 million contract with the subsidiaries in the utility company. Therefore, prior to the disposal it was essential that a formal contract was implemented, along with more stringent service levels. The duration of the contract was three years from the disposal date. The incorporation of performance bonuses and penalties into the contract created incentives for improvement and made a significant difference to the relationship once the spin-off was disposed of. In particular, the relationship was based on a firm contractual arrangement with formal protocols for changes in processes and payment rates. This led to significant improvements in the service being delivered to the subsidiaries in the utility company. The standard protocols that exist in any commercial relationship were implemented, which led to problems being resolved more quickly and in a formal manner.

Illustration 8.3 Theoretical perspectives on outsourcing and the spin-off arrangement

The experiences of the utility company have shown that an appreciation of perspectives from strategy, entrepreneurship and economics are important for understanding outsourcing and spin-off arrangements. The motives of the utility company in spinning off parts of their operations mirror closely the logic of the resource-based view.[a] The company had been under pressure to meet the needs of the regulator and shareholders and focus on its core energy business. This led the company to externalise areas of its operations that were non-core. Through spinning off a number of business functions the company believed it would exploit valuable internal capabilities. Decoupling these functions into a spin-off business would allow it to compete in external service markets and achieve the benefits of specialisation through servicing other clients. However, the experiences of the company have illustrated the dangers of externalising certain functions that lack the necessary capabilities and scale to compete in external service markets. Services outside the IT portfolio lacked the scale and required performance levels to compete, and warehousing, logistics and debt collection had to be brought back in-house.

An entrepreneurial perspective is also an important aspect of the spin-off arrangement.[b] In the case of the spin-off, most of the staff were accustomed to working in a hierarchical organisation where there was little incentive to improve performance. Stimulating an entrepreneurial culture in the spin-off involved introducing an incentive structure that encouraged management and employees to rapidly grow its client base. In effect, staff were moving from a risk-averse environment to one where risks had to be taken to grow the business. The recruitment of management from the private sector allowed the spin-off to identify opportunities for certain contract sizes in IT services in the public sector. The knowledge of the IT services market possessed by these managers allowed the spin-off to exploit existing capabilities and supplement these capabilities through acquisitions. However, the experiences of the spin-off in its acquisitions strategy highlighted the need for striking a balance between risk-taking and achieving a profitable growth path. Senior management in the spin-off expanded the business too quickly via acquisitions, without due diligence and putting the necessary financial controls in place.

The findings from the research also highlight the explanatory power of transaction cost economics in outsourcing and spin-off arrangements.[c] Some of the difficulties encountered by the company in the sourcing of services from the spin-off company could have been avoided if transaction cost considerations had been taken into account. For example, the fact that staff in the spin-off business had highly specific knowledge of the processes and requirements of the subsidiaries in the utility company meant that it was extremely difficult to transfer these processes to another vendor. It was only prior to disposing of the spin-off business that the company began to develop a formal approach to understanding the processes and its requirements rather than relying solely on staff in the spin-off business. Indeed, the findings here have shown that it is not enough to consider capabilities alone in outsourcing decisions. The case has illustrated the risks of companies outsourcing activities defined as 'non-core' without understanding transaction costs. Many companies often employ the distinction between core and non-core as the primary basis for outsourcing without understanding the supply context. However, the experiences of the utility company in this study illustrate the importance of transaction cost considerations in outsourcing and spin-off arrangements.

Notes:
[a] For key reading on the resource-based view, see Peteraf, M. A. (1993). The Cornerstones of Competitive Advantage: A Resource-Based View, *Strategic Management Journal*, 14, 179–91; and Barney, J. B. (1991). Firm Resources and Sustained Competitive Advantage, *Journal of Management*, 17(1), 99–120.
[b] For further reading on entrepreneurship, see Wickham, P. (2006). *Strategic Entrepreneurship*, 4th edn, Harlow: FT Prentice Hall; and Timmons, J. (2004). *New Venture Creation: Entrepreneurship in the 21st Century*, 6th edn, Homewood, Ill.: Irwin.
[c] For key reading on transaction cost economics, see Williamson, O. E. (1985). *The Economic Institutions of Capitalism: Firms, Markets and Relational Contracting*, New York: Free Press; and Williamson, O. E. (1975). *Markets and Hierarchies*, New York: Free Press.

8.9 Summary implications

The analysis presented in this chapter has identified a number of important implications for outsourcing and spin-off arrangements.

Spin-off functions with strategic potential

It is essential that functions included in a spin-off have the strategic potential to compete in the markets targeted. Analysis of the vendor market and the level of competition can provide valuable insights into internal capabilities and the potential to compete as separate businesses. The spin-off company in this chapter identified the areas of local government and education as under-developed markets and used its capabilities, strengthened through acquisitions, to exploit these opportunities. However, it found it difficult to compete in a number of other target markets. The utility services market was more fully developed, and the spin-off company was unable to compete with other utility service providers that already had well-established positions. Moreover, in other areas such as call handling it did not have the necessary scale to compete in the market-place for these services. Therefore, in-depth analysis has to be undertaken of the capabilities of functions affected prior to considering a spin-off arrangement. This involves benchmarking these capabilities with those of competitors and vendors. This analysis can also be a valuable opportunity to learn from potential vendors and assess whether the potential exists to create a spin-off operation. Careful consideration should be given to the following issues:

- What level of competence does the parent company have in the functions relative to external vendors?
- How standardised are the services and can they be offered to clients in other business sectors?
- How much scale is required in order to compete effectively in the target markets?
- What strategies can be employed to supplement existing capabilities?

Plan and implement an achievable growth path

The parent company must establish an achievable growth path for the spin-off operation and its future direction. The key to success for any spin-off business is its ability to generate sales from new clients. The growth in its client base will allow the spin-off company to achieve the benefits of specialisation and also offer competitive services to subsidiaries in the parent company. The spin-off company in this chapter achieved a stunning growth path in the first three years of operation. One of the key drivers of growth during this period was the ambitious acquisitions strategy, funded largely by the parent company. The acquisitions strategy allowed the company to exploit the opportunities that the company identified in under-developed markets such as local government and education. However, this rapid growth was achieved at a cost. The company acquired six companies within a two-year period and encountered significant integration problems, which became a critical issue during the downturn in the IT market. The rapid growth in IT services also diverted management attention from achieving performance improvements in other areas within its service portfolio, which affected the service levels being provided to subsidiaries in the company. Part of the growth plan for a spin-off should include targets and actions on service level improvements in the services offered to the parent company. Therefore, a growth path must be established which allows a spin-off to grow its client base whilst still delivering and improving services required by the parent company.

Establish effective governance structures between the parent and spin-off

There must be effective governance arrangements both at parent level and in the service relationship between a spin-off and its parent company. Senior management in the parent company in this chapter allowed the spin-off operation to embark upon an aggressive acquisitions strategy, without paying adequate attention to the viability of the acquired companies. Although the acquisitions strategy was a critical ingredient for success, insufficient attention was given to planning and integrating these companies into the business. In addition, there were no clear service lines between the spin-off and the subsidiaries in the utility company to which it provided services.

Understand processes and interdependencies

As is the case with any outsourcing arrangement, it is important to understand clearly the processes and associated interdependencies prior to establishing a spin-off business. The spin-off arrangement offers an attractive option for the parent company, as it can source services from a vendor with intimate knowledge of its requirements. It does not have to untangle the processes involved as it would if it were transferring them to an independent vendor. However, there are dangers with pursuing such a strategy, as evidenced by the experiences of the utility company in this chapter. Although the utility company had carried out extensive re-engineering post-privatisation, many of the processes transferred to the spin-off company were highly specific to the needs of the subsidiaries of the utility company. Prior to the disposal of the spin-off it would have been difficult to transfer the processes to another vendor without extensive re-engineering. This situation was further compounded as staff with important process knowledge had been transferred to the spin-off. However, it is essential to understand the processes involved and associated interdependencies with other parts of the business prior to transfer. This involves drawing up clear specifications of the service requirements of the parent company. Deriving clear service requirements will enable performance levels to be assessed throughout the relationship. Furthermore, when managing the staff transfers, key staff who possess important knowledge associated with each process should be retained. Prior to the disposal of the spin-off, the utility company invested resource in redesigning and improving processes using Six Sigma tools, which allowed it to develop more effective SLAs. Crucially, this exercise was important in reducing the specific nature of its requirements and making it possible for processes to be transferred to other vendors in the future.

Establish formal governance arrangements

A formal contract must be established at the outset between the parent company and a spin-off company for the services being provided. In the case of the utility company, the commercial agreement with the spin-off business was an important source of stability for the spin-off and allowed it to establish its position and seek new business in its target markets. However, as it developed, it lost focus on the relationship with subsidiaries in the parent company and took for granted the business with its largest client. The lack of a formal contract meant that the parent company found it difficult to sanction the spin-off company for under-performance. This problem would have been prevented if a formal contract with agreed service levels, performance penalties and bonuses had been established at the outset. In fact, once the spin-off was disposed of and a formal contract was introduced, service levels improved and the vendor became more responsive to the needs of the parent company. The introduction of a contract much earlier would have stimulated improvement and might have helped the spin-off to be more competitive in areas that it had struggled to sell to other clients outside its IT services portfolio.

Recruit new talent

The recruitment of external expertise has significant implications for the success of a spin-off arrangement – right from idea generation through to full implementation. Prior to considering a spin-off arrangement, recruiting talent can introduce a different perspective to the business and identify important capabilities and commercial potential that are not obvious to internal management in the parent company. In the case of the utility company, senior management were more concerned with dealing with the industry regulator than exploiting internal capabilities. A number of new recruits to the company were pivotal in championing the development of new revenue streams from existing internal capabilities. The recruitment of a senior management team to the spin-off business with extensive experience of winning public sector contracts was important in ensuring its development in the IT services market. The recruitment of talent throughout the process can also limit the potential difficulties encountered. The lack of expertise in the spin-off company in acquiring and integrating companies led to significant problems. The recruitment of talent with outsourcing expertise prior to establishing the spin-off would have limited the problems in a number of areas including poorly defined processes and SLAs and the transfer of people with important knowledge. Prior to the spin-off the utility company had only limited experience with outsourcing. Many of the shortcomings in measuring service levels and managing the relationship would have been avoided if external expertise in the area of outsourcing and contracting had been recruited. The introduction of expertise in the area of process improvement techniques to redesign processes much earlier would have limited some of the problems that arose in the relationship between the parent company and the spin-off.

Notes and references

1 Moncada-Paterno-Castello, P., Tübke, A., Howells, J. and Carbone, M. (1999). The Impact of Corporate Spin-offs on Competitiveness and Employment in the European Union, IPTS Technical Report Series, European Commission, Brussels (December).

2 Kakabadse, N. and Kakabadse, A. (2000). Critical Review – Outsourcing: A Paradigm Shift, *Journal of Management Development*, 19(8), 670–728.

3 Lacity, M., Willcocks, L. and Feeny, D. (2004). Commercialising the Back Office at Lloyds of London: Outsourcing and Strategic Partnerships Revisited, *European Management Journal*, 22(2), 127–40.

4 Lacity, M. and Willcocks, L. (2001). *Global Information Technology Outsourcing*, Chichester: Wiley.

5 See Lacity *et al.* (2004) in note 3 above.

6 The analysis presented in this chapter is based on study of a utility organisation. Data were gathered to obtain insights into the historical perspective of the utility company, and understand fully the process through which the utility

spun off the relevant functions into a separate business. A number of sources were used for data collection. The primary source was semi-structured interviews. In-depth interviews were carried out with senior and middle managers in both the utility and the spin-off company. The interviews were conducted in person and were tape-recorded and transcribed. Archival data in the form of internal memoranda, annual reports, strategy documents, trade and internal company magazine articles were also collated.

7 In 1999, the UK government embarked upon an initiative – entitled *Modernising Government* – to promote greater use of information technology in the public sector. The aim of this initiative was to fundamentally change the way in which information technology was used, and 'to achieve joined up working between different parts of government and providing new, efficient and convenient ways for citizens and businesses to communicate with government and to receive services' (*Modernising Government* (1999), London: HMSO, p. 45).

8 Williamson (1975) uses the term *information impactedness* to explain this difficulty in outsourcing arrangements. This occurs when one of the parties in a relationship is much better informed than the other, and the other cannot achieve information parity without incurring a considerable cost. See Williamson, O. E. (1975). *Markets and Hierarchies*, New York: Free Press.

Recommended key reading

Hammer, M. (2002). Process Management and the Future of Six Sigma, *Sloan Management Review*, 43(2), 26–32. This paper provides a useful overview of the Six Sigma approach and introduces practical illustrations throughout.

Lacity, M., Willcocks, L. and Feeny, D. (2004). Commercialising the Back Office at Lloyds of London: Outsourcing and Strategic Partnerships Revisited, *European Management Journal*, 22(2), 127–40. This paper discusses how a number of organisations have transformed their back-office operations into commercial enterprises. These new firms have reduced back-office costs, improved service levels and generated additional revenue through selling services to other clients.

Mack, D. and Quick, J. (2002). EDS: An Inside View of a Corporate Life Cycle Transition. *Organizational Dynamics*, 30(3), 282–93. This paper focuses on the spin-off of EDS from GM. It examines EDS from a historical perspective and provides insights into the development of EDS.

Learning from failure and strategies for recovery in business process outsourcing

9.1 Introduction

Senior executives continue to express disappointment with outsourcing, and fail to achieve the anticipated benefits despite considerable investments of time and effort. Many organisations have found that outsourcing has increased complexity and costs, and required a wider range of management competencies than initially anticipated.[1] Business process outsourcing (BPO) is one area where organisations have had difficulties and encountered failure. BPO involves transferring responsibility for delivering and managing a business process to an external vendor. Rather than involving the relatively smooth transfer of standard processes with clear interfaces to a vendor, BPO arrangements are often characterised by a high level of complexity and uncertainty. The business processes involved are tightly coupled with other organisational processes, and complexity arises from outsourcing the technological, workflow and human resource elements.[2] The presence of both idiosyncrasies and inefficiencies in the processes transferred makes it difficult for the vendor to achieve anticipated cost savings and performance improvements. Uncertainty and changing requirements from the client further increase the difficulties for the vendor, and often lead to costly contract renegotiations.

This chapter considers common causes of failure in BPO and outlines a number of strategies for recovery. The analysis is presented through outlining the experiences of a global software provider in a major BPO arrangement.[3] The company initially outsourced its revenue processing services to three vendors. However, over time the BPO arrangement failed to deliver the desired results. The experiences of the software company in this arrangement, along with illustrations from the existing literature, are used to outline the common causes of failure in BPO. The chapter focuses on potential strategies for transforming failing BPO arrangements by outlining how the software company transferred the revenue processing services to a single vendor arrangement. These strategies involved developing an effective sourcing strategy, business process analysis and redesign, knowledge management and employing formal contracting and collaboration as complements. Illustrations are provided on how knowledge management tools, information technology applications and continuous improvement techniques can be employed in the pre- and post-contract phases of BPO arrangements to reduce transaction costs.

9.2 Business process outsourcing: a case of failure

This case focuses on the European operation of a global software company that marketed software products to a range of customers including large corporations, small companies, government organisations, academic institutions and individuals in Europe. A key role of this operation involved processing revenue from its European customers. The total cycle time for processing revenue and dealing with customer queries was used at corporate level to evaluate the performance of the operation. The company outsourced a number of elements of revenue processing including order processing, customer care and rebates to three vendors. Because of the importance of the processes, the company decided that the three vendors should be located on the same site, as this would allow for greater control. Employees involved in revenue processing were transferred from the software company to the relevant vendors. An overview of the outsourcing arrangement is shown in Figure 9.1.

There were a number of challenges associated with revenue processing. Revenue processing involved a lot of manual work such as data entry and document scanning, which often led to errors in areas such as invoice accuracy, invalid contract agreements and incomplete documents. The software company had complex licensing agreements and pricing and rebate rules, which created complication and often slowed down the total cycle time for processing revenue. Rather than opting for standard product options, customers such as large corporations often required a different suite of the company's software products for each of its European sites, which led to different licensing agreements and pricing rules being applied. The software company frequently changed aspects of licensing agreements, which had knock-on effects for

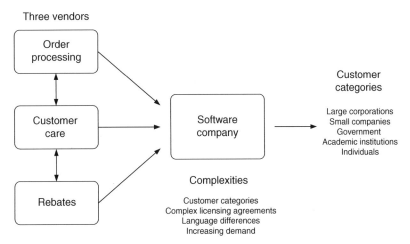

Figure 9.1   Structure of the BPO arrangement

processing. A further layer of complexity was the need to employ employees with different languages to deal with customers from countries across Europe.

After operating successfully for a number of years, the outsourcing arrangement encountered significant difficulties for a number of reasons. The arrangement with the three vendors had grown on an incremental basis. Although the services provided by the vendors were closely related, there were poor communication interfaces between each vendor. There were informal communication channels between the software company and the vendors, which meant that customer queries were not being formally recorded and dealt with. For example, when a customer logged a contract query with the software company, it set off a series of informal telephone conversations between people in the software company and vendors, which often led to the query not being dealt with quickly enough. The interdependencies between the processes in each of the vendors were not fully understood which meant no one vendor was taking responsibility for problems that arose. This created a blame culture among the vendors and the software company. This was all taking place in the context of increasing demand for the software company's products and changing licensing agreements as shown in Figure 9.2.

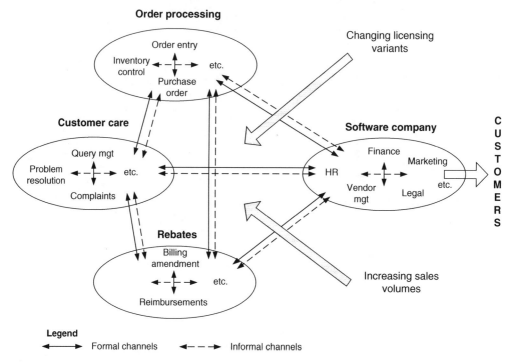

Figure 9.2   Poorly understood and informal interdependencies

---

Illustration 9.1 The influence of process interdependence and complexity in BPO

Process interdependence

Process interdependence complicates outsourcing because interdependencies among processes increase the difficulties of unbundling one process from other processes. The functionality of a process influences the number of interdependencies. Processes such as payroll and benefits management specific to a single function are often self-contained and can be adapted with little impact on other processes. In contrast, adapting cross-functional processes such as order fulfilment will have considerable knock-on effects across the organisation, and therefore outsourcing such processes will require considerable organisation-wide involvement to co-ordinate and manage the outsourcing relationship. Key questions to assess process interdependence include:

- To what extent does the process have standard interfaces with other organisational processes?
- To what extent do changes to the process impact other organisational processes?
- How difficult is it to assess performance in the process independent of the performance of other processes?

- To what extent can the process be split into sub-processes that can be performed independently?

Process interdependence creates several outsourcing challenges:

- Changes in the outsourced process may impact multiple functions and processes. The wider the impact, the more communication and co-ordination is required with the vendor.
- As the breadth of vendor involvement in organisational processes increases, the potential for losing important information also increases.
- Interdependent components of the outsourced process create problems of shared ownership, and a skilled integrator is required to manage the interrelated components.

Process complexity

Process complexity refers to the difficulty in analysing and understanding the inner workings of the process and measuring and verifying the output. Complex processes can lead to incomplete contracts and vendor opportunism because the client cannot precisely define tasks, allocate tasks or specify performance measures. As performance measures have to evolve, the client and vendor have to spend considerable time renegotiating service standards and requirements throughout the relationship. Key questions to assess process complexity include:

- To what extent does a clearly defined body of knowledge guide the effective functioning of the process?
- How quickly do managers know whether or not the process has executed successfully?
- To what extent are the activities and methods in the process common across different inputs and parameters (for example, across different categories of clients)?
- How often do staff involved in the process have to adopt different methods or procedures to do their work?

Process complexity creates these outsourcing challenges:

- Costly and incomplete contracts with few measurable outputs.
- Lack of industry standards and benchmarks.
- Increased co-ordination and communication costs.

Source: Mani, D., Barua, A. and Whinston, A. (2006). Successfully Governing Business Process Outsourcing Relationships, *MIS Quarterly Executive*, 5(1), 15–29.

As well as having poorly understood and informal interdependencies, many of the processes were inefficient, which impacted performance. The vendors lacked the necessary capabilities to redesign and improve processes, and no effort had been made to define processes. The lack of formal

Table 9.1 How problems in the BPO arrangement impacted transaction costs

Transaction cost variable	Problems in the BPO arrangement
Asset specificity	Lack of understanding of processes involved. Poorly understood interdependencies meant neither the client nor vendor was sure who was responsible for each process and sub-process, which led to shirking and disputes between the software company and vendors.
Knowledge loss	High employee turnover in vendors led to a loss of knowledge. Process definitions or rules for dealing with specific customers were not formally documented. Vendors were spending too much time training newly recruited staff and taking too long to process revenue and deal with customer queries.
Performance measurement	The lack of process definitions and poorly understood interdependencies meant performance management was poor. Service levels were poor and often out of date as the arrangement grew. Therefore, the client was not in a position to sanction vendors for under-performance.
Uncertainty	Changing licensing variants and increasing volumes were creating difficulties for vendors to meet the requirements.

process definitions meant that there were poor service level agreements (SLAs) in place. The lack of clearly defined processes and informal process interdependencies meant that many of the performance measures in the SLA were largely irrelevant. Therefore, the software company was not in a position to penalise the vendor for under-performance. A further problem in the arrangement was high employee turnover in the vendors leading to the loss of important knowledge on how to deal with complex licensing agreements and rebates. Queries from customers of the software company were taking too long to resolve, as new employees in the vendors had to undertake lengthy on-the-job training to learn the procedures involved.

Employee retention was a problem for a number of reasons including the lack of career development opportunities in the vendors and the transient nature of foreign-language employees being recruited. All of these difficulties created a situation where managers in the software company were spending a considerable amount of time addressing any problems that arose with each of the vendors. This problem was further exacerbated as there were separate vendors involved. Although the vendors were located on the same site, managers in the software company were afraid to let go of the process and were operationally managing the vendors. Table 9.1 illustrates how the problems with this BPO arrangement were impacting transaction costs.

Illustration 9.2 Causes of outsourcing failure

Outsourcing continues to present challenges for organisations, and there are many cases of failure documented in the popular media and academic journals. This illustration provides an outline of seven common causes of outsourcing failure drawn from the existing literature.

Lack of a formal strategy

Many organisations still experience considerable difficulties with outsourcing, and fail to achieve their desired objectives. Organisations continue to be motivated by short-term cost savings, and fail to consider the implications of outsourcing for long-term competitiveness. The problem with making the outsourcing decision on the basis of costs is further exacerbated by the fact that many companies have inadequate costing systems. Many organisations have not taken a holistic approach to creating an outsourcing strategy that best fits their outsourcing context and objectives. Organisations often choose an outsourcing relationship which is not aligned with the objectives of outsourcing.

Outsourcing the core

Many organisations have unknowingly relinquished their core competencies by cutting internal investment in what they mistakenly thought were 'cost centres' in favour of external vendors. Determining which processes can be best performed by external vendors requires a good understanding of where competitive advantage resides. Rather than using outsourcing to build competitive advantage, companies are employing outsourcing to offload problem processes. In certain circumstances, where poor performance is a result of a lack of scale economies or superior knowledge of the process, outsourcing may be appropriate. Where a vendor can realise significant scale economies in a process through serving a number of clients, it is very difficult for the client to replicate such a position. However, where poor performance is a result of poor management that can be addressed through an internal improvement initiative, then outsourcing can be fraught with risks. Such processes may be of significant value to the company currently, and in the future, and potentially contribute to the organisation's competitive advantage.

Unbundling processes

Organisations often do not fully understand the difficulties of transferring responsibility for an internal process to an external vendor. There are complex, and often misunderstood, interdependencies between the process and other internal processes and functions. Even when a process is considered to be non-core, there can be implicit and tacit interdependencies with processes that are considered to be core. Indeed, most processes have elements that belong to the core business and elements that do not, making the distinction between core and non-core business processes difficult. For example, when outsourcing a process an organisation may fail to account for both the formal and informal co-ordinating mechanisms that have allowed the organisation to perform the process internally in the past. The outsourcing of such a process can also have a detrimental effect upon the performance of core processes that remain internal.

Under-estimating the transaction costs

Transaction costs can often offset the gains from vendor labour savings. Examples of transaction costs are the extra project management resource required to manage the vendor, which adds to the total cost of outsourcing. Highly specific and idiosyncratic client requirements increase transaction costs. Where the vendor is not delivering a standard process, the client has to expend additional resource to ensure that the vendor understands the specific requirements and idiosyncrasies associated with the process. There are a number of important components of transaction costs, including: monitoring the agreement with the vendor to ensure that contractual obligations are being met; bargaining with the vendor and imposing penalties when the vendor fails to fulfil its contractual obligations; and negotiating changes to the contract in the case of any unexpected changes in the business environment. The failure to understand transaction costs is further compounded because companies do not commit sufficient resource to managing the vendor and believe responsibility for the process resides solely with the vendor. Moreover, the sourcing organisation often lacks the necessary skills and capabilities to manage the vendor.

People issues

Organisations often fail to take account of the people issues associated with outsourcing. Many outsourcing strategies are based primarily on reducing costs regardless of the damage that it causes to employees that remain in the client organisation. Outsourcing adversely impacts an employee's sense of job security, and creates an environment where there is a lack of loyalty. Internal fears and resistance can lead to tactics being employed to ensure the outsourcing initiative fails, which in turn limits the likelihood of the organisation outsourcing other parts of the business. A further cause of outsourcing failure is when important knowledge is lost through key employees being transferred to the vendor. Often, prior to outsourcing, a process has been performed internally for a long period of time, and some employees possess crucial knowledge on how the process should be carried out. This is an important consideration in the case of processes that have highly specific requirements and the vendor therefore requires the specific knowledge of the employees to ensure the process is performed properly. In addition, heavy turnover of key employees – whether transferred or not – can significantly impact upon service quality, ultimately leading to additional costs for the client.

Vendor selection

Organisations often do not give sufficient attention to the vendor selection phase of outsourcing, which can lead to outsourcing failure. Failure to allocate sufficient attention to gathering information to identify and evaluate the most suitable vendor creates difficulties in a number of areas. Vendors often exaggerate their capabilities when given the opportunity by the client to tender for the contract. For example, vendors may be short of business, or want to enter a new outsourcing market to lock out competitors, and thus will over-sell their capabilities. Some vendors often tender unrealistic low bids in order to win the business – sometimes referred to as the Winner's Curse.[a] As the contract develops and the vendor fails to achieve a profit margin on the contract, service quality will be affected and the client will incur additional costs.

Ineffective contracts

Although contracting is recognised as a crucial aspect of outsourcing, poorly drafted contracts are a common cause of outsourcing failure. Poor contracting stems from the inability of the client to specify clearly its requirements to the vendor. Internal personnel with knowledge of the outsourced process are not consulted in establishing requirements. The lack of clearly defined requirements also means that it is difficult to incorporate effective performance measures into the contract. Ineffective contracting is particularly difficult in the case of highly specific and idiosyncratic processes, which are more difficult to transfer in the event of vendor failure. There are a number of common weaknesses in contracts: contracts often lack precision in terms of client requirements and service levels; the lack of incentives in the contract means that the vendor is unlikely to advance upon the service levels established in the contract; the lack of flexibility clauses in the contract to allow for changes; and the lack of balance in the contract means that either the client or vendor is disadvantaged, which ultimately damages the outsourcing relationship.

Note:
[a] The Winner's Curse involves vendors making unrealistic bids to ensure they win an outsourcing contract. However, they already know, or subsequently discover, that they cannot recover their tendering, business and operational costs during the contract. Vendors take this risk in the expectation that they can recover their costs by offering additional services that merit additional fees during the contract. For an illustration of the Winner's Curse in IT outsourcing, see Kern, T., Willcocks, L. and van Heck, E. (2002). The Winner's Curse in IT Outsourcing: Strategies for Avoiding Relational Trauma, *California Management Review*, 44(2), 47–69.

Sources: Shi, Y. (2007). Today's Solution and Tomorrow's Problem: The Business Process Outsourcing Risk and Management Puzzle, *California Management Review*, 49(3), 27–44; McIvor, R. (2005). *The Outsourcing Process: Strategies for Evaluation and Management*, Cambridge: Cambridge University Press; Barthélemy, J. (2001). The Hidden Costs of IT Outsourcing, *Sloan Management Review*, 42(3), 60–9.

9.3 Strategies for recovery

The software company was faced with a number of options to recover the situation. The first option involved addressing the problems in the outsourcing arrangement, and continuing with the three vendors. This option appeared attractive as it would involve less change than terminating the contract and moving to an alternative arrangement. However, the three vendors lacked the capabilities and necessary capacity to meet the requirements of the software company. Relationships between staff in the software company and the vendors had deteriorated to such an extent that radical improvement would not have been possible through continuing with the current arrangement. Terminating the contract with the three vendors, and bringing the processes back in-house, was also considered. However, this option was deemed unsuitable for a number of reasons including the lack of internal capabilities to redesign and manage the services internally. Senior management were unwilling to allocate scarce resource to an area that they felt could be better managed by external vendors. Terminating the contract with the three vendors and transferring the processes to another vendor arrangement was considered to be the most appropriate option. The following sections provide an outline of the key strategies involved in transitioning the processes to the new outsourcing arrangement.

9.4 Effective sourcing strategy

The software company developed a sourcing strategy that involved clearly defining its requirements from the BPO arrangement, and then selecting a vendor that would meet these requirements. Determining its requirements involved analysing the problems with the previous outsourcing arrangement. The complexity of the processes meant that it was not feasible to continue with an arrangement where the processes were performed by three separate vendors, as there would have been considerable difficulties with co-ordinating and managing multiple vendors to ensure the integrated processes were performed effectively. It was decided that it would be more appropriate to outsource the processes to a single vendor. Once it determined its requirements it was clear that the software company needed a vendor that possessed significant business improvement capabilities, and had experience of offering these services to other clients. The software company would have to work closely with the vendor in transferring and consolidating the processes, reducing process complexity and driving out process inefficiencies. The presence of highly specific requirements associated with some processes, and the need for continuous improvement, necessitated a collaborative relationship with the selected vendor.

The software company conducted extensive evaluations and negotiations with three vendors. A global BPO vendor was selected that already had close links with the software company at corporate level. The vendor had sufficient capacity and skills to deal with the increasing requirements of the software company, and offered a number of standard processes in revenue processing that it provided to other clients. The successful vendor had a number of capabilities that allowed the software company to attain its outsourcing objectives:

- The vendor had the capability to develop staff through training programmes, and offered a career progression structure. This was important in the case of transferred employees whose morale was low and performance was suffering as a result. The vendor had a track record of training, managing and motivating people.
- The software company required a vendor that offered standard processes and the associated scale economies, while possessing specialised skills and experience that delivered performance improvement in processes that were specific to its business.
- The vendor was expected to automate many manual elements of the processes, and use its knowledge management capabilities to retain knowledge and limit the effects of employee turnover. In addition, it was anticipated that the vendor would quickly deploy its capabilities in IT to meet and improve service levels.
- Process redesign capability was a critical consideration for the software company, and the selected vendor possessed specialist capabilities in continuous improvement techniques. Significant skills were necessary for removing inefficiencies, reducing complexity and improving process performance.
- The vendor had experience of working with large clients in a range of BPO arrangements, and operated a number of sourcing arrangements for managing relationships. The vendor had a service review board that defined, tracked and evaluated performance. This involved having reporting mechanisms to ensure that the relevant personnel in the client and vendor were properly informed, and there were procedures for expediting and dealing with problems.

Illustration 9.3 Vendor capability analysis in BPO

The BPO phenomenon has created a supply market of vendors with an array of capabilities. Some vendors offer lower-cost services through scale economies and lower labour costs, whilst other vendors offer specialist business improvement capabilities to transform performance in a range of business processes. In this environment, the vendor selection process is both complex and challenging for the client. There are two important elements to vendor selection in BPO: (1) determining the requirements from outsourcing; and (2) evaluating carefully whether a vendor can meet these requirements. Determining the requirements involves addressing some of these questions:

- Does the client need a vendor that can deliver the highest level of performance in the process?
- Does the client need a vendor that can transform performance in the process?
- Does the client require standard processes that can be sourced in the supply market, or is the process highly specific to the needs of the client?
- In the case of highly specific requirements, does the client wish to develop a long-term, collaborative relationship with the vendor?

Evaluating whether a vendor can meet the client's outsourcing requirements involves answering some of these questions:

- How does the vendor achieve lower costs in the service, for example, through lower labour rates or experience?
- How quickly can the vendor deploy its capabilities to meet the client's required performance levels in the process?
- What specialist capabilities does the vendor possess that enable it to transform performance in the process?
- Does the vendor have a track record of managing and motivating people to deliver high performance?

Feeny *et al.* have developed a valuable framework for understanding the required vendor capabilities in BPO.[a] Regardless of their area of expertise, every BPO vendor possesses competencies in these areas.

- *Delivery competency.* How well the vendor can respond to the client's requirements for operational services. Consideration should be given to the scope and complexity of the vendor's services including levels of costs, quality, robustness and flexibility. The client should be confident that the vendor can meet the minimum performance standards throughout the contract.
- *Transformational competency.* The ability of the vendor to improve service performance in areas such as cost, quality and functionality. Some vendors possess specialist capabilities for delivering radical change and improvement. However, this is an area where vendor capabilities can differ significantly.
- *Relationship competency.* The extent to which the vendor is willing to develop a 'win–win' relationship where the client's and vendor's goals are

aligned, and risks and rewards are shared equally. Although the client may negotiate the best price at the beginning of the contract, once the contract is signed the vendor may seek greater control and build switching costs into the relationship. Therefore, the client should assess carefully whether the vendor is willing to develop a 'win–win' relationship.

• Feeny *et al.* have identified twelve capabilities from these three competencies as shown in Table 9.2.[a] The client should assess vendors against these capabilities depending upon their specific requirements.

Table 9.2 Twelve vendor capabilities

Capability	Description
Domain expertise	The vendor's capability to apply and retain process knowledge to meet client requirements. The vendor can acquire process knowledge through employee transfers. The vendor can adjust capacity, eliminate poorly performing employees and unlock the potential of the better employees.
Business management	The vendor must be able to consistently meet the client's service-level agreements and its own business plans. This involves allowing the vendor to make a fair margin. Clients often fail to give their vendors credit for items in the bundle of services that are priced quite competitively compared with external benchmarks and other vendors.
Behaviour management	Clients should evaluate the vendor's capability to motivate and manage people. Indicators of behaviour management capability include the track record of the vendor in training, managing and motivating people.
Sourcing	This involves the client tapping the vendor's capacity to meet its service-level objectives. The client's requirements depend on the type of service, and the level of change required. Some clients require standard services to access the vendor scale economies; whilst others require the specialised skills in functional areas.
Technology exploitation	Vendors that invest considerable resource in new technology are often a major attraction to clients, as it allows them to reduce capital expenditure in process technology. Clients should evaluate how quickly and effectively vendors can deploy this technology to meet service improvement levels.

Table 9.2 (*cont.*)

Capability	Description
Process re-engineering	The vendor must have the ability to redesign and improve processes, which involves the following issues. Who has the critical skills? Who will own the redesigned process? How is improvement measured? And who benefits?
Customer development	Client users of services should be viewed as 'customers', as they specify the service requirements and make choices on service levels, functionality and costs. The vendor should establish personal contacts with users to understand how they want to use the service. Secondly, the vendor should work with client managers to define the required service.
Planning and contracting	A vendor must have the capability to develop and implement business plans that deliver benefits to both the client and vendor. The plan can include a vision of projected cost savings, and a structured process for achieving these benefits. The contract provides a framework for understanding how rewards are shared between the client and vendor.
Organisation design	The client must determine whether the vendor has the capabilities to deliver on the objectives in the business plan. An important aspect of organisation design is resource allocation. Where a client seeks service transformation, vendors must have capabilities in important areas such as technology and process re-engineering.
Governance	The vendor must have a service review committee to define, track and evaluate performance. This committee should consider the following: the type of reporting mechanisms to ensure that each part of the governance structure is properly informed, procedures for dealing with problems, and powers and sanctions in the governance arrangement.
Programme management	Programme management involves prioritising, co-ordinating and mobilising the organization, and driving interrelated change projects. This is likely to involve developing transferred employees, moving from a user- to a customer-orientation, and possessing technology- and process-based projects that deliver improvements.

Table 9.2 (*cont.*)

Capability	Description
Leadership	Effective vendors will exercise leadership, which involves identifying, communicating and delivering the activities required for success. The relationship between the vendor leader and top management in the vendor is crucial, as access can be gained to key resources required to deliver on client requirements.

Note:
[a] Feeny, D., Lacity, M. and Willcocks, L. (2005). Taking the Measure of Outsourcing Providers, *Sloan Management Review*, 46(3), 41–8.

9.5 Business process analysis and redesign

Business process analysis and redesign was an important part of transferring the processes to the new outsourcing arrangement. The software company recognised that some of the difficulties with the previous outsourcing arrangement were created by its own internal processes and procedures, and these issues would have to be dealt with prior to moving to the new outsourcing arrangement. In particular, it needed to understand more fully the processes involved to determine what it required from the new outsourcing arrangement. This would assist with communicating its requirements more clearly to the selected vendor, and facilitate the smoother transfer of the processes. Understanding more fully the process complexities and interdependencies would make it less difficult to assign responsibility for execution of certain tasks between the client and vendor. Moreover, understanding the processes requirements would allow more effective performance measures to be derived and also amended throughout the contract as requirements changed.

There were a number of important elements to business process analysis and redesign. The first element involved analysing internal processes in the software company and the linkages with the three outsourced processes – order processing, customer care and rebates. It embarked on an extensive workflow mapping exercise to document and understand the processes, and the internal and external linkages with the outsourced processes. This initiative involved redesigning and driving out inefficiencies from some

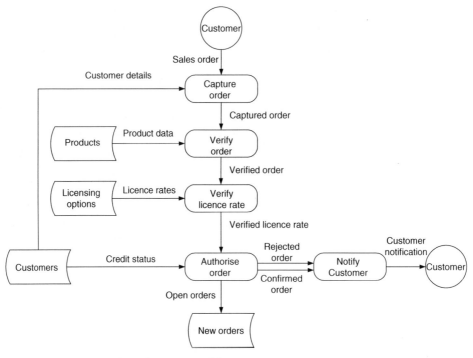

Figure 9.3   Sample order entry workflow map

of its internal processes, by deploying its expertise in business improvement tools such as Six Sigma. Figure 9.3 shows a sample workflow map for order entry. This exercise provided valuable insights into the working of complex processes, and assisted in identifying areas for performance improvement. In addition, the continuous improvement exercise involved simplifying some of the complex licensing agreements, and reducing the number of customer categories in order to reduce the complexities in revenue processing. This required working with staff at corporate level to reduce the number of potential licensing options, and establishing clear rules for dealing with exceptions.

Preparing for the new outsourcing arrangement involved mapping out and documenting the outsourced processes – order processing, customer care and rebates. This analysis revealed significant process inefficiencies and complex, poorly understood interdependencies. Benchmarking was used to make comparisons with external sources, and also determine baseline performance levels it expected from the vendor in the new outsourcing arrangement. Prior to establishing the outsourcing arrangement, the software company reduced some of the complexity and interdepend-encies among the processes, and applied continuous improvement tech-niques to improve performance in some areas. However, it recognised that it lacked the capabilities to reduce the inefficiencies and complex-ities entirely, owing to its highly specific requirements, and that it would have to rely on the vendor to improve performance during the outsour-cing arrangement.

9.6 Knowledge management

Managing knowledge was an important consideration in both the pre- and post-contract phases of the new outsourcing arrangement.[4] A key part of the transitioning phase involved transferring people from the three ven-dors to the new arrangement via the TUPE framework.[5] Although there had been performance problems with the previous arrangement, the vendor viewed the transfer of staff as essential to the success of the new outsourcing arrangement, and spent considerable time dealing with this issue. These staff had extensive experience of working in revenue pro-cessing and had built up valuable knowledge of the associated rules and procedures. Effective transfer of this knowledge would assist the vendor with operationalising the processes. Some key personnel with exten-sive experience negotiated improved salaries as a result of the transfer. Without transferring the staff it would have taken an additional nine months to get the project up and running. The TUPE negotiations were viewed as successful, with 90 per cent of staff transferring to the new arrangement. Many of the staff viewed the new arrangement positively, as they would receive better training and more opportunities for career development.

Illustration 9.4 Transitioning in BPO

Transitioning involves transferring the processes and associated equip-ment, staff and knowledge to the vendor. Many organisations fail to realise the effort involved and the complexity of transitioning. There are a number of factors that increase the complexity of the transitioning phase.

Characteristics of the process. Where the service requirements are com-plex and highly specific to the needs of the client, it will take time for the vendor to understand and meet the required service levels. Alternatively, where the services involved are highly standardised with low levels of com-plexity, the vendor can quickly get up to speed with the process through experience developed with other clients.

Number of service users. The number of service users in the client will increase the transitioning time, and where they are from different client functions it is likely that their needs will be different, thus requiring greater attention.

Number of transferred staff. It will take time to manage the transfer of staff from the client to the vendor operation. As well as dealing with changes to staff terms and conditions, motivation and morale issues have to be considered in order to ensure the vendor can improve performance.

There are a number of important issues that should be considered in effectively managing the transitioning phase.

Establish a team. The client will normally establish a team comprising staff with different skills and perspectives. These will include the manager of the internal function affected by outsourcing, service users, vendor management and contracting. The team will work closely with the vendor and be responsible for a number of issues including location change, transfer of staff, selection and installation of equipment, and transfer and the establishment of the new service. The skills, experience and personal qualities of the team members are an important consideration in the selection of team members from the client and the vendor. The team leaders should have experience of the functions involved, sufficient technical knowledge and the ability to develop relationships and foster an ethos of continuous improvement. There will be frequent formal and informal interaction between client and vendor staff to ensure that client service needs are met, problems are addressed and changes to performance measures or the contract are agreed.

Manage expectations. The expectations of both the client and vendor staff involved in transitioning the processes and the client service users has to be managed carefully. For those involved in transitioning, they must be aware that operationalising the processes will require a significant amount of work, with problems likely to arise in the initial phases of service delivery. The transitioning team leaders should ensure that staff in both the client and vendor work together to resolve any problems, and foster realistic expectations of vendor performance among service users. Client service users must be made aware of likely service disruptions in the early phases of the service going live.

Manage the transfer. As well as dealing with staff terms and conditions, another important aspect of managing the transfer involves transferring knowledge to assist the vendor with operationalising the processes. The client should identify staff with key knowledge that should be transferred to ensure the smooth transfer of the service to the vendor. A further consideration is maintaining the goodwill of transferred staff, which is particularly important where client requirements are highly specific and include idiosyncratic elements.

> Additional important factors in transitioning include client experience with outsourcing and resource allocation. As with any phase of the outsourcing process, there is a high correlation between outsourcing experience and success in transitioning. Where the transitioning phase is not managed effectively, it is likely that any problems that existed when the process was performed internally by the client will remain.

Knowledge management was also a critical aspect of improving service and reducing costs in the post-contract phase of the outsourcing arrangement. Under the previous arrangement, high employee attrition rates meant that important knowledge was lost, and additional costs were incurred with recruiting and training new employees. No one was taking responsibility for documenting and retaining knowledge. Changing rules for licensing agreements and rebates were not updated, and often resided in the heads of individuals across different teams in the vendor. Crucially, the whole area of revenue processing had become increasingly dependent upon a number of key individuals with tacit knowledge built up over a number of years – referred to as key knowledge-holders.

Therefore, the software company and vendor put in place a strategy for managing knowledge, as shown in Figure 9.4. The first part of the strategy involved gaining a fuller understanding of the processes and rules for processing revenue. This assisted with identifying important unstructured and disparate knowledge that had never been formalised. Working with 'key knowledge-holders', the vendor began to formalise and document the most important knowledge. Much of this exercise involved working with the software company to document the rules for licensing agreements and rebates.

There were a number of facilitators of this strategy, as shown in Figure 9.4. Incentives were offered to key knowledge-holders to ensure they shared knowledge, which involved linking the knowledge management strategy with the performance and bonus structure of the relevant team. This motivated individuals to share their knowledge with other less experienced individuals in the team, and to allow it to be documented, as it would enhance the overall performance of the team. Moreover, where knowledge was shared and documented it reduced the difficulties and costs associated with individuals leaving a team.

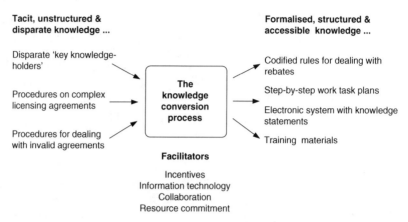

Figure 9.4   Knowledge management strategy

Information technology was used to codify and store much of the unstructured and tacit knowledge gathered from the key knowledge-holders. Rules for dealing with rebates were codified and stored electronically, which meant that this knowledge could be shared and accessible to all individuals in the team. This knowledge was also useful for developing training materials, and meant that new recruits did not have to spend as much time learning the job from incumbent employees.

Managing knowledge was a continuous process and required close collaboration between the software company and vendor. Formalising and documenting knowledge involved both formal and informal interaction between staff in the two organisations. The software company changed its rules for licensing agreements and rebates, which often had knock-on effects for stored knowledge. Codified and stored knowledge that was affected by these changes had to be updated, or deleted in some cases. Moreover, when the software company introduced new products or upgrades, it worked closely with the vendor to communicate clearly licensing agreements, rebates and the relationship with its existing product portfolio. The vendor convened monthly forums with each team to ensure that knowledge was kept as current and as accessible as possible. This was found to be a valuable means of identifying how rules could be simplified or inefficiencies removed from processes. Throughout the knowledge management process, both companies committed significant resource to ensure that managing knowledge was at the heart of the relationship.

Illustration 9.5 Knowledge management and outsourcing

Although the link between outsourcing and knowledge management is well recognised, organisations often lack the experience and capability to assess the value of the knowledge they are transferring and receiving in outsourcing arrangements. Organisations do not understand how knowledge can be created and exploited in outsourcing relationships with vendors. Studies of information technology outsourcing have shown that organisations have had disappointing experiences with managing knowledge.[a] Many clients have been frustrated with endless debates on cost and service levels, and have lost control over their knowledge on information technology. In turn, vendors fail to deliver on their promises of innovation, as a result of a lack of knowledge of the client's long-term business strategy. Knowledge management has implications for a number of aspects of the outsourcing process.

Making the decision

Knowledge is a critical asset of any organisation, and has the potential to generate long-term and sustainable competitive advantage. This issue is particularly relevant to professional services organisations that rely on the knowledge of their employees to serve the needs of their clients, and differentiate their service offerings from competitors. Outsourcing can lead to the transfer of important knowledge to vendors, who in some cases have the potential to become competitors in the future. Therefore, organisations should be careful not to outsource processes and associated knowledge that are important to competitive advantage. In addition, organisations should ensure that outsourcing certain processes frees up resource to invest in developing knowledge associated with more critical processes that are performed internally.

Transitioning

Knowledge is an important consideration in the transitioning phase of outsourcing. The vendor requires knowledge of the process involved and the operating procedures of the client to understand and deliver on the requirements of the client. Whilst not critical in the case of processes with standard requirements, and where there are a high number of vendors available, it is important in the case of processes where the needs of the client are specific and include idiosyncratic requirements. In such circumstances, it will take the vendor time to understand and gain knowledge of the specific requirements of the vendor in the initial phases of the outsourcing arrangement. One strategy for dealing with this issue involves transferring employees from the client to the vendor in the initial phases of the outsourcing arrangement. This allows the vendor to gain knowledge of the process and have access to staff who understand the requirements and idiosyncrasies of the client's operations.

The client has to be careful to retain employees who have knowledge on how to specify their requirements, and the ability to deal with non-routine problems and the historical complexities of the process and linkages with other internal processes. A risk of many outsourcing arrangements occurs when the client loses control over the process, and knowledge asymmetries develop in favour of the vendor. This is of particular importance in the case of processes where the client has specific requirements and where there are high switching costs in moving to another vendor. Often, such processes are based on tacit knowledge which has never been formalised and fully understood. Prior to outsourcing, the client should employ mechanisms to gain a better understanding of the process and convert the associated tacit knowledge into a more explicit format. This will open up the opportunity for transferring the process to another vendor in the event of any difficulties, and also mitigate the risks associated with transferred employees with specific knowledge leaving the vendor, or the vendor withholding knowledge for opportunistic purposes.

Managing the outsourcing relationship

There are a number of aspects to the knowledge dimension in managing the outsourcing relationship.

Accessing existing knowledge. The client should ensure that it is fully accessing the knowledge that many specialist vendors possess. One important benefit of accessing knowledge is that it can be employed to redesign and improve performance in the outsourced processes. Of course, there must be clauses in the contract to ensure that there is an incentive for vendors to share knowledge, which will also include a structure for sharing any associated benefits between the parties in the relationship.

Exploiting new knowledge. New knowledge can be created in the outsourcing relationship. In longer-term collaborative outsourcing relationships, the potential exists for both the client and vendor to develop knowledge to transform process performance, and also exploit process innovations in other areas. This involves creating a learning culture in the relationship in which there is an emphasis on acquiring and developing new knowledge. Such arrangements can strengthen the competitive position of the client, as it can develop specific knowledge and capabilities with a vendor that competitors will find difficult to imitate. However, there must be incentives in both the client and vendor to ensure that individuals are motivated to both share knowledge and acquire new knowledge.

Retaining knowledge. This is also a vital consideration during the outsourcing relationship. The client should consider ways of documenting and storing process knowledge as the relationship develops. This is particularly important in the case of processes with both specific and changing requirements throughout the outsourcing relationship. Retaining

> some knowledge reduces the risks of overdependency on the vendor, and allows the client to transfer the process to another vendor or back in-house.
>
> *Note:*
> [a] Willcocks, L., Hindle, J., Feeny, D. and Lacity, M. (2004). IT and Business Process Outsourcing: The Knowledge Potential, *Information Systems Management*, 21(3), 7–15; and Cullen, S. and Willcocks, L. (2003). *Intelligent IT Outsourcing: Eight Building Blocks to Success*, Oxford: Butterworth.

9.7 Employing contracting and collaboration as complements

Formal contracts and collaboration were important complements in managing the outsourcing arrangement.[6] The software company and vendor put extensive efforts into developing and agreeing performance measures and improvement targets in contract negotiations. Collaboration was particularly important in the early phases of the outsourcing arrangement when difficulties emerged. The vendor had struggled to deliver some of the services, and did not fully understand the complexity of outsourced processes, and the linkages with internal processes. In addition, the vendor did not commit sufficient resource to get the arrangement fully operational, and was relying too much on staff transferred from the three vendors to deal with problems, as evidenced by a comment from a vendor manager in the software company. The vendor had staffed the project with staff from its consultancy division rather than those with experience in implementing and managing BPO arrangements. It was also felt that the vendor had spent too much time on managing employee transfers via the TUPE framework, and could have spent more time understanding the process prior to the beginning of the contract.

Vendor staff believed that the software company contributed to the difficulties and had not sufficiently documented a number of key processes, and expected performance improvement too quickly from processes that had been causing problems. Some junior staff with important knowledge and experience had taken redundancy prior to the new outsourcing arrangement, which created further difficulties. Throughout these difficulties, service users in the software company had become increasingly frustrated with service levels, having expected a seamless transition to the outsourcing arrangement. The software company acknowledged that the service expectations of users could have been better managed in the early phases of the outsourcing arrangement. Moreover, staff in the vendor felt that the software company was placing too much emphasis on measuring performance and highlighting service deficiencies, rather than working with the vendor to address the causes of poor performance.

The software company and the vendor recognised that these problems had to be resolved together, rather than terminating the contract. Both parties had been contributing to the difficulties and senior management in both companies became involved in addressing these issues. During these discussions, the vendor accepted that it under-estimated the complexity of the processes involved, and had not committed sufficient and appropriately skilled resource to deliver the services. In turn, the software company acknowledged a number of key processes were not sufficiently documented, and service users were demanding service improvement too soon.

Therefore, senior management in both organisations, and those responsible for managing the outsourcing arrangement, put in place a number of practices to address the difficulties. Staff in the software company agreed to work with the vendor both to understand and improve processes that were causing problems. The software company implemented more quickly changes that had been implemented at corporate level to reduce the complexity of licensing agreements and rules for rebates, reduce the manual elements of some processes and introduce more information technology to automate some of the processes, and thereby reduce the number of errors. The vendor committed additional resource to deal with some of the difficulties that had arisen in the transitioning phase. These people had experience of working with other large BPO arrangements and possessed skills in continuous improvement and knowledge management.

The software company also conducted meetings with internal service users to manage expectations of service levels and formalise procedures for dealing with service problems. Previously, service users raised problems informally with staff in the vendors, and no one was formally tracking whether problems were being resolved. The vendor addressed some of the staff attrition issues. Although it was recognised that attrition was always going to be a challenge, the vendor found that 'over-recruiting' had been happening, where recruits had been over-qualified and were leaving within a short period of time. Therefore, it placed more emphasis on matching the requirements of the job with the person's qualifications and prior experience. This involved improving the training and induction process, and establishing a clear career development path. Also, cross-training took place in teams to reduce problems of staff attrition.

Collaboration was important throughout the relationship, and was employed to build flexibility into the relationship and compensate for any gaps in the contract when reacting to changing circumstances. For example, the software company had to adapt its approach to monitoring performance. It reduced the number of metrics used, and recognised that metrics had to be changed as processes were changed. Moreover, in order to make the relationship work, the software company worked with the vendor, where possible, to understand the causes of performance problems. In addition, collaboration was also necessary for driving process improvement. Through deploying its skills in Six Sigma, the vendor consolidated and eliminated inefficiencies from a number of processes that had been previously performed by the three vendors.

Both the software company and the vendor recognised the importance of having an effective governance model to manage the relationship. Weekly meetings were held to deal with service level issues and address any problems. Monthly meetings were held to deal with process changes and process improvements, which in some cases required some amendments to the contract. Quarterly meetings were held between senior managers to deal with strategic issues such as resource allocation and the future direction of the outsourcing arrangement. The governance model was an important model for agreeing and reaffirming the long-term objectives of the relationship. In the early phases of the outsourcing arrangement, much of the improvement was incremental and the vendor had difficulties with implementing more radical improvements due to highly specific requirements, and the number of process changes coming from the software company. Therefore, the software company agreed to reduce the level of process change to allow the vendor to drive process improvement and also introduce standard processes that it uses with other clients.

9.8 Summary implications

• Planning and implementing BPO arrangements poses considerable challenges to organisations. Organisations often rush into BPO without adequate preparation, and all too often experience disappointing results. Common causes of BPO failure include the lack of a formal outsourcing strategy, outsourcing core processes, difficulties with unbundling processes, under-estimating the transaction costs of managing vendors, failing to manage people issues, poor vendor selection and ineffective contracting.

• An effective sourcing strategy in BPO involves determining the requirements from outsourcing and evaluating whether a vendor can meet these requirements. Determining the requirements involves considering issues such as the level of process improvement required, the level of specific client requirements and the type of outsourcing relationship required. Vendor evaluation involves considering issues such as how the vendor can reduce process costs, its capabilities to improve performance and how it manages and motivates people.

• Careful preparation is essential in transferring responsibility for processes to vendors. The presence of interdependencies between processes and process complexity increases the difficulties of unbundling processes. The client should identify and untangle unnecessary complexity and reduce the number of interdependencies. Continuous improvement techniques can be employed to reduce process complexity and process inefficiencies prior to outsourcing. Understanding and documenting processes will help in communicating its requirements and allow the vendor to meet the required performance levels more quickly.

• Knowledge management has important implications for planning and managing BPO arrangements. The client should be careful to retain important process knowledge when making the decision, whilst the vendor can access key process knowledge through staff transfers in the transitioning phase. Knowledge management tools can be employed to formalise and retain important process knowledge throughout the BPO arrangement. Retaining knowledge can reduce the risks of overdependency on the vendor, and allow the client to transfer the process to another vendor or back in-house.

• Formal contracts and collaboration are important complements in BPO arrangements. A detailed contract can serve as an impetus for action and performance improvement. Collaboration can work alongside formal contracts through building flexibility into the client–vendor relationship, and compensate for any gaps in the contract when reacting to changing circumstances. Resolving performance problems via collaboration is more effective than resorting to the contract, which should be a last resort.

• The complexity of BPO necessitates a broad set of skills and management capabilities. As well as requiring skills in contracting and vendor relationship management, the client requires skills in continuous improvement tools such as process mapping, knowledge management and Six Sigma. The experiences of the software company in this chapter have shown how continuous improvement tools can be used to reduce transaction costs in BPO arrangements, as shown in Table 9.2.

Table 9.3 How continuous improvement tools can reduce transaction costs in BPO

Transaction cost variable	Application of continuous improvement tools
Asset specificity	Process mapping tools were used to map out and understand the processes and identify inefficiencies and complex interdependencies. Clearer process definitions meant clear lines of responsibility could be established between the processes involved. Continuous improvement techniques were employed to reduce interdependencies, and where possible reduce specific process requirements to deploy standard processes offered by the vendor.
Knowledge loss	Knowledge management tools were employed to derive clear task specifications and licensing agreement rules that could be stored electronically and clearly documented. This exercise assisted with training and limited the impact of employee turnover and knowledge loss.
Performance measurement	Clearer process definitions and better understood interdependencies led to improved performance measurement. The adoption of a formal approach to documenting process change in the BPO arrangement meant that performance measures were kept relevant, and where necessary amended or removed.
Uncertainty	The client simplified the licensing variants and rules for rebates, which reduced uncertainty for the vendor.

Notes and references

1 Mani, D., Barua, A. and Whinston, A. (2006). Successfully Governing Business Process Outsourcing Relationships. *MIS Quarterly Executive*, 5(1), 15–29.
2 Tan, C. and Sia, S. (2006). Managing Flexibility in Outsourcing, *Journal of the Association for Information Systems*, 7(4), 179–206.
3 Much of the material presented in this chapter is based on the experiences of a global software provider in a BPO arrangement. Data were collected via semi-structured interviews. In-depth interviews were carried out with managers in both the software company and the vendors. A longitudinal approach was applied to the analysis. Firstly, data were gathered to obtain insights into the development of the BPO arrangement with the three vendors. Secondly, data were obtained on the motives and outcomes of the software company moving to a single-vendor BPO arrangement.
4 Useful sources on knowledge management include Birkinshaw, J. and Sheehan, T. (2002). Managing the Knowledge Life Cycle, *Sloan Management Review*, 44(1), 75–83; Gupta, A. K. and Govindarajan, V. (2000). Knowledge Management's Social Dimension: Lessons from Nucor Steel, *Sloan Management Review*, 42(1), 71–80; Hansen, M., Nohria, N. and Tierney, T. (1999). What's Your

Strategy for Managing Knowledge? *Harvard Business Review*, 77(2) 106–16; and Nonaka, I. (1994). A Dynamic Theory of Organizational Knowledge Creation, *Organization Science*, 5(1), 14–37.

5 In the European Union, employee regulations, such as the Transfer of Under-takings (Protection of Employment) Act (TUPE), require procedures to be completed before staff can be transferred to the vendor. The objective of this legislation is to ensure continuity of employment for staff, and guarantee their existing terms of service.

6 For a useful study testing whether relational contracting and formal con-tracts act as complements or substitutes, see Poppo, L. and Zenger, T. (2002). Do Formal Contracts and Relational Governance Function as Substitutes or Complements? *Strategic Management Journal*, 23, 707–25.

Recommended key reading

Barthélemy, J. (2003). The Seven Deadly Sins of Outsourcing, *Academy of Management Executive*, 17(2), 87–98. Based upon a survey of outsourcing contracts in the USA and Europe, this paper highlights seven common reasons for outsourcing failure.

Feeny, D., Lacity, M. and Willcocks, L. (2005). Taking the Measure of Outsourcing Providers, *Sloan Management Review*, 46(3), 41–8. This paper provides a frame-work for helping organisations evaluate the capabilities that vendors require to meet their requirements from BPO.

Mani, D., Barua, A. and Whinston, A. (2006). Successfully Governing Business Process Outsourcing Relationships, *MIS Quarterly Executive*, 5(1), 15–29. This paper argues that insufficient attention to governance is the key reason why BPO rela-tionships fail. The authors propose a model for successful BPO, which is based on the premise that three key requirements of the outsourced process – process interdependence, complexity and strategic importance – should determine the three governance capabilities – the outsourcing contract, relationship manage-ment and technical capabilities.

Shi, Y. (2007). Today's Solution and Tomorrow's Problem: The Business Process Outsourcing Risk and Management Puzzle, *California Management Review*, 49(3), 27–44. This paper provides a comprehensive review of the different types of risks that a client has to deal with in BPO arrangements.

Conclusion

10.1. Introduction

The analysis in this book has focused on planning, implementing and managing services outsourcing arrangements, and has shown that services outsourcing involves a range of issues including continuous improvement, change management, stakeholder management, knowledge management, information technology, contracting and performance management. Outsourcing services to foreign locations includes a number of additional concerns such as language, culture, service quality, political factors, time zone and company reputation. The book has highlighted the difficulties and risks, as well as the reasons for failure. The complexity of services outsourcing means that failure is likely, and, of course, failure cases will generate more headlines than successful outsourcing. In spite of outsourcing failure, there is no discernible trend towards organisations bringing processes back in-house during or at the end of contracts. Indeed, the drivers of services outsourcing such as corporate restructuring programmes, developments in information and communication technologies (ICTs) and more demanding consumers will continue to operate. This chapter summarises some of the key challenges of services outsourcing, and outlines key aspects of effective services outsourcing based upon the analysis presented in the book.

10.2. Challenges of services outsourcing

Conflicting incentives

A difficulty at the heart of any outsourcing arrangement is the conflicting motivations of the client and vendor. A key objective of the client in outsourcing is to obtain a service at a lower cost from the vendor. The aim of staff in the client is to demand more services from the vendor without having to pay more.[1] Conversely, the aim of staff in the vendor is to squeeze as much profit as possible from the contract with the client, or to sell additional services to increase its revenue. The difficulty with conflicting incentives is further exacerbated where client requirements are difficult to specify or where there is a high level of uncertainty and frequent changes in the contract. Where changes are required by the client, the vendor is likely to resist because of the impact upon its profit margin. It is extremely difficult to develop an effective contract in a situation where the needs and goals of the client and vendor are not aligned or where the client cannot specify clearly its requirements.[2] Partnerships and joint ventures between the client and vendor have been employed to reduce the problems of conflicting incentives in outsourcing arrangements. However, these types of relationship can be often difficult to develop and sustain over the long term. Moreover, clients and vendors have attempted to develop partnerships without amending the internal incentive structures that create the problem of conflicting incentives in outsourcing relationships.

Scale and complexity

Outsourcing is a daunting prospect for organisations, as they are faced with shrinking budgets and pressures to improve performance. These pressures are particularly pronounced for those running back-office functions with processes and people dispersed across different departments and locations.[3] Legacy systems, disjointed processes and duplication of effort create a strong pressure from the corporate level for performance improvement either through internal improvement programmes, or by outsourcing. Outsourcing offers some attractive features, including vendor continuous improvement capabilities, better technology utilisation, and cost savings through economies of scale and vendor presence in lower labour cost regions. However, managers are often reluctant to get involved in large-scale outsourcing, as it involves considerable upheaval and internal changes. Many organisations do not fully understand the complexity or the weaknesses in existing systems or processes. Transferring responsibility for such systems and processes is fraught with risk and a high potential for failure. These are only some of the fears; yet these are enough to deter organisations from even contemplating large-scale outsourcing arrangements. In the face of these fears, organisations often consider 'less risky' options such as partial outsourcing or attempting internal improvement through the insourcing option.

Skills deficit

Many organisations start at a major disadvantage when entering into outsourcing contracts, as they lack the necessary skills and experience.

Mistakenly, clients rely on vendors to assist them in areas such as contracting and performance improvement, which places them in a weak position in relation to the vendor. In such a situation, the client can lose control over the process, and knowledge asymmetries develop in favour of the vendor. Large-scale outsourcing arrangements involve high levels of uncertainty and risk. The scale and complexity of some outsourcing arrangements means that clients lack the skills to determine requirements and a detailed outline of the service delivery model. In some cases, organisations are implementing new and innovative outsourcing solutions that have never been attempted before. Although vendors offer significant capabilities to transform performance, organisations still require significant in-house skills in project management, continuous improvement, vendor management and change management. People management skills are required to manage vendors and drive the necessary change and performance improvement in the internal functions impacted by outsourcing.

Unbundling service processes

Some have argued that the services outsourcing phenomenon – both locally and globally – will accelerate more quickly than that of manufacturing outsourcing, primarily as a result of developments in ICTs allowing service processes to be unbundled digitally. However, there are significant challenges with outsourcing service processes which are not present in manufacturing outsourcing. Outsourcing service processes involves redrawing the boundaries between internal functions, processes and people. Unbundling non-core processes can adversely affect the performance of core processes. Once organisations embark on an analysis of existing systems and processes prior to outsourcing, they discover high levels of complexity and interdependencies among other processes and functions. An organisation's information technology (IT) infrastructure further compounds this difficulty. In many organisations, the IT application driving the business process is highly customised and tightly integrated with the organisation's IT infrastructure including the operating systems and hardware.[4] Over time, IT professionals develop tightly coupled solutions that integrate processes across multiple and disparate IT systems.[5] Standardising and modularising processes with links to tightly coupled systems is extremely time-consuming and expensive. Although developments in IT such as enterprise systems have led to standardised processes, many organisations are still relying on legacy systems with tightly coupled IT and business processes.

10.3. Key aspects of effective services outsourcing

Deciding whether to outsource

The starting point for effective services outsourcing is the decision to out-source. Rather than adopting outsourcing to follow the lead of competitors or in response to vendors marketing their services, outsourcing should be considered for the right reasons. When implemented effectively, outsour-cing can deliver significant cost reductions through vendor scale economies and experience, allow management to focus on core business areas and achieve flexibility through keeping fluctuating capacity outside the com-pany. However, outsourcing will fail where it is used to offload a problem process or squeeze lower costs from the vendor through a contract imbal-anced in the client's favour. Organisations should establish clear objectives linked with overall corporate strategy. Developing a business case is a key aspect of deciding whether to outsource a process. A business case should describe the problems with an existing internal process, and outline how these problems can be overcome through retaining the process internally or through outsourcing. Where outsourcing is considered appropriate, there should be a convincing rationale and clear benefits to win the support of key stakeholders.

Deciding where to outsource

Organisations now have a range of location options when deciding where to outsource. Understanding the influences on location choice allows an organisation to maximise the benefits and mitigate the risks of outsourcing. Key location factors include geographic distance, culture, language, gov-ernment policy, labour issues, infrastructure and legal matters. Domestic outsourcing still offers many advantages over foreign outsourcing, includ-ing geographical and cultural closeness. Selecting domestic vendors allows organisations to outsource complex processes, and have the frequent face-to-face communication necessary for developing collaborative relationships. When opting for remote offshore locations it is difficult to assess fully the costs of factors such as cultural distance on service quality. However, select-ing an appropriate sourcing model can mitigate some of the risks of global services outsourcing. The captive model allows organisations to maintain control over complex service processes, whilst fee-for-service models can be used to outsource standard services with clearly defined rules. Moreover, the nearshore location option allows organisations to transfer services to lower labour cost foreign locations that are geographically and culturally close, rather than to remote offshore locations. The dynamics of potential locations should also be considered. Increasingly, vendors in offshore locations have been upgrading their capabilities to offer more complex and knowledge-intensive services. Developments in ICTs, business process methodologies and project management will further drive the modularisation and standardisation of many service processes, allowing companies to use domestic vendors for customer contact processes that require local knowledge and cultural closeness, whilst leveraging the cost and specialist knowledge skills of vendors in remote offshore locations.

Determining requirements from outsourcing

Although determining requirements is extremely challenging, particularly in large and complex outsourcing arrangements, it is a task to which organisations should give considerable attention. There are a number of aspects to determining requirements. Existing systems and processes should be analysed and documented, which involves understanding the interdependencies, complexity and level of changes required in the processes. A key part of this analysis involves assessing how specific the organisation's requirements are if it enters into an outsourcing arrangement. Efforts should be made to determine current internal performance levels, and comparisons with vendor performance levels through external benchmarking should be undertaken. Engaging with vendors prior to outsourcing is a valuable means of exploring potential sourcing options, gaining ideas and refining requirements. Specialist vendors have superior levels of knowledge and experience, and engaging with vendors offers the potential to exploit these capabilities to improve the performance.

Determining requirements is valuable for a number of reasons. It will identify the scale of the challenge and potential sourcing options for improving performance. Where performance is marginally weaker than that of external vendors, it may be prudent to improve performance internally and retain the process in-house. Where performance is considerably weaker than that of vendors, outsourcing is likely to be the most suitable option for improving performance. This type of analysis is crucial to making an effective vendor selection decision. The scale of performance deficiencies will provide an indication of the vendor capabilities required to transform performance, and how quickly the vendor can deploy its specialist capabilities to deliver the required performance levels.

Assessing the level of specific requirements and process complexity allows the client to address a number of important issues prior to outsourcing. The client has to decide whether it will retain its specific requirements, or adopt the standard offerings of the vendor. Transferring processes with highly specific requirements to the vendor will inhibit the vendor from delivering significant cost reductions. Standardising requirements will deliver cost reductions, whilst leading to internal upheaval and resistance where internal functions have to relinquish long-held practices and idiosyncratic processes. Understanding the level of improvement required and specific requirements will also inform the choice of outsourcing relationship. Where client requirements are highly specific and performance transformation is required, a relational contracting outsourcing relationship will be appropriate.

Supplementing internal skills

The scale and complexity of outsourcing means that organisations lack the necessary skills internally to effectively evaluate the potential sourcing options and implement services outsourcing arrangements. Organisations can address this challenge through employing external consultants and recruiting people with the necessary skills and experience. In developing a business case, specialist consultancy expertise in the functional areas affected can be employed to identify potential sourcing options for improving performance. Where an organisation's processes and performance measurement systems are weak, legal advice and performance measurement and procurement expertise should be sought to assist with developing a robust contract that creates incentives for vendor performance improvements. The additional complexity of global services outsourcing also requires significant external expertise. Differences in legal systems, as well as geographical, time zone and culture differences, require specialist expertise to reduce the difficulties of contracting in global services outsourcing. The increasing scope of services outsourcing requires a broad set of skills and range of management capabilities. As well as requiring skills in traditional outsourcing areas such as contracting and vendor relationship management, organisations increasingly require skills in business process redesign, knowledge management, change management and continuous improvement.

Stakeholder management

Outsourcing involves considerable change, often including the redesign of organisational structures and processes. Such changes can lead to employee resistance and attempts to block change, particularly where it involves relinquishing idiosyncratic practices and employing standard vendor processes. Engaging with stakeholders throughout the outsourcing process is a valuable mechanism for winning the support of powerful stakeholders, and also for obtaining co-operation from less enthusiastic stakeholders. Gaining the support of senior management in the initial evaluation phase of outsourcing is important for securing the necessary resource for implementation. Senior management can be used to win the support of less enthusiastic stakeholders at lower levels in the organisation. Key mechanisms for engaging with stakeholders include timely and properly directed communication and involving potential opponents in decisions and tasks throughout the outsourcing process. The effectiveness of stakeholder engagement activities should be monitored throughout implementation, which involves consulting stakeholders on the effectiveness of communications and monitoring how the support of stakeholders is changing.

Performance management

Organisations must understand the many dimensions of performance management in the outsourcing process. Prior to outsourcing, it is important to understand why internal process performance is weaker than that of vendors or competitors. Such analysis is important in the case of processes that are critical to competitive advantage, as outsourcing can lead to a loss of skills in strategically important areas. Moreover, the analysis may reveal that an internal improvement programme is more appropriate. Where outsourcing is considered, the client must understand how the vendor delivers better performance, and how long it will take for the vendor to meet the required performance levels. Organisations often assume that vendors will deliver better performance than internal functions, and that performance improvement will occur in the early phases of the contract. When determining requirements from outsourcing and during contract negotiations, the client and vendor should agree baseline performance targets for the start of the contract and how these will be changed as the contract matures. Of course, in complex contracts with highly specific requirements and uncertainty, flexibility is necessary to allow changes in performance measures and targets.

Managing performance throughout the outsourcing relationship has a number of dimensions. Where vendors are delivering services to client employees, the client must have formal mechanisms for measuring vendor service quality. Where employees' experiences with the vendor are poor, it will lead to employee resistance and threaten the success of the outsourcing relationship. The client should put in place mechanisms to ensure that any performance problems are addressed quickly with the vendor. Senior management view outsourcing as a means of allowing retained functions to move from transaction-intensive tasks to more value-adding tasks.

Moreover, retained functions are facing competition from vendors to offer additional services, and can no longer rely on their traditional monopoly position as a provider for services in their functional area. Some organisations have been employing service level agreements (SLAs) to assess the performance of retained functional areas. Such developments have been placing pressure on internal functions to create more value and improve performance, lest they become a target for further outsourcing.

Formal and relational contracting as complements

Detailed contracts are an essential ingredient for success in services outsourcing. Drafting a tight contract can act as an important complement to building an ethos of collaboration in the outsourcing relationship. It is often assumed that partnering and collaboration alone can deal with any difficulties in the relationship. However, a carefully drafted contract can serve as an impetus for action and improvement. In particular, the contract allows the client and vendor to establish expectations and make commitments to short-term objectives. There is much rhetoric in the academic literature and in practice in relation to collaboration and partnerships in outsourcing relationships. Some argue that partnerships can be readily developed with vendors for leveraging skills and resources that are unobtainable by competitors. However, collaboration and partnership relations are a long-term commitment, and consume a considerable amount of resource on the part of the client and vendor.

Rather than collaboration being used to achieve competitive advantage, it can be employed to build flexibility into the relationship, and compensate for any gaps in the contract when reacting to changing circumstances. Services outsourcing arrangements involve reconfiguring and changing the relationship between outsourced processes and internal processes. In some cases, it is possible to deal with these changes through renegotiating the contract. However, collaboration can act as another important mechanism for allowing changes to be made to processes without renegotiating the contract. Collaboration is also an important mechanism for dealing with difficulties in the early phases of an outsourcing arrangement. This is particularly important in a case where the vendor cannot meet the required service levels because the client has outsourced a poorly performing internal process without understanding the causes of poor performance prior to outsourcing. Resolving performance problems via collaboration can be a much more effective means of addressing weaknesses in the outsourcing arrangement than terminating the contract.

Project management

Project management skills are an essential part of services outsourcing arrangements. Outsourcing arrangements require many of the factors associated with successful project management including clearly defined objectives, leadership and top management support, competent project managers and team members, sufficient resource commitment, adequate communication channels, and mechanisms for dealing with problems and project change. Large-scale outsourcing, such as shared services, involves a wide range of tasks that have to be scheduled and co-ordinated within a structured project management framework. The need for project management skills is further amplified in the case of global services outsourcing. Differences in geographic distance, time zone and culture increase complexity and the potential for failure. The lack of face-to-face interaction between the client and vendor can lead to breakdowns in communication and misunderstandings of client requirements. Moreover, culture and geographic distance have increased the challenges of developing a collaborative and team ethos in global services outsourcing. Organisations have been employing features of project management to address these challenges including defining clear objectives, designing effective client–vendor communication structures and selecting team members with a mix of skills, language and cultural background.

Notes and references

1 Lacity, M., Willcocks, L. and Rottman, J. (2008). Global Outsourcing of Back Office Services: Lessons, Trends, and Enduring Challenges, *Strategic Outsourcing: An International Journal*, 1(1), 13–34.

2 Tadelis, S. (2007). The Innovative Organisation: Creating Value through Outsourcing, *California Management Review*, 50(1), 261–77.

3 Hesketh, A. (2008). Should It Stay Or Should It Go? Examining the Shared Services or Outsourcing Decision, *Strategic Outsourcing: An International Journal*, 1(2), 154–72.

4 Hagel, J. and Brown, J. (2005). *The Only Sustainable Edge: Why Business Strategy Depends Upon Productive Friction and Dynamic Specialization*, Boston: Harvard Business School Press.

5 Tanriverdi, H., Konana, P. and Ge, L. (2007). The Choice of Sourcing Mechanisms for Business Processes, *Information Systems Research*, 18(3), 280–99.

Glossary

asset specificity – refers to the level of customisation associated with an outsourcing arrangement. Investments in highly specific assets have little or no value outside the outsourcing arrangement and create switching costs for the client.

asynchronous communication – the sending and receiving of information in which there is a time delay between the sending and receiving.

back-office services – consist of processes that require little or no contact with the customer.

backsourcing – involves bringing an outsourced process back in-house.

benchmarking – a continuous process of measuring and comparing performance in processes against organisations that are world leaders.

build–operate–transfer model – the vendor owns, builds, staffs and operates a facility in a foreign location on behalf of the client. The client has the option of taking ownership of the facility in-house from the vendor in the future.

business case – describes a business problem and outlines a proposal on how it should be overcome.

business process – a collection of activities that takes a number of inputs and creates an output.

business process outsourcing – involves the vendor taking responsibility for executing a business process, and delivering it to the client as a service.

business process redesign – the redesign of business processes, organisational structures and information technology systems to achieve radical performance improvements.

Capability Maturity Model – developed as a global standard for software development processes. It has been employed to measure progress in software development and compare one software vendor's processes with another's.

captive model – the client builds, owns, staffs and operates a facility in a foreign location.

change management – involves the management of significant organisational change and business process redesign.

codification – the extent to which tasks associated with a process can be described completely in a set of written instructions.

continuous improvement – an approach to improving process performance through frequent, regular and incremental improvement steps.

core process – refers to a process that is critical to competitive advantage and therefore should be performed internally.

critical success factors – represent those areas of an organisation or project on which management needs to focus in order to create high levels of performance.

economies of scale – occur when the unit costs of creating and delivering a service decrease as volume increases.

enterprise system – a set of applications capable of integrating and managing business functions and operations for an entire, multi-site organisation.

explicit knowledge – knowledge that can be formalised, represented in words and numbers and readily communicated.

fixed-price contract – the client pays a pre-negotiated, fixed price for the service, which is linked to clearly defined deliverables.

follow-the-sun development – involves exploiting time zone differences to produce and deliver services around the clock, thus speeding up development and enhancing customer service.

foreign direct investment – a strategy where an organisation establishes a physical presence in a foreign location via the acquisition of assets such as capital, technology, labour, land and equipment.

front-office services – consist of processes that are performed while the customer is present. Customers actively interact and are involved directly in the delivery of front-office services.

governance structure – refers to the structures and procedures in place to manage an outsourcing relationship.

group support system – software system that supports decision-making in a group or team environment.

hierarchical governance – involves performing a process internally within the firm.

information and communication technologies – include telecommunications technologies, such as telephony, cable and satellite, as well as digital technologies, such as computers, networks and software.

insourcing – the use of internal business functions to deliver products or services that could be provided by external vendors.

intellectual property – refers to the rights given to a creator for the exclusive use of a creation over a certain period of time, and can include patents, copyrights, trademarks and trade secrets.

intranet – a secure internal organisational network that uses Internet tools such as web browsers and Internet protocols.

knowledge intensity – the extent to which a service is based on knowledge.

knowledge management – involves capturing, storing, updating, interpreting and using knowledge whenever necessary.

labour arbitrage – the large gap between labour costs in developed economies and emerging economies.

legacy systems – older information technology applications that may still be capable of meeting the needs of the organisation, although they may require updating to meet future needs.

modularisation – involves breaking large and complex business processes into component modules and activities so that organisations and vendors can specialise in certain modules and activities.

multi-sourcing – integrates in-house service delivery with outsourced solutions such as business process outsourcing.

nearshoring – involves outsourcing a process to a location that is both geographically and culturally close.

non-core process – refers to a process that is not critical to competitive advantage, and therefore is a potential candidate for outsourcing.

non-specific contracting – involves a relatively short-term client–vendor contract, where the primary objective of the client is to achieve cost reductions. The needs of the client are non-specific, which enables the vendor to achieve economies of scale on production costs.

offshoring – involves outsourcing a process to a location that is both geographically and culturally remote.

opportunism – involves the vendor shirking on responsibilities agreed in the contract with the client. Factors that influence opportunism potential include high asset specificity, performance measurement difficulties, uncertainty and changes in client requirements.

outsourcing – the use of an external vendor to provide products or services previously provided by internal business functions.

outsourcing evaluation – refers to the analysis involved in determining whether it is appropriate to outsource a process.

outsourcing management – refers to implementing and managing the outsourcing contract once an organisation has decided to outsource a process.

outsourcing relationship – refers to activities involved in managing the client–vendor relationship throughout the outsourcing contract.

process idiosyncrasies – refers to processes that are performed in a specific or highly customised way by the client. Such processes create high asset specificity in outsourcing arrangements.

process interdependencies – refers to the interconnections among processes, business units and tasks. Complex interdependencies among processes can increase transaction costs.

process mapping – refers to the activities involved in defining what a business process does, who is responsible, to what level of performance the process should be completed and how performance should be measured.

production costs – the direct costs involved in creating a product or service, including labour and infrastructure costs.

recurrent contracting – involves a contract where there are moderate levels of asset specificity. Excessive dependence on a single vendor is avoided, and the client can incorporate a number of mechanisms that allow it to switch to another vendor in the event of contract termination.

relational contracting – involves a contract where there are high levels of asset specificity. The focus in relational contracting is moving beyond a contractual mindset and developing a trust-based and mutually beneficial relationship.

requirements analysis – systems development phase where the outputs of the system are assessed in relation to the needs of users.

selective outsourcing – involves outsourcing a limited number of activities associated with a business process.

service disaggregation – involves splitting a process into a number of sub-processes for outsourcing purposes.

service level agreement – an agreement between the client and vendor that specifies the service levels required by the client.

shared services – involves consolidating and standardising common tasks associated with a business function across different parts of the organisation into a single services centre.

stakeholders – individuals or groups of individuals who can influence the strategy of an organisation.

standardisation – the extent to which the tasks in a process can be executed using a set of consistent and repeatable steps.

synchronous communication – the simultaneous sending and receiving of messages.

systems analysis – systems development phase involving the analysis of existing processes and systems to identify weaknesses and areas for improvement.

tacit knowledge – knowledge that is based on subjective and experiential learning and is highly personal and difficult to formalise.

time-and-materials contract – refers to a contract for the sourcing of services on the basis of direct labour hours at a specified rate.

total outsourcing – involves outsourcing an entire process to a service provider.

transaction costs – the costs of selecting vendors, negotiating prices, writing contracts and monitoring performance.

transactional outsourcing – involves outsourcing a process that is not critical to competitive advantage, has limited interdependencies with other processes, and has low complexity.

transformational outsourcing – involves using outsourcing to achieve a rapid, sustainable, step-change improvement in organisational and process performance.

transitional outsourcing – involves outsourcing a process to a service provider on a temporary basis.

unbundling – is another term used to refer to outsourcing a process to an independent vendor.

workflow – the movement of information associated with the work procedures of an organisation.

workflow mapping – involves determining the tasks required to accomplish the process objectives, choosing the ideal sequence that tasks should follow, and determining who should be responsible for performing each task.

Index